# THE WORLD OF
# SPORT
# *examined*

## PAUL BEASHEL
## JOHN TAYLOR

Nelson

Thomas Nelson and Sons Ltd.
Nelson House
Mayfield Road
Walton-on-Thames
Surrey KT12 5PL UK

©Paul Beashel and John Taylor 1997

Published by Thomas Nelson and Sons Ltd. 1997

I(T)P® Thomas Nelson is an International Thomson Publishing Company

I(T)P® is used under licence

ISBN 0-17-438719-9
NPN 987654

Printed in Croatia

ACKNOWLEDGEMENTS
The authors would like to thank John Coghlan, Jenny Filbey, Kate Kerr, Janet Kendrik, Andy Sibson, John White and, most importantly, Liz and Marilyn.

PHOTOGRAPH ACKNOWLEDGEMENTS
Pictures supplied by All Sport, with thanks to R. Mayston. Every effort has been made to trace all the relevant copyright holders but if any have been inadvertently overlooked the publishers will be pleased to make the necessary arrangements at the first opportunity.

Acquisitions: Brenda Eisenberg
Administration: Eileen Regan
Design: The Junction
Editorial: Joanne Ely
In house designer: Lorraine Inglis
Marketing: Jeremy Warner
Production: Tony Warner

# The World of Sport Examined

The world of sport is an ever changing one. It is change which makes sport so attractive. Millions of pounds change hands to bring football to our television screens, fully professional basketball players win gold at the Olympics and athletes of all types go faster, higher and further.

The world of sport is uplifting. It brings inspiration and hope for the future. The Faroe Islands have won at football and Frank Bruno has worn a champion's crown.

The world of sport demands our attention. It is a powerful force in the world today, and it will not go away.

We have both been sports addicts for as long as we can remember. There seems to be no cure. We hope our enthusiasm comes through in this new edition. More importantly, we hope you find it a good read and helpful for your exam course.

*Paul Beashel*

*J Taylor.*

# Contents

Introduction                      6

**1  Our Body Systems        8**
Our skeletal system               10
Our muscular system               18
Our circulatory system            26
Our respiratory system            32
Our nervous system                36
Our hormonal system               38
Our digestive system              39
Our excretory system              39

**2  Energy in Action        42**
Creatine phosphate system         44
Lactic acid system                45
Aerobic system                    46

**3  Fitness for Health and Performance    50**
What is aerobic capacity?         54
What is strength?                 56
What is muscular power?           57
What is muscular endurance?       58
What is body build?               59
What is flexibility?              62
What is speed?                    64
What is agility?                  65
What is coordination?             66
What is reaction time?            67
What is balance?                  68

**4  Training for Success    70**
Principles of training            72
Planning a training programme     74
Training programme - phases       74
Training methods                  76
Long term effects of training     81
Age and training                  83
Gender and training               84

**5  Skill in Sport          86**
What is skill?                    88
How do we learn skills?           96
Competitive sport and skill       100

**6  Care of our Body        104**
Sensible eating                   106
The right lifestyle               114
Limiting alcohol                  116
Don't smoke!                      117
Don't misuse drugs!               118

**7 Safety in Sport** 124

Planning for safety 126
How can we make sure we are safe? 128
Sports injury 130
Emergency procedures 132
Soft and hard tissue injuries 136

**8 The Changing Face of Sport** 140

Developments in British sport 142
The changing Olympics 146
The role of the performer 154
New technology 160

**9 Providing for Sport** 164

What are the Sports Councils? 166
What are the national governing bodies of sport? 168
What is the Central Council of Physical Recreation? 169
Other major organisations 170
Who controls international sport? 172
Who provides sports facilities? 174
Funding for sport - an overview 178

**10 Taking Part in Sport** 188

Leisure time 190
Benefits 191
Home influences 192
School influences 194
School and community links 196
National campaigns 197
Gender and sport 198
Black and ethnic minorities and sport 199
Disability and sport 200
Older people and sport 201
Careers in sport 202

**11 Sport as a Spectacle** 204

Sponsorship 206
The media 212
Television 214
Sport, sponsorship and television - the future? 215

**Glossary** 220

**Index** 223

# Introduction

## Energy in Action

We need efficient energy systems for everyday living, but sport makes extra demands on our energy.

## Our Body Systems

We need all our body systems to be in good working order for healthy living and our best sports performances.

FOUNDATION

PARTICIPATION

**The Sports Development Continuum**

## Providing for Sport

We need facilities of all types at a fair price. Clubs provide the organisation and opportunities for us to take part. Private enterprise is replacing Government support in sport.

## Sport as a Spectacle

The entertainment industry, sponsoring companies, and the media have taken control of much of sport. The excitement offered by sport makes it compulsive viewing.

## Taking Part in Sport

Playing sport is a popular activity. Our reasons for taking part are many and varied. The influence of our family and teachers is critical. Some people are disadvantaged through gender, race, disability and age.

# Fitness for Health and Performance

Everyone needs basic fitness for health. Sportspeople must build up special fitness for their chosen sport.

# Training for Success

Improving our performance depends on the effort we put into training. Our body responds to strenuous exercise.

# Skill in Sport

Skilled performances need basic ability, sound techniques and good skills. Teaching skills is an art based on understanding the learning process.

EXCELLENCE

PERFORMANCE

# Care of our Body

Our bodies need looking after. We should exercise regularly, eat sensibly, watch our weight and resist drugs of all kinds.

# Safety in Sport

Preventing accidents and injuries is better than dealing with them. We should prepare our bodies for sport and respect our opponents. First aid knowledge can return us to sport quickly and may even save a life.

# The Changing Face of Sport

Sport has developed through the ages from the village feast days to the Olympic spectacle. Gentlemen amateurs have been replaced by wealthy television sports stars. Modern technology has made dramatic changes but sport is still built on the amateurs playing in the parks and halls of Britain.

# 1 Our Body Systems

What do we need to stay alive? We need air, food, sleep, shelter, clothes. We need to breathe, move about and know what is going on around us. We need to get supplies of energy into our bodies and convert them so we can use them. We then need to get rid of any waste products.

Our bodies have developed special systems so that these and other life-preserving activities can be carried out. Although we will look at a number of these body systems separately, it is important to remember that they all work together to keep our bodies working.

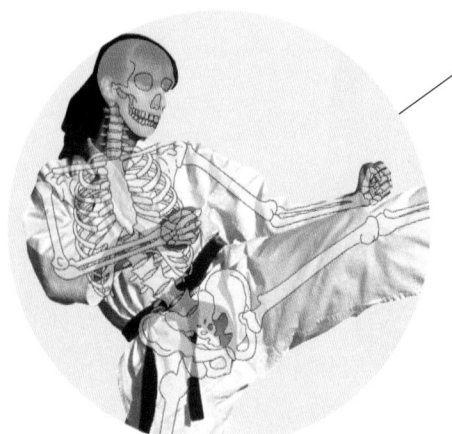

## Our skeletal system page 10

Bones give shape to our bodies and protect vital organs. They also provide attachments for muscles and allow movement to take place through the joints.

## Our muscular system page 18

All our movements need muscular action. Skilful movement results from many skeletal muscles working smoothly together. Our muscles work non-stop in order to keep the body working, even when it is at rest.

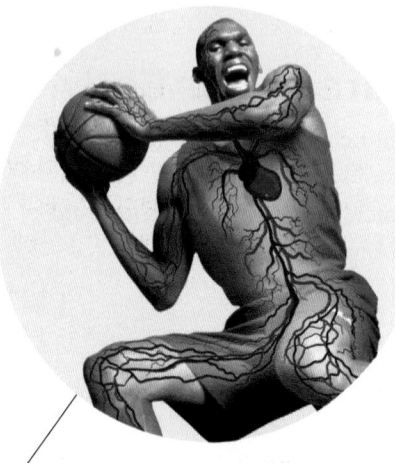

## Our circulatory system page 26

Our heart and its blood vessels ensure that oxygen and nutrients are carried to all cells of the body. At the same time, waste products are removed.

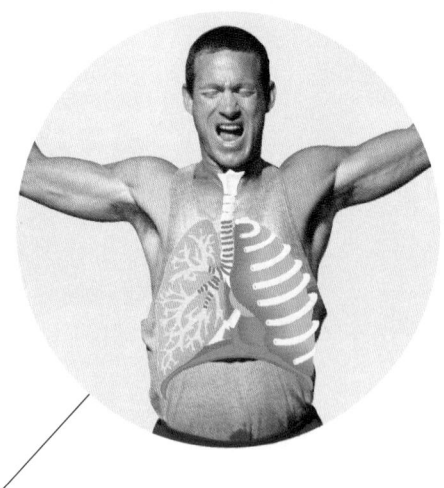

## Our respiratory system page 32

Our bodies need oxygen to be able to make use of the energy available in food. Our lungs allow oxygen from the air to be exchanged with waste products from the body.

Our bodies are designed for action. Nowhere is this more apparent than in sport. Different sports make different demands on our bodies. Our bodies are machines which learn and are able to change to meet a wide variety of different stresses. They do this by improving and combining our separate body systems effectively.

## Our nervous system page 36

Our senses tell us what is going on around us. Information about what is going on around us is sent through our nervous system to our brain. Also, our brain sends instructions along our nervous system to tell our working muscles what to do.

## Our hormonal system page 38

Hormones are chemical messengers. They are released into the bloodstream so that they can send messages around our bodies. These messengers control the workings of our bodies.

## Our digestive system page 39

All our energy for muscular work is provided by the food we eat. We need a balanced diet for good sporting performance and a healthy body.

## Our excretory system page 39

When in action, our bodies produce more waste products. These have to be removed. Gases are dealt with by the lungs, and other products by the kidneys.

# Our skeletal system

Without our skeletal systems we would look very different indeed. Our bodies would have no framework, our delicate organs would be unprotected, and we would be unable to move.

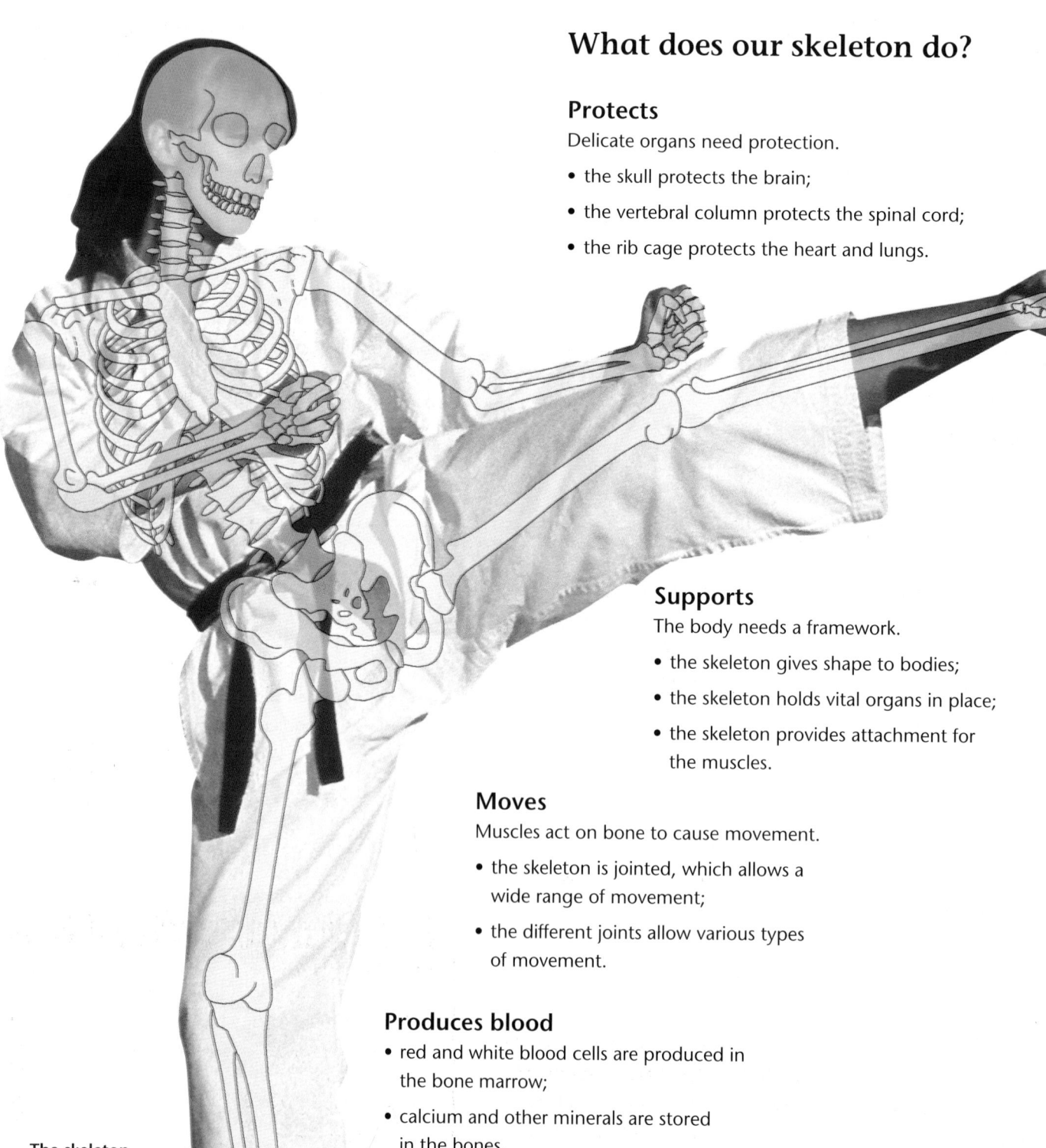

## What does our skeleton do?

### Protects

Delicate organs need protection.

- the skull protects the brain;
- the vertebral column protects the spinal cord;
- the rib cage protects the heart and lungs.

### Supports

The body needs a framework.

- the skeleton gives shape to bodies;
- the skeleton holds vital organs in place;
- the skeleton provides attachment for the muscles.

### Moves

Muscles act on bone to cause movement.

- the skeleton is jointed, which allows a wide range of movement;
- the different joints allow various types of movement.

### Produces blood

- red and white blood cells are produced in the bone marrow;
- calcium and other minerals are stored in the bones.

**The skeleton**

The skeleton

Skull

Clavicle
(collar bone)

Ribs

Sternum
(breast bone)

Vertebrae

Sacrum

Fibula

Tibia
(shin bone)

Tarsals

Metatarsals

Phalanges

Scapula
(shoulder blade)

Ulna

Phalanges

Femur
(thigh bone)

Patella
(kneecap)

Humerus

Radius

Carpals

Metacarpals

# Bone types

There are four basic types of bone (see diagram left). Their size and make up are linked to how we use them.

## Long

- These are the large bones in our legs and arms. They are used in the main movements of the body.

## Short

- These are the small bones at the joints of our hands and feet. They are used in the fine movements of the body.

## Flat

- These are the bones of the skull, shoulder girdle, ribs and pelvic girdle. They protect organs of the body. Large muscles can be attached to the flat bones.

## Irregular

- These are the bones in the face and vertebral column. They give the body protection and shape.

# How do our bones grow?

### In the embryo

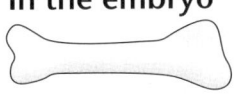

Cartilage with start of bone growth

In the embryo (our state before birth) most of the skeleton is made up of **cartilage**, which is a firm but elastic material.

### Young person

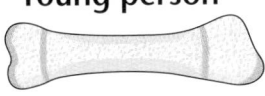

Bone continues to grow

As the embryo grows, the cartilage is changed to bone. The development of bone from cartilage is called **ossification**. Ossification also continues through childhood until adulthood.

### Adult

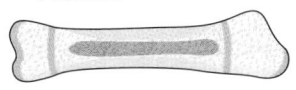

Mature bone

Bones are hard, rigid non-elastic materials. They are made up of calcium compounds which give them hardness. Collagen fibres make them strong and light.

# Bone growth and sport

Exercise helps the development of the skeleton in young people. Injuries to bone need careful treatment to avoid damage to growth areas.

## ⊙ EXTENSION

Ossification occurs in three ways:
1. Normal bone growth from embryo (before birth) to maturity.
2. Replacement of bone worn through normal daily activity.
3. Repair of bone damaged by accident or over-use.

# What are the main parts of our skeleton?

The skeleton is divided into the **axial skeleton** and **appendicular skeleton**.

**Axial skeleton**
Skull
Vertebral column
Ribs
Sternum

**Appendicular skeleton**
Arms
**Shoulder girdle**
Legs
**Hip girdle**

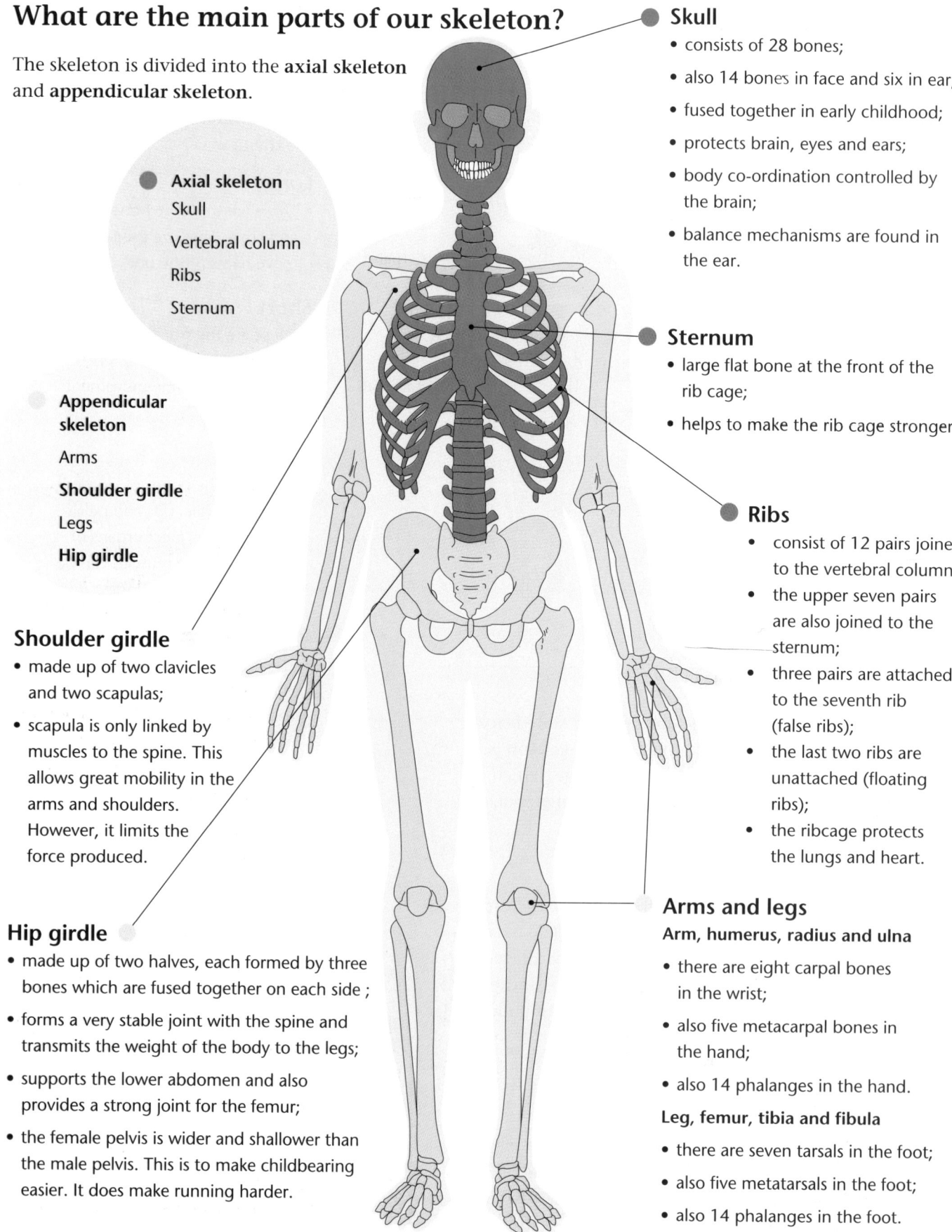

### Skull

- consists of 28 bones;
- also 14 bones in face and six in ear;
- fused together in early childhood;
- protects brain, eyes and ears;
- body co-ordination controlled by the brain;
- balance mechanisms are found in the ear.

### Sternum

- large flat bone at the front of the rib cage;
- helps to make the rib cage stronger.

### Ribs

- consist of 12 pairs joined to the vertebral column;
- the upper seven pairs are also joined to the sternum;
- three pairs are attached to the seventh rib (false ribs);
- the last two ribs are unattached (floating ribs);
- the ribcage protects the lungs and heart.

### Shoulder girdle

- made up of two clavicles and two scapulas;
- scapula is only linked by muscles to the spine. This allows great mobility in the arms and shoulders. However, it limits the force produced.

### Hip girdle

- made up of two halves, each formed by three bones which are fused together on each side ;
- forms a very stable joint with the spine and transmits the weight of the body to the legs;
- supports the lower abdomen and also provides a strong joint for the femur;
- the female pelvis is wider and shallower than the male pelvis. This is to make childbearing easier. It does make running harder.

### Arms and legs

**Arm, humerus, radius and ulna**

- there are eight carpal bones in the wrist;
- also five metacarpal bones in the hand;
- also 14 phalanges in the hand.

**Leg, femur, tibia and fibula**

- there are seven tarsals in the foot;
- also five metatarsals in the foot;
- also 14 phalanges in the foot.

**Axial and appendicular skeleton**

# Our vertebral column

The **vertebral column** is also known as the spine or spinal column. It is made up of 33 small specialised bones called vertebrae. The vertebral column is divided into five regions, each of which have their own type of vertebrae and individual functions. Between each vertebra is a disc of cartilage called a **vertebral disk**. This cartilage is a thick circle of tough tissue. It acts as a shock absorber throughout the vertebral column and allows movement between vertebrae.

> ## ⮕ KEY POINT
>
> **The vertebral column:**
> - protects the spinal cord;
> - supports the upper body;
> - allows a wide-range of movement;
> - is important for posture;
> - transmits force to body parts.

Our vertebral column has many joints, making it flexible but strong

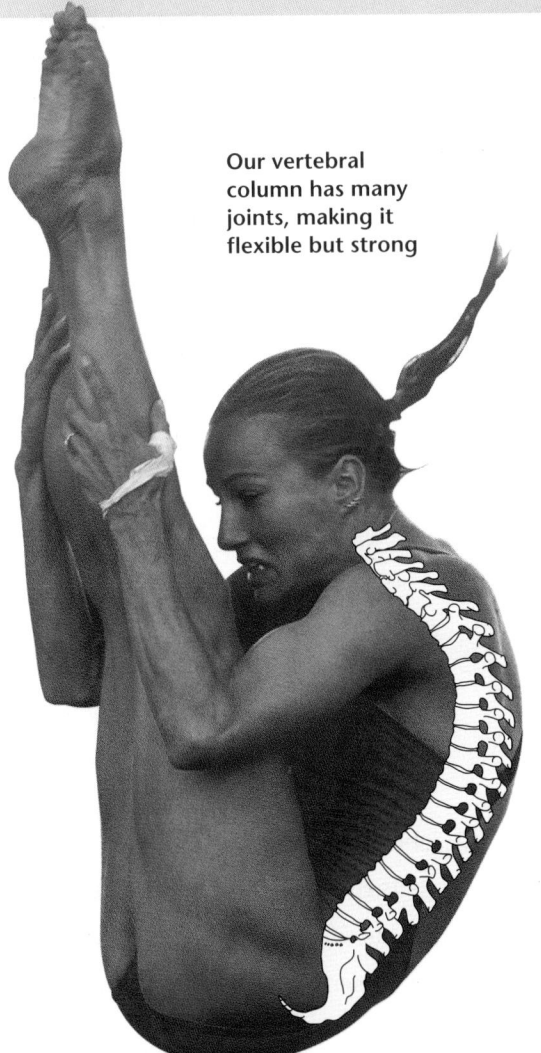

# The vertebral column and sport

The vertebral column is important in all sporting movement. Its large number of joints allows for an extreme range of movement. Its structure also makes injury possible. As spinal injuries may be disabling, or even life threatening, we should treat them all very seriously.

- ## Seven cervical vertebrae
  - these provide attachment for the neck muscles;
  - the top vertebra, the **Atlas**, fits into the skull and allows the head to be nodded;
  - the second vertebra, the **Axis**, allows the head to be rotated.

- ## 12 thoracic
  - the thoracic vertebrae are connected to the ribs;
  - they also support the rib cage;
  - the thoracic vertebrae allow some bending forward, backward and from side to side and rotation.

- ## Five lumbar
  - these are larger vertebrae which provide attachment for the back muscles;
  - they allow bending forward, backward and from side to side;
  - this large range of movement makes the area liable to injury.

- ## Five sacral
  - the sacral vertebrae are fused together. In turn they are joined to the pelvic girdle;
  - the sacral vertebrae provide a very strong structure which supports the weight of the body;
  - they also transmit force from the legs and the hips to the upper body.

- ## Four coccyx
  - the four bones of the coccyx are fused together and have no special use.

Gymnasts, demonstrating flexibility

# How do we move?

The skeleton is jointed so that the muscles can move the bones and so cause movement. There are over 100 different joints within our bodies. They can be put into three different groups based on the amount of movement they allow. These groups are: immovable joints; slightly movable joints; and freely movable joints.

**1. Immovable joints (fibrous)**
- immovable joints are fixed joints;
- with them, no movement is possible between the bones;
- examples are found between the flat bones of the skull (suture) and between the bones of the pelvic girdle.

**2. Slightly movable joints (cartilaginous)**
- the bones in slightly movable joints are linked by cartilage;
- this allows for slight movement;
- examples are found in the joints of the vertebral column and the joints between the ribs and the sternum.

**3. Freely movable joints (synovial)**
**Synovial joints** are complex joints.
- there are a number of types of freely movable joints;
- they make possible a wide variety of movement;
- examples are found throughout the body including in the knee, hip and shoulder.

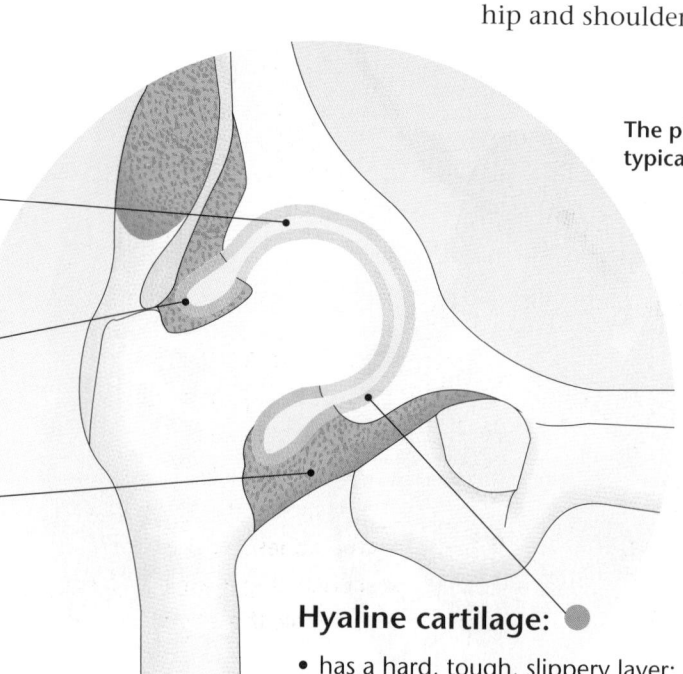

The picture shows a typical synovial joint

**Synovial fluid:**
- is found within the joint;
- lubricates the joint;
- allows friction free movement.

**Synovial membrane:**
- is a layer on the inside of the capsule;
- secretes the synovial fluid.

**Ligaments:**
- are bands of tough, fibrous tissue;
- vary in shape and size;
- hold bones together at the joints;
- limit the range of movement;
- prevent dislocation;
- are joint capsules which surround the joint.

**Hyaline cartilage:**
- has a hard, tough, slippery layer;
- covers the head of bones forming the joint;
- protects the bone;
- reduces friction within the joint.

## How is hyaline cartilage different?

Hyaline cartilage is found in all synovial joints and is different from other forms of cartilage found in the body. For example, cartilage in the knee and vertebral column are pads of tough cartilage which act as shock absorbers.

## Types of synovial joint

There are six basic types of synovial joint:

- Ball and socket
- Pivot
- Hinge
- Gliding (plane)
- Saddle
- Condyloid (ellipsoidal)

The individual structure of each joint makes it possible to look at some joints in more than one way. For example, our knee joint is constructed as a condyloid joint but actually works as a hinge joint. In other words, the knee joint can fit into more than one category of synovial joint.

### 2. Pivot joint

Only rotation is possible. This is due to its ring on peg structure, for example between the axis and atlas in the neck.

### 4. Gliding joint

One bone slides on top of another. The movement is limited only by the strong connecting ligaments, for example the carpal bones in the hand.

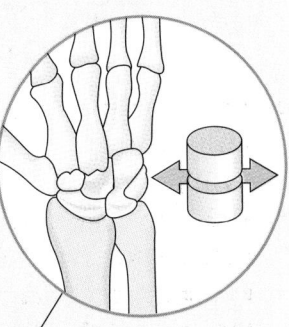

### 1. Ball and socket joint

The ball and socket joint moves freely in all directions. Stability is provided by ligaments for example the hip.

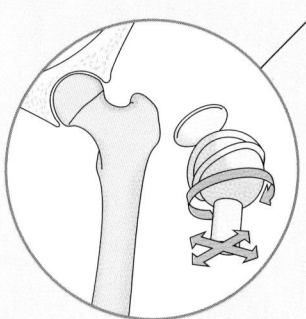

### 3. Hinge joint

The hinge joint moves in one plane only. Movement is limited because of the shape of the bones and the strong connecting ligaments, for example the elbow.

### 5. Saddle joint

This joint allows movement in two planes at right angles to each other. Movement is limited because of the shape of the bones, for example the thumb.

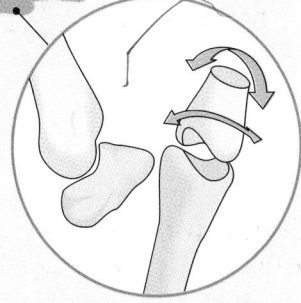

### 6. Condyloid joint

Movement is possible in two planes. The ligaments prevent rotation, for example the wrist.

# How does our body move?

Our bodies have many joints which enable us to move in different ways. We use special words to describe these movements.

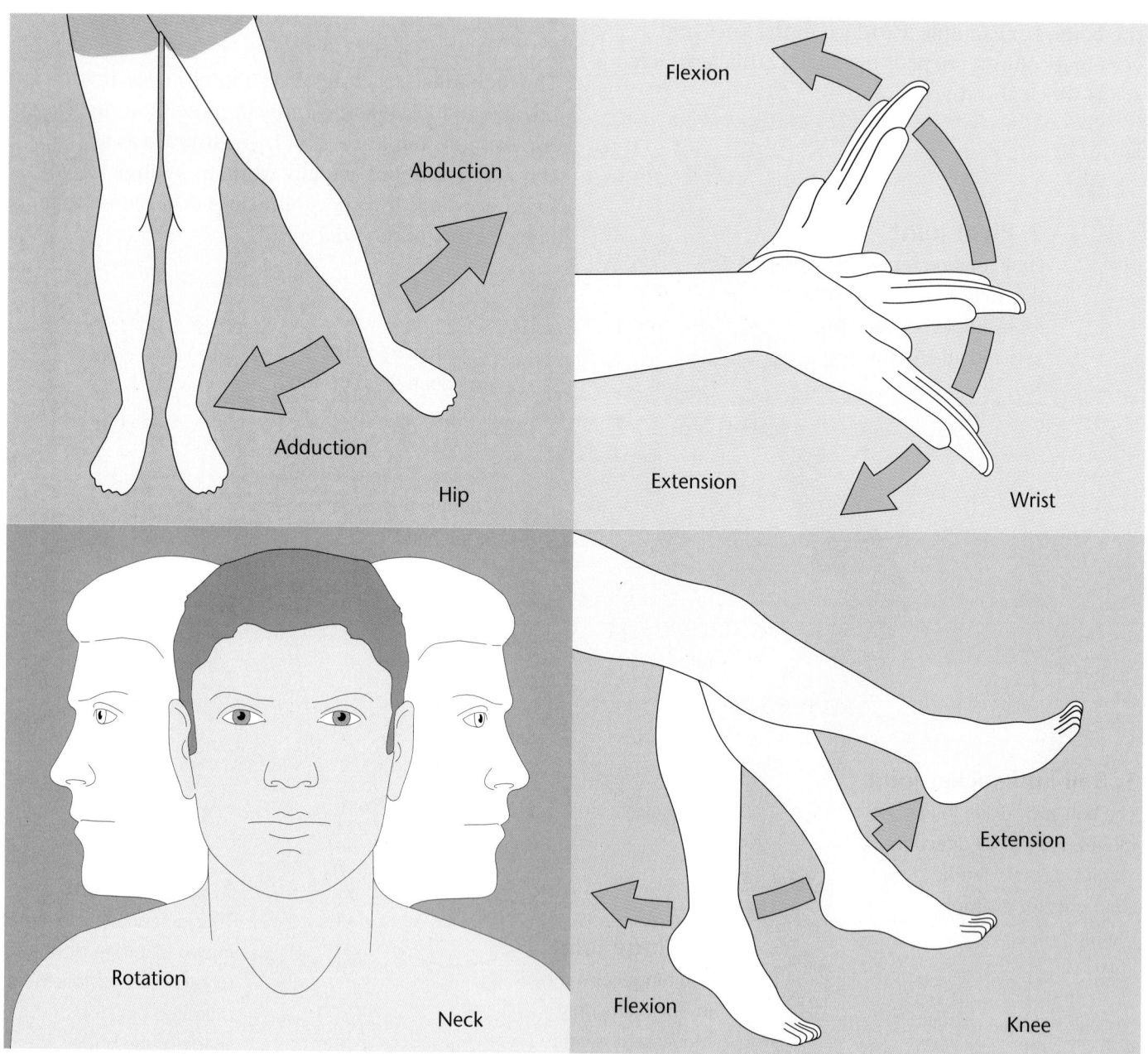

# What happens to our skeletal system as we exercise?

**Exercise** is essential for proper bone growth. It will increase bone width, bone density and, therefore, bone strength. It appears to have no effect on bone length. Lack of physical activity will lead to loss of both bone mass and density and will, therefore, weaken bones.

# Questions

## Our Body Systems

### The skeletal system

1  **a** Name two functions of the skeleton.
   **b** Bones belong to either the axial or appendicular skeleton. Look at the labels on a skeleton. Write them out under the headings 'Axial' and 'Appendicular'.

2  **a** Name two types of bone and describe their function.
   **b** Name one of the bones of the forearm.
   **c** Give one example of a slightly movable joint.

3  The anatomical name for the kneecap is:
   **i** Cranium
   **ii** Femur
   **iii** Patella
   **iv** Tarsus

4  Which of the following has a ball and socket joint?
   **i** Ankle
   **ii** Hip
   **iii** Knee
   **iv** Skull

5  **a** What name is given to the end of the long bones where growth takes place?
   **b** What purpose does calcium serve in the growth of bone?
   **c** Name the tough membrane that surrounds a bone.

6  **a** Give the main function of the vertebral column.
   **b** What is unusual about the sacral region of the spine?
   **c** The sacral region is one region of the vertebral column. Name two others.

7  Define the term 'joint'.

8  Name the type of joint at the following parts of the body:
   **i** Elbow
   **ii** Neck (atlas and axis)
   **iii** Thumb
   **iv** Vertebrae

9  Identify the main bones of the shoulder girdle involved in the throwing of a cricket ball.

10  Name three types of movement possible at the hip joint.

# Our muscular system

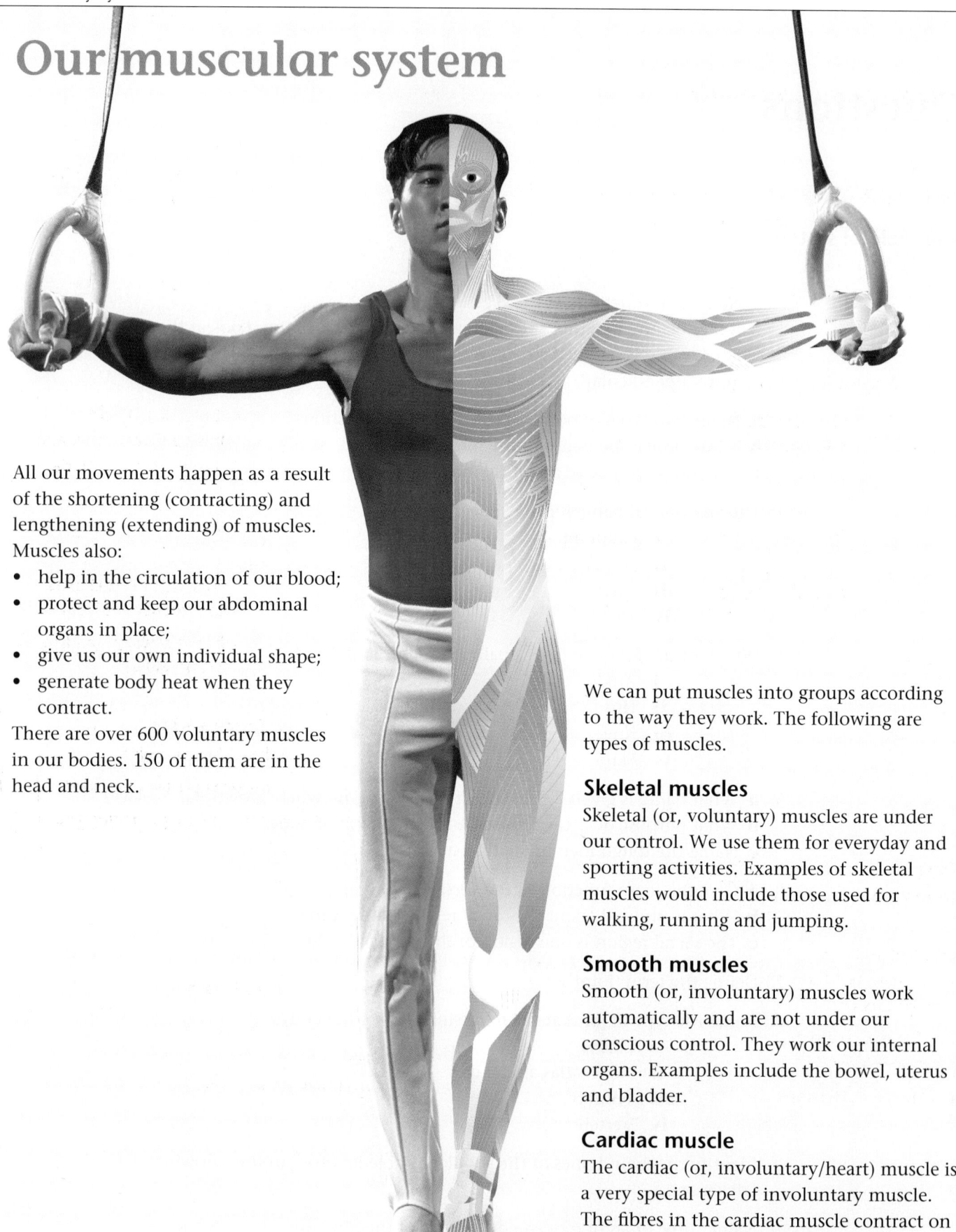

All our movements happen as a result of the shortening (contracting) and lengthening (extending) of muscles. Muscles also:

- help in the circulation of our blood;
- protect and keep our abdominal organs in place;
- give us our own individual shape;
- generate body heat when they contract.

There are over 600 voluntary muscles in our bodies. 150 of them are in the head and neck.

We can put muscles into groups according to the way they work. The following are types of muscles.

## Skeletal muscles

Skeletal (or, voluntary) muscles are under our control. We use them for everyday and sporting activities. Examples of skeletal muscles would include those used for walking, running and jumping.

## Smooth muscles

Smooth (or, involuntary) muscles work automatically and are not under our conscious control. They work our internal organs. Examples include the bowel, uterus and bladder.

## Cardiac muscle

The cardiac (or, involuntary/heart) muscle is a very special type of involuntary muscle. The fibres in the cardiac muscle contract on their own and they work all the time without tiring. The heart muscle is under constant nervous and chemical control.

**Our main muscles**

# Our muscles in action

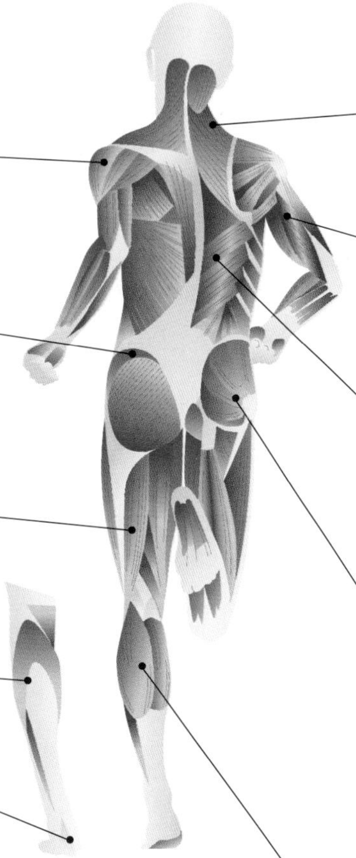

**Deltoids**
- these move the arm in all directions at the shoulder (depending on which part of the arm is working).

**Gluteus medius**
- this abducts the hip joint;
- it is used in walking.

**Hamstrings**
- these extend the hip joint;
- they flex the knee joint.

**Soleus**

**Achilles tendon**

**Trapezius**
- this helps to control the shoulder girdle.

**Triceps**
- these extend the forearm at the elbow;
- they extend the arm at the shoulder.

**Latissimus dorsi**
- these adduct and extend the arm at the shoulder;
- they are involved in coughing.

**Gluteus maximus**
- this extends the hip joint;
- it is used when standing and climbing.

**Gastrocnemius**
- this flexes the knee joint;
- the plantar flexes the ankle joint;
- it is used in walking, running and jumping.

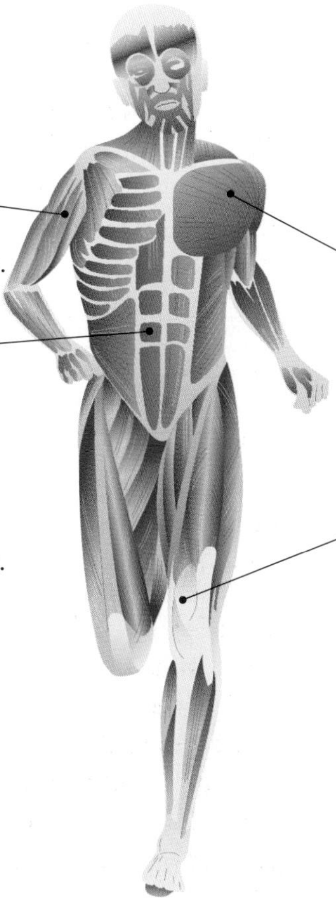

**Biceps**
- These rotate and bend the forearm at the elbow.

**Abdominals**
- these strengthen the abdominal wall;
- they flex and rotate the vertebral column;
- they help with breathing.

**Pectorals**
- these move the arm and shoulder;
- they are also involved in deep breathing.

**Quadriceps**
- these straighten the leg at the knee.

# Do our muscles all work in the same way?

There are three types of muscular contraction:

1. isometric;
2. isokinetic;
3. isotonic (these can be eccentric or concentric).

## Isometric contraction

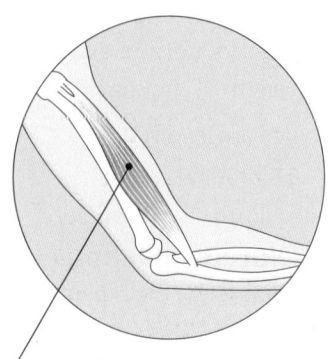

Tension is high but there is no movement

**Isometric contraction** takes place when the muscles remain the same length throughout the contraction. Many of our stabilising muscles work in this way. They hold parts of the body steady as other parts move.

In a tug of war where there is little movement, our muscles work isometrically

## Isokinetic contraction

**Isokinetic contraction** occurs when the speed of the movement stays the same throughout the range of movement. Although the muscles work at their maximum, the force they produce will vary. We need specialised equipment to exercise in this way.

## Isotonic and eccentric contraction

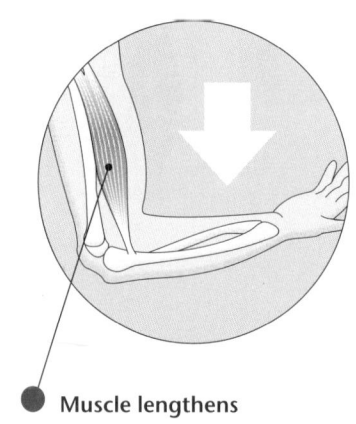

Muscle lengthens

## Isotonic and concentric contraction

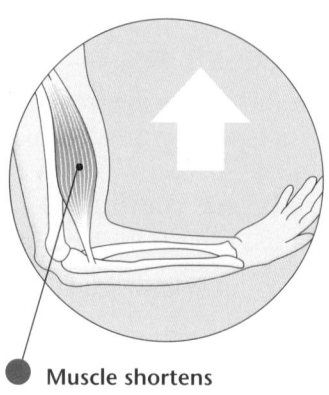

Muscle shortens

- **Isotonic contraction** takes place when a muscle is working concentrically or eccentrically.
- **Eccentric contraction** takes place when the muscles are under tension as they lengthen. The ends of the muscles move further apart.
- **Concentric contraction** takes place when the muscle shortens as it contracts. The ends of the muscles move closer together.

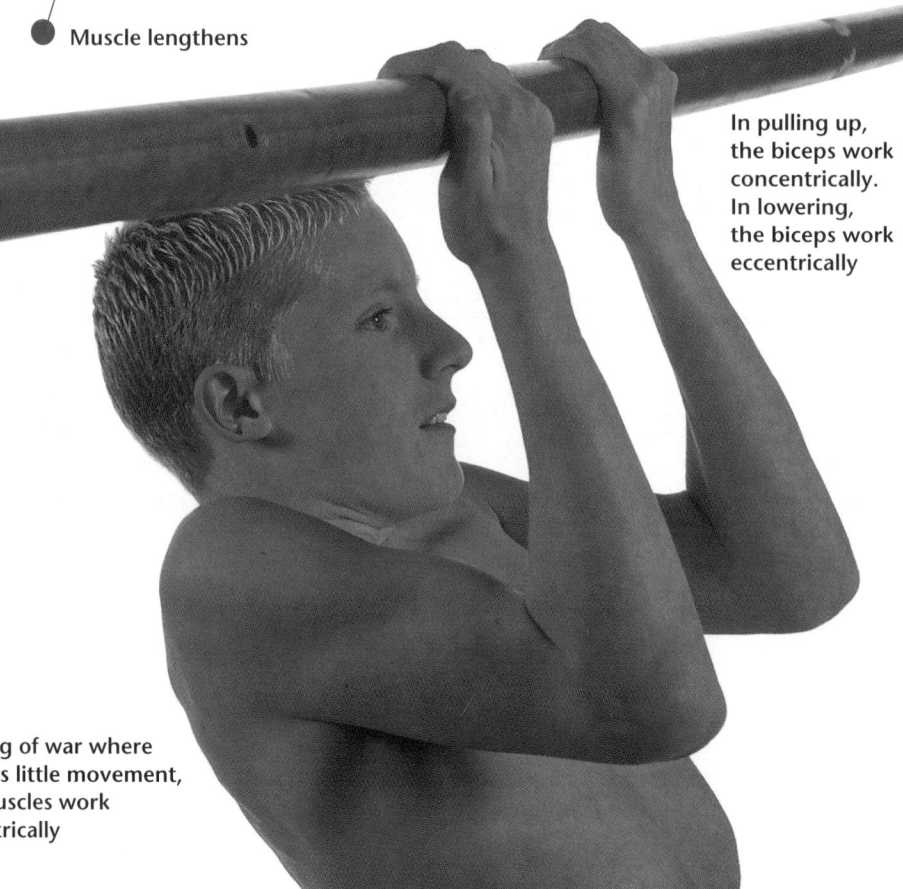

In pulling up, the biceps work concentrically. In lowering, the biceps work eccentrically

# What are the different types of fibres we find in muscle?

There are two different types of muscle fibres which we find in muscles: fast twitch and slow twitch muscle fibres.

**Slow twitch muscle fibres** have a very good oxygen supply. They work for long periods of time without tiring. Slow twitch fibres are not as big or as strong as the fast twitch muscle fibres. They also take longer to contract. Slow twitch fibres are used in all types of exercise.

**Fast twitch muscle fibres** contract very quickly. They are bigger and stronger than the slow twitch fibres. They are used whenever rapid, powerful movements are needed. They work anaerobically. They do not have a good oxygen supply and get tired very quickly. Fast twitch fibres are only used in high intensity exercise.

There are two types of fast twitch fibres: fast twitch glycolytic and fast twitch oxidative.

The fast twitch oxidative fibres have a better oxygen supply than the fast twitch glycolytic fibres. We can train the fast twitch oxidative fibres better for aerobic activities (see also chapter 3).

# How do these different types of fibre work together?

When we walk or jog slowly, only a few of our slow twitch fibres will be working. If we increase our speed we will use more slow twitch fibres so that our muscles can cope. If we are working too hard for the slow twitch muscles then some of our fast twitch oxidative muscle fibres will also start to work. More and more will start to work as we work harder and harder. When we are working at our maximum then our fast twitch glycolytic fibres will also be working. Slow twitch fibres are important for aerobic work. Fast twitch fibres are important for high intensity anaerobic work (see chapter 3).

# Do we all have the same amount of fast and slow twitch fibres?

Our muscles are made up of both fast and slow twitch fibres. Most of us have about 50% fast and 50% slow twitch fibres. The amount we have does vary and appears to be fixed at birth. Good long distance runners, cyclists, rowers and cross-country skiers have more slow twitch fibres in the leg and shoulder muscles. Good sprinters, jumpers, throwers have more fast twitch fibres. If we wish to train the fast twitch fibres we must work hard enough to use them (see page 56).

**Both our fast twitch and slow twitch fibres will be contracting when we are cycling very fast**

# Muscles working together

Our muscles can pull by contraction but they cannot push. If one muscle contracts across a joint to bring the two bones together, then another muscle is needed to pull them apart. In other words, muscles always work in pairs. Even simple body movements need a large number of muscles to work together in different ways.

Our muscles work as prime movers, antagonists, fixators and synergists at different times. Their action is linked to the movements taking place.

**Prime movers** (or agonists) produce the movement.

**Antagonists** are muscles which work against the prime movers.

**Synergists** reduce unnecessary movement when the prime mover contracts. They can also fine tune the movement.

**Fixators** steady parts of the body to give the working muscles a firm base.

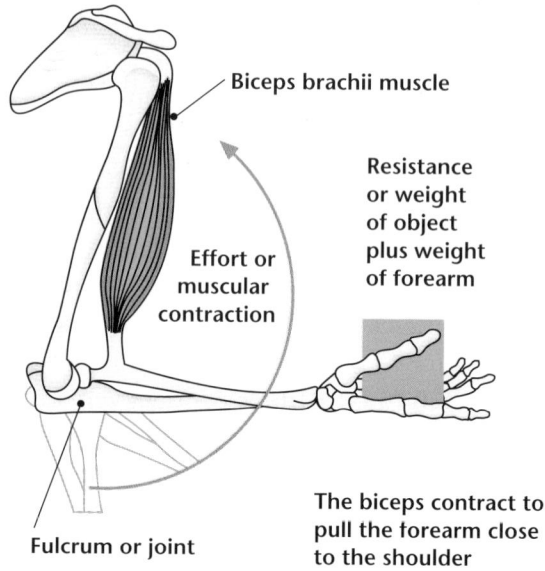

Biceps brachii muscle

Resistance or weight of object plus weight of forearm

Effort or muscular contraction

Fulcrum or joint

The biceps contract to pull the forearm close to the shoulder

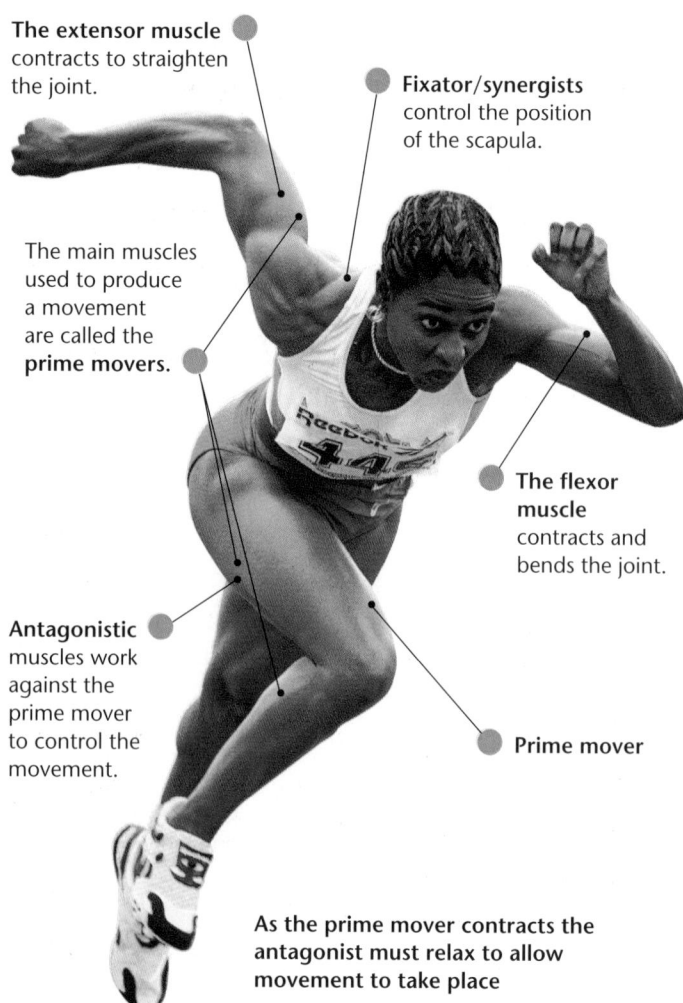

The extensor muscle contracts to straighten the joint.

Fixator/synergists control the position of the scapula.

The main muscles used to produce a movement are called the prime movers.

The flexor muscle contracts and bends the joint.

Antagonistic muscles work against the prime mover to control the movement.

Prime mover

As the prime mover contracts the antagonist must relax to allow movement to take place

## How do our muscles work in pairs?

When the prime mover contracts, the antagonist must relax to allow movement to take place. The antagonist muscle will keep some fibres contracting. This is to stop the prime mover moving the joint so fiercely that the antagonists are damaged. It can also control the action of the agonists.

## Muscle tone

All the time, some muscle fibres in our bodies are contracting whilst others are relaxed. This is true even when no limb movement is taking place. These contractions tighten the muscles but are not strong enough to cause movement. Different fibres contract at different times to prevent fatigue. This is called **muscle tone**. It is very important for good posture.

## Tendons

Tendons:
- attach muscle to bone;
- vary in size and shape;
- attach one end of a muscle to a fixed point (the origin);
- attach the other end of the muscle to the moving part of the body (the insertion).

# What is good posture?

Our bodies are unstable when we are in an upright position. This is because we have a high centre of gravity and a small base of support. If we have good **posture** we can keep our bodies upright easily by keeping our centre of gravity over our base of support. Most of the weight of our bodies will be supported by our bones. We need only a little help from muscles such as the gluteals soleus, abdominals and trapezius, which hold us upright. When we slouch, our upper back muscles must contract to move the body to the correct posture. If we continue to slouch the muscles will gradually adapt to that position. Our poor posture may then become permanent.

**Poor posture**

**Good posture**

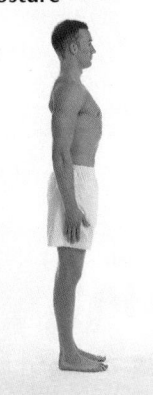

**Poor posture**

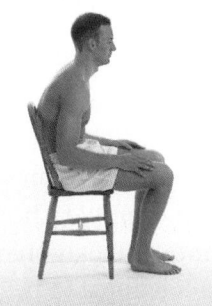

**Good posture**

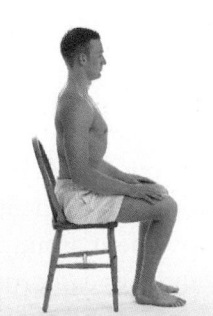

**Poor posture**

**Good posture**

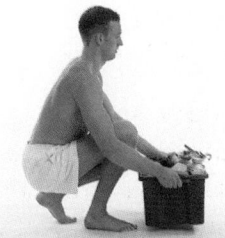

## How can we have good posture when standing and walking?

- stand with head up;
- keep shoulders straight and chest forward;
- balance weight evenly on both feet;
- flex one hip by supporting one foot higher than the other, if standing still for a long time;
- wear sensible shoes.

Poor body posture when standing results in the body being out of line. This means the muscles have to work harder.

## How can we have good posture when sitting?

- choose chairs that support the small of the back;
- sit back in the chair to support the lower back;
- ensure working surfaces are at the correct height;
- try to have knees higher than hips;
- have a break after 20 minutes and gently exercise arms and shoulders.

## How can we have good posture when lifting?

- never bend forwards without bending the knees;
- keep the back flat and straight;
- try to avoid lifting anything above the level of the elbows;
- keep objects as close to centre of gravity as possible;
- extend legs in order to lift objects;
- keep head up and eyes looking forward.

A long arm allows force to be applied over a wide range of movement.

## How are muscles and leverage linked together?

Muscles and **leverage** are linked together in the following way. Movement takes place when the skeletal muscles pull hard enough on the bones to make them move. They use the bones as levers. Levers have a hinge at one point and forces are applied to them at two other points.

In our bodies, the joint is the hinge. One of the forces operating on it is the weight of the body, another may be an object like a ball or discus.

The other force is the **muscular power** we use to move our bodies or throw the object.

The length of the limb has a definite effect on the movement around the joint. For example, short arms and legs can produce speed more quickly than long limbs. However, long limbs allow force to be used over a greater distance. Our physical build will determine which sports we have an advantage in.

## What happens to our muscular system as we exercise?

- there is an increased flow of blood to working muscles;
- more oxygen is taken up from the blood at the working muscles;
- there are more muscular contractions;
- more muscle fibres in the working muscles contract;
- the temperature of working muscles increases;
- stores of **ATP** and **CP** are reduced (see chapter 2);
- stores of muscle glycogen are reduced (see chapter 2).

# Questions

## Our body Systems

### The muscular system

1 Muscles work together to produce and control movement. Explain how this happens and give an example to illustrate your answer.

2 Write out the following definitions and match them to the terms provided below.

    **i** Muscles that straighten a limb at a joint
    **ii** Muscles that are used to produce movement
    **iii** Muscles that bend a limb at a joint
    **iv** Muscles that relax to allow movement to take place

PRIME MOVERS; EXTENSORS; FLEXORS; ANTAGONIST

3 **a** Describe three forms of muscle contraction.
  **b** Whilst you are doing a press up, what type of muscular contraction is taking place in your triceps as you:
    **i** raise yourself off the floor?
    **ii** hold the press up position?

4 Consider the action of an athlete running. Identify the main muscles of the legs involved in the movement.

5 Name three different types of muscle and give one example of each.

6 Describe what is meant by the following types of muscle movement and give an example of each in your answers.
    **i** Contraction
    **ii** Relaxation

7 Where is cardiac muscle found? What is unique about it?

8 "Muscles are always ready for action. They remain in a state of very slight tension." What is being described?

9 Describe slow and fast twitch muscles. Explain how they relate to prolonged and explosive types of physical activity.

10 Name the two major movements that occur at the knee and name the main muscle involved in each.

# Our circulatory system

The circulatory system is made up of blood, blood vessels, **pulmonary** and **systemic circulation**, and the heart.

Our **systemic circulation** carries oxygenated blood and nutrition around the body. It returns with waste products that have to be removed from our body.

Our **pulmonary circulation** carries deoxygenated blood from the heart to the lungs. Here carbon dioxide is exchanged for oxygen. Oxygenated blood is then carried back to the heart.

## The circulatory system

The circulatory system:

- *takes* oxygen and nutrients to every cell;
- *removes* carbon dioxide and other waste products from every cell;
- *carries* **hormones** from the **endocrine glands** to different parts of the body;
- *maintains* temperature and fluid levels within the body;
- *prevents* infection from invading organisms.

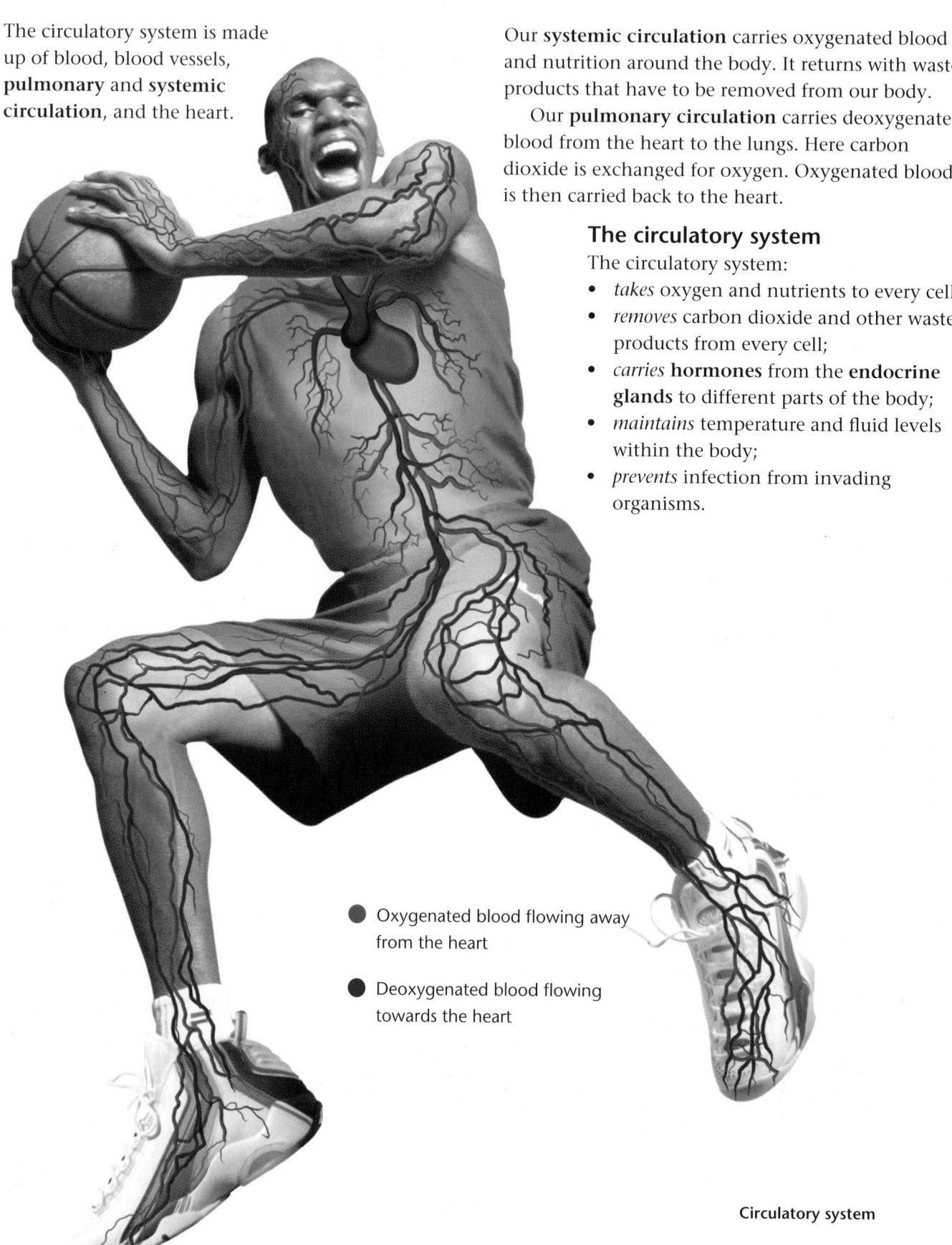

● Oxygenated blood flowing away from the heart

● Deoxygenated blood flowing towards the heart

**Circulatory system**

# How does our heart work?

Our heart works in the following way:

1 • when we are at rest, our heart pumps between 50 and 80 times a minute. The heart pumps 4.7 litres or so of blood around the body. At rest, our blood will take about 20 seconds to go around once;

• during hard physical work, our heart rate can increase to over 200 beats per minute. The heart of a trained athlete can pump up to 45 litres of blood a minute;

• deoxygenated blood enters the right atrium through the two vena cava. In its journey around the body the blood has lost or given up much of its own oxygen. It has picked up a number of waste products, including carbon dioxide. It is a dull red colour;

• the newly oxygenated blood enters the left atrium. At this point the heart is between beats and the atrium is relaxed;

2 • the atrium muscles contract to pump the blood through the tricuspid valve and into the right ventricle;

• the atrium muscles contract and the blood is pushed into the left ventricle;

3 • the ventricle muscles contract and the blood is pumped out of the heart. It goes through the semilunar valves, in the pulmonary artery, to the lungs. In the lungs, the blood releases carbon dioxide and is supplied with fresh oxygen. The blood is now scarlet in colour. It returns to the heart in the pulmonary vein;

• the ventricle muscles contract. The blood is pumped out of the heart and into the largest artery, the aorta. It then goes on another journey around the body.

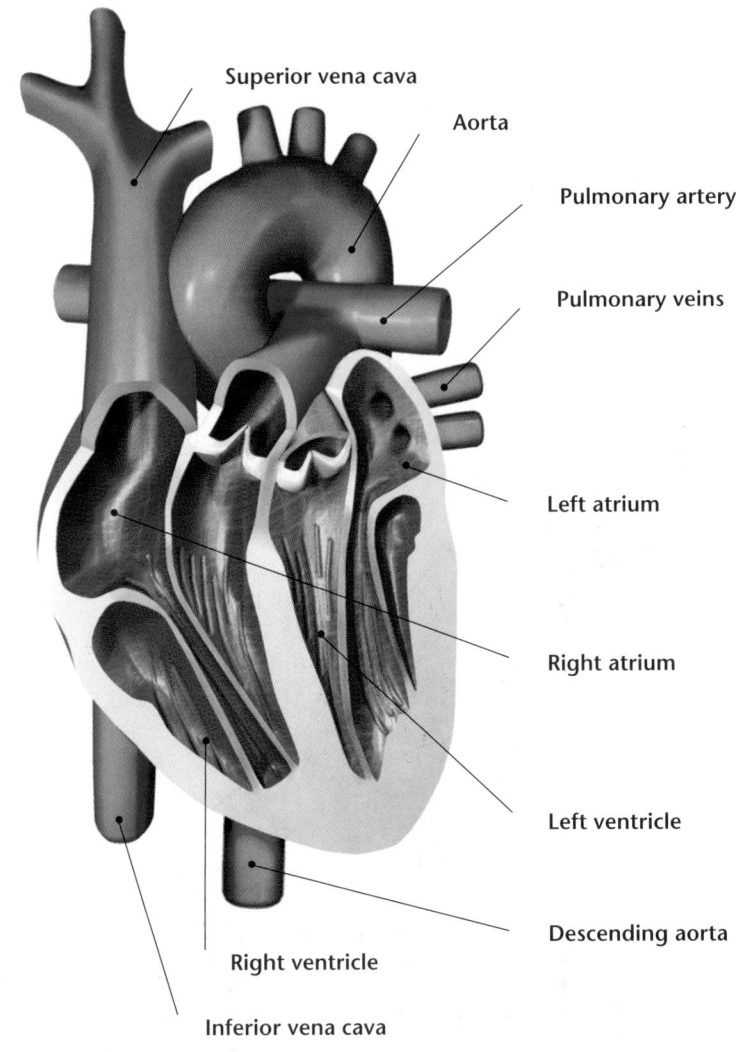

The structure of our heart

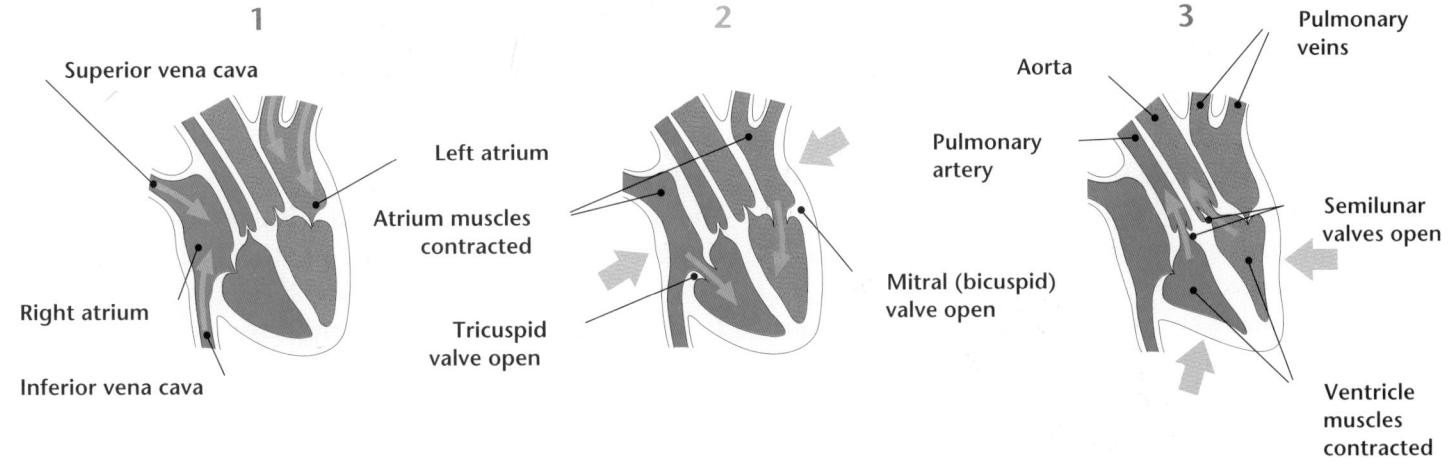

Our heart in action

# How is blood carried around our bodies?

Blood vessels carry the blood from our hearts to the tissues and back. The blood is freshly oxygenated.

Arteries are used to carry this blood from our hearts. The arteries become smaller and smaller. The smallest arteries are called arterioles. These join up with the smallest vessels called capillaries.

## Blood vessels

### The structure of our arteries:

Arteries carry blood away from the heart. The blood is under high pressure. Artery walls are very elastic; they can expand to carry the blood pumped by the heart. Artery walls can contract – they force the blood towards the capillaries.

### The structure of our veins:

The walls of veins are quite thin and non-elastic. Some veins have valves to ensure that blood flows only in one direction.

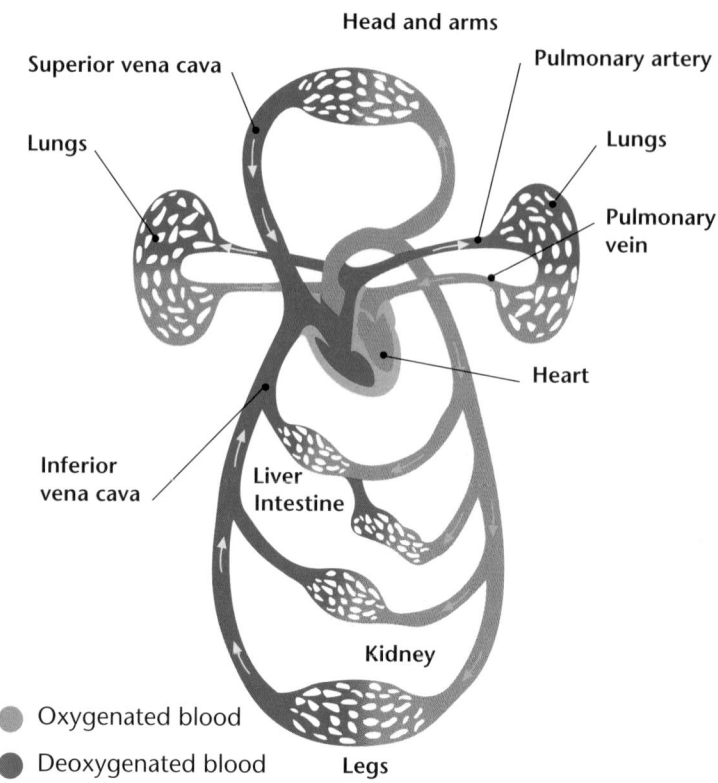

General plan of the circulaton

- Oxygenated blood
- Deoxygenated blood

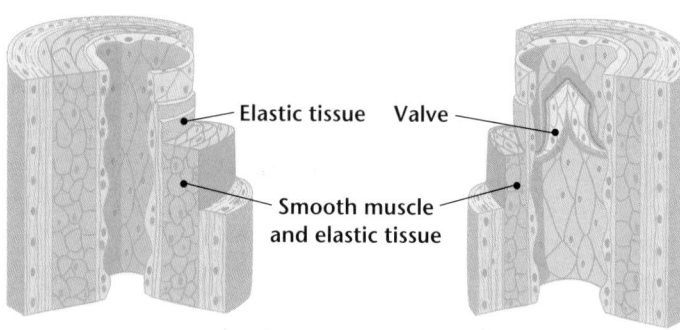

Structure of an artery — Elastic tissue, Smooth muscle and elastic tissue

Structure of a vein — Valve

## Valves

The deoxygenated blood (without oxygen and dull red in colour) moves from the capillaries into the tiniest of veins, called venules. They join together to form larger and larger veins which carry the blood back to the heart. Deoxygenated blood enters the heart from the largest veins, the vena cava. As the blood is at low pressure in the veins, the veins are supplied with valves at short distances along their length. The valves keep the blood flowing in one direction only. It is not able to flow backwards.

## Capillaries

Capillaries are tiny vessels with walls only one cell thick. Oxygen passes through these thin walls into the tissues. Carbon dioxide, dissolved food and other products are exchanged for the oxygen. They go from the tissues into the capillaries. The capillary network is extremely large. In active tissues, such as muscle and the brain, it is also fine and dense. It is less dense in less active tissue.

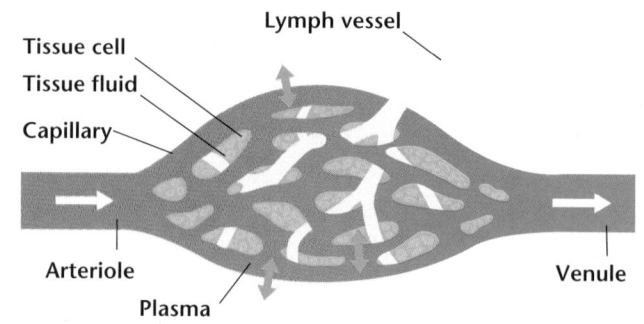

Tissue cell, Tissue fluid, Capillary, Arteriole, Plasma, Lymph vessel, Venule

Plasma and oxygen from the red blood cells pass through the capillary walls and into the tissue fluid. Waste products pass from the lymph cells through the tissue fluid back into the capillaries or the lymph vessels.

A great deal of the food and oxygen reaching the cells is carried by a colourless liquid called lymph. Lymph is made up of plasma and white cells which squeeze out of the capillaries. Lymph bathes all cells and tissues.

# What is blood?

Our blood is a fluid which links all the other tissues and the organs
of the body. Its three main functions in sporting activities are:

* *transportation*. For example it carries oxygen to the working muscles;
* *temperature regulation*. The heat given off by the working muscles is
  reduced as it is spread throughout the body;
* *acidic balance*. The blood can reduce the effect of lactic acid in
  the muscles. This will allow physical activity to continue.

# What makes up blood?

The total volume of blood varies a lot from one
person to another. It depends mainly on our body
size. The average amounts are five to six litres in men
and four to five litres in women. Amounts are higher
in people who train for endurance.

Blood is made up of plasma (a watery liquid), solid
cells and parts of cells known as formed elements.
Blood plasma makes up about 55% of blood volume.
This percentage can be increased by 10% or more by
endurance training.

The formed elements make up about 45% of blood
volume. They are made up of red blood cells
(erythrocytes), white blood cells (leucocytes) and
platelets (thrombocytes).

**55% plasma**

90% water

7% plasma
proteins

3% other

**45% formed
elements**

99% red
blood cells

1% white blood
cells and platelets

## Red blood cells (Erythrocytes)

**Red blood cells:**

* give the blood its colour;
* are produced in the red
  marrow of the bones,
  such as the sternum, the
  ribs and vertebrae;
* contain haemoglobin,
  which transports oxygen
  from the lungs to the cells.
  It is the iron in the
  haemoglobin which
  binds oxygen to the red
  blood cells;
* have no nucleus and last
  for about 120 days;
* are replaced by the body
  in very large numbers.

## White blood cells (Leucocytes)

**White blood cells:**

* are made in the bone
  marrow, the lymph
  nodes and the spleen;
* are three times the size
  of red blood cells;
* are a mobile guard and
  repair system to deal
  with disease and damage
  to the body.

## Platelets (Thrombocytes)

**Platelets:**

* are formed in the bone
  marrow;
* help to produce clotting
  when a blood vessel is
  damaged;
* work with fibrinogen to
  make blood clot.

# What is blood pressure?

Each time it beats, our heart pumps blood through the arteries. Pressure can be felt in the arteries as they expand to allow blood to flow through them. The pulse can be felt at points on the body where our arteries are near to the surface.

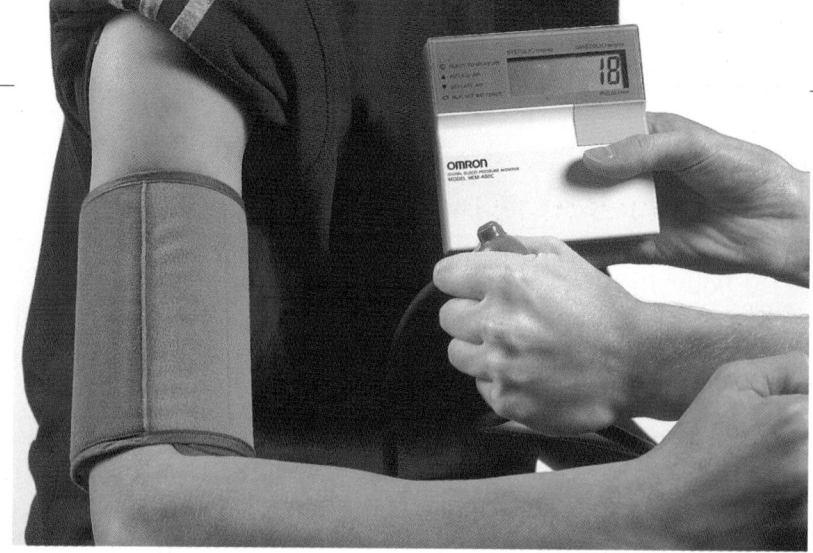

Athlete having blood pressure taken

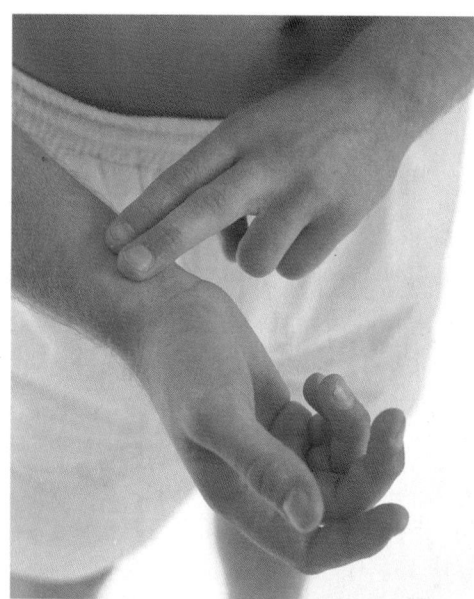

You can feel the pulse in your wrist

# How do we measure blood pressure?

We use a special instrument to measure the pressure needed to stop the flow of blood through an artery. Two readings are taken: the systolic and the diastolic. The systolic pressure is the maximum reading as the heart contracts and pumps blood into the arteries. The diastolic pressure is the minimum reading as the heart is relaxed and fills with blood. Our blood pressure should be taken when we are relaxed and resting. It will therefore be at its lowest.

# Why do we measure blood pressure?

Our blood pressure tells us how hard the heart has to work to push the blood through the arteries, capillaries and veins. It also tells us about the health of our arteries, capillaries and veins.

# What will affect blood pressure?

**Blood pressure** can be affected by:

### Age
Blood pressure increases as we grow older. The arteries of older people are less elastic. They do not expand so much when blood is pumped through them.

### Exercise
Our blood pressure increases when we exercise. This is because the heart has to beat faster to supply more oxygen to the working muscles. It returns to normal after exercise. Regular exercise helps to lower our resting blood pressure. It helps prevent cardiovascular disease.

### Stress and tension
Stress and tension increase blood pressure. This is because the 'fight or flight' hormones are released into the bloodstream.

### Cigarette smoking
Cigarette smoking increases blood pressure, because nicotine reduces the efficiency of our capillaries. The effects last for at least 20 minutes after each cigarette.

### Diet
A diet which is high in fat, or salt, may lead to a permanent increase in blood pressure. Fatty deposits block up and harden the artery walls so that they become less elastic and narrower.

# What does high blood pressure mean?

A person has high blood pressure (or **hypertension**) if both systolic and diastolic readings stay high over a long period of time. High blood pressure may be caused by blockages in the smaller blood vessels. The heart has to work harder to force the blood around the body. The heart responds to this extra work by increasing in size. The greater pressure from the heart puts even more strain on the now less springy artery walls. If they rupture in the brain, a stroke will occur. The arteries taking blood to the heart muscles can also become blocked. They may become less elastic as fat builds up on their walls. If, for example, a person runs for a bus, there will be a sudden demand on the heart. The heart muscles may not get sufficient blood because of the blocked arteries. They will become starved of oxygen. They may feel a sharp pain called angina. In very severe cases, a heart attack may occur.

The main factors linked to heart disease are high blood pressure, diabetes, being overweight, a family history of heart disease and strokes, lack of exercise and too much stress.

The circulatory system speeds up during exercise

# What happens to our circulatory system as we exercise?

Even before we start to exercise, our bodies release the hormone adrenalin. This prepares us for action by stimulating the circulatory and respiratory systems.

The circulatory system speeds up. It sends greater amounts of blood (and therefore oxygen) to the working muscles.

The pumping action of the muscles forces more deoxygenated blood back to the heart.

The heart receives a greater amount of blood into the left atrium. The heart reacts by contracting more vigorously. It sends out a greater amount of blood with each contraction.

Adrenalin in the bloodstream causes the heart to beat more rapidly. Blood flow is reduced to the areas of the body not in urgent need. Blood flow is increased to the areas in greatest need.

The blood vessels to the skin are dilated (made larger). This allows excess heat to be lost from the body's surface. During extremely strenuous activity these blood vessels will be constricted (made smaller). The body temperature then rises very quickly. This can cause overheating and fatigue.

The muscles receive up to three times the resting amount of oxygen. Blood flow can be increased up to 30 times. Because the blood flow has increased, the working muscles can receive up to 90 times the resting amount of oxygen.

# Our respiratory system

Our bodies are made up of millions of cells, all of which use oxygen. Our cells need oxygen to break down the sugars from food and free the energy needed to work. Oxygen is taken from the air and into our bodies through our lungs. It is then carried to our body cells by our circulatory system. Carbon dioxide is collected from our cells and removed by our lungs. The process of getting energy from food is called respiration.

Our lungs are two, thin-walled elastic sacs lying in the thorax (chest). The thorax is an airtight cavity enclosed by the ribs at the side and the diaphragm below. Any change in the volume of the thorax affects the volume of the lungs. The lungs are surrounded by smooth, double skins called the pleural membranes. These membranes slide against one another as the lungs expand and contract. The pleural membranes reduce friction between the lungs and the wall of the thorax.

## What happens as we breathe?

Air enters the body through the nose and mouth.

1. The **nasal cavity** removes large dust particles using coarse nasal hairs.

2. The **cilia** (tiny hairs) trap dust and bacteria in the air and send them down the throat to be swallowed.

3. The **palate** separates the nasal cavity from the mouth so that we can chew and breathe at the same time.

4. The **epiglottis** (flap at the back of the throat) closes when we swallow to stop food from going down the trachea.

5. The **trachea** (windpipe) has hoops of cartilage to prevent it from collapsing. It divides into two bronchial tubes behind the breastbone. These then branch out again into smaller bronchi which in turn become bronchioles.

8. The **diaphragm** is a muscle which forms the internal floor of the chest.

6. The **bronchioles** split up into alveoli. There are a vast number of these thin, walled air sacs. Most of our lung tissue is made up of alveoli. When the lungs expand or contract these tiny air sacs fill and empty.

7. A **pulmonary artery** carries blood directly from our heart into each of the lungs. This artery divides again and again until a network of capillaries surrounds each group of alveoli. There is direct contact between the walls of the alveoli and the capillaries.

The haemoglobin in the blood of the capillaries takes up oxygen from the alveoli. At the same time carbon dioxide is passed out of the bloodstream and into the lungs. The carbon dioxide is then breathed out into the air.

# How do we breathe?

When breathing in (also called **inspiration**), our diaphragm contracts, descends and flattens out the floor of our rib cage. At the same time, the intercostal muscles across our ribs contract and pull the ribs upwards. Our lungs increase in size. This lowers the pressure inside them. The higher external (atmospheric) pressure pushes air into our lungs through our nose and mouth.

When breathing out (also called **expiration**), our diaphragm and intercostal muscles relax. Our diaphragm is pushed back into a domed position by the organs beneath it. Our ribs move down under their own weight. The space in our lungs is now smaller and the pressure inside increases so that it is higher than the external pressure. Air is therefore forced out of the lungs through our nose and mouth. When our body is at rest, we can breathe just by using our diaphragm on its own.

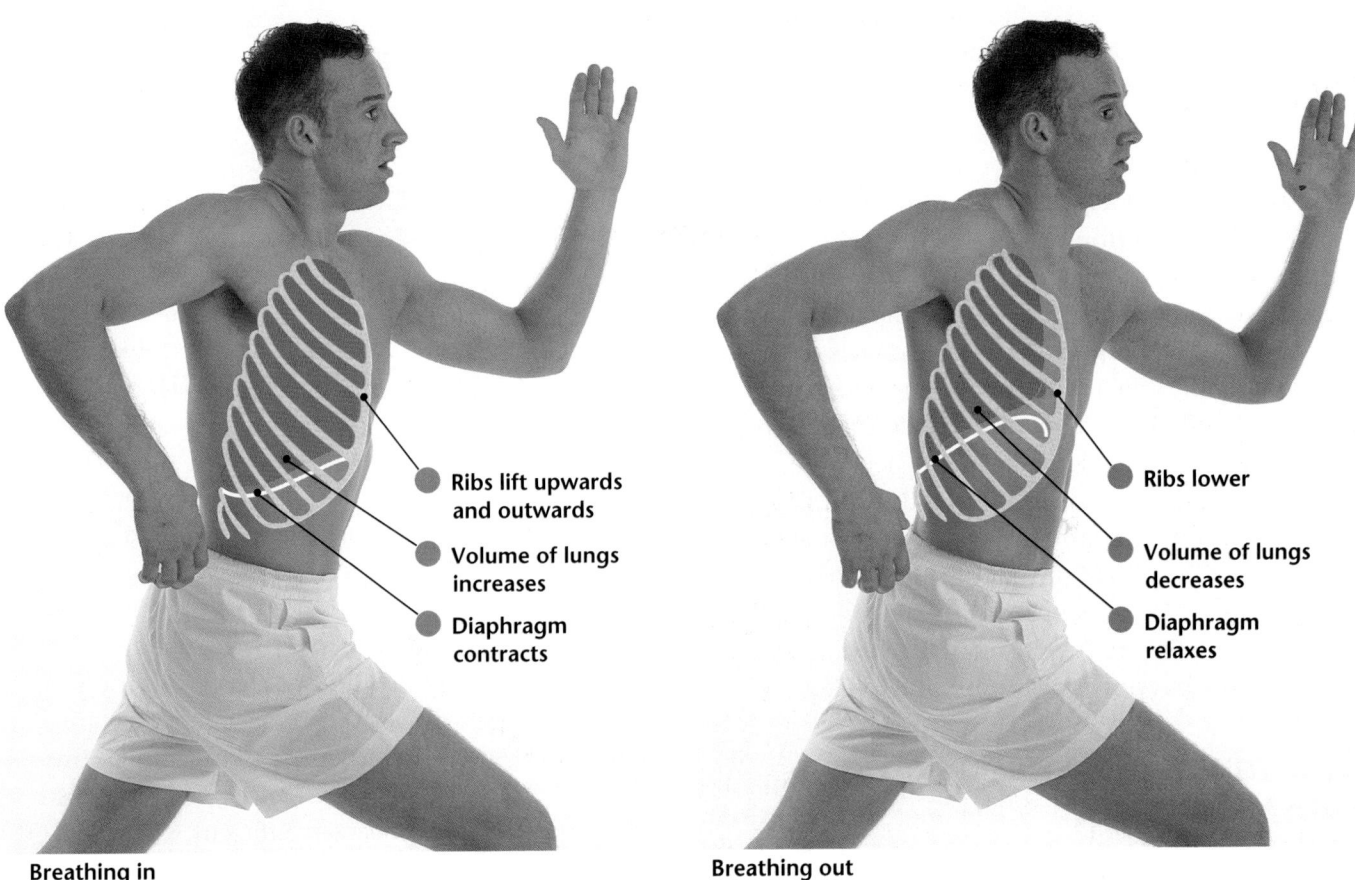

Ribs lift upwards and outwards

Volume of lungs increases

Diaphragm contracts

**Breathing in**

Ribs lower

Volume of lungs decreases

Diaphragm relaxes

**Breathing out**

# How is our breathing controlled?

We breathe to supply our cells with oxygen. The harder our muscles have to work, the more energy they will use up and therefore the more oxygen they will need. Our breathing is controlled by the respiratory centre in the brain. Carbon dioxide levels increase during hard physical activity. Carbon dioxide enters the blood stream from the muscles. The respiratory centre checks this increased level of carbon dioxide. It makes our body take more frequent and deeper breaths. This helps to get rid of the carbon dioxide through the lungs and at the same time take in much needed oxygen.

# How does oxygen get to our working muscles?

The air we breathe in passes through the trachea, into the bronchi and through the bronchi into the bronchioles, and from there into the tiny air sacs called alveoli. There is direct contact between the walls of the alveoli and the capillaries. The haemoglobin in the blood of the capillaries takes up oxygen from the alveoli. The oxygenated blood is carried through the pulmonary veins to the left side of the heart.

From the left side of the heart the oxygenated blood is pumped through the aorta to the body tissues. The oxygen is carried in the blood by red cells. When the blood arrives in the capillaries at the tissues it gives up the oxygen, as well as nutrients such as glucose. It picks up the waste products carbon dioxide and water. In our body cells, the oxygen is used to release the energy from glucose. This process is called **cell respiration**.

Glucose + Oxygen → Energy + carbon dioxide and water. The carbon dioxide is carried back to the heart and then to the lungs. Here it is released into the alveoli and breathed out of the body. Not all the carbon dioxide is removed. The brain checks the amount of carbon dioxide in the bloodstream. It uses this information to control our rate of breathing.

The air we breathe in (inspire) contains about 79% nitrogen, 21% oxygen and 0.04% carbon dioxide. The air we breathe out (expire) contains about 79% nitrogen, 16% oxygen and 4% carbon dioxide.

# How much air can our lungs hold?

When we are resting about 500 ml of air moves in and out of our lungs with each breath. This is called the **tidal volume**. Our lungs never completely empty, there is always some air left. The air that is left is called the **residual volume**.

Our **vital capacity** is the largest amount of air that can be forced out of our lungs after we have taken in as much air as we can in one breath.

**Total lung capacity** = vital capacity + residual volume.

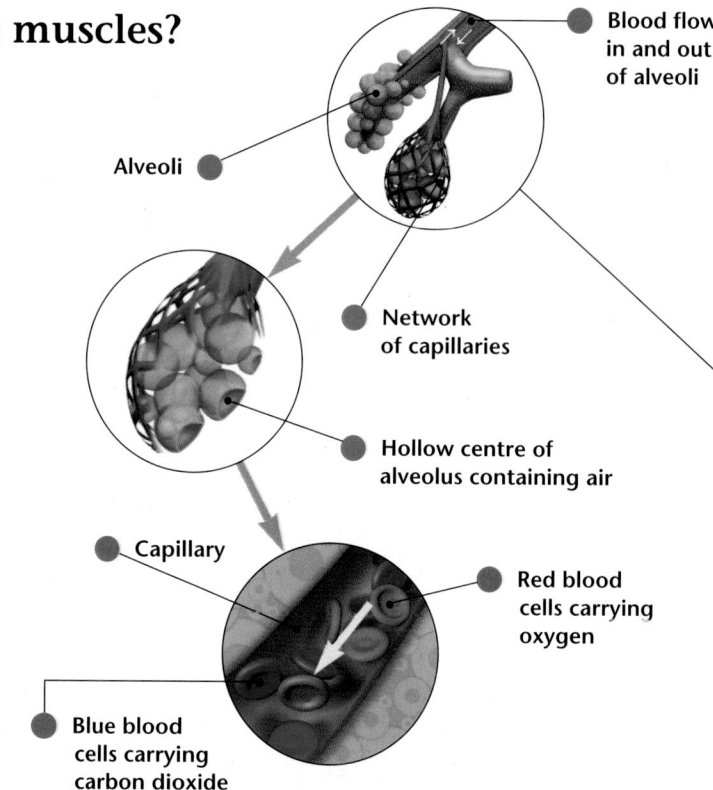

Blood flow in and out of alveoli

Alveoli

Network of capillaries

Hollow centre of alveolus containing air

Capillary

Red blood cells carrying oxygen

Blue blood cells carrying carbon dioxide

# Is lung capacity important for sporting success?

Lung capacities differ according to age, sex, body type and aerobic fitness. Because we have a large lung capacity, it does not mean that we will have aerobic fitness.

Two athletes could have exactly the same lung capacity but totally different levels of fitness. The fitter athlete will be able to make much greater use of the oxygen which is breathed in through the lungs. The exchange of oxygen and waste products in the fitter athlete will be very efficient. The fitter athlete will have a better **$VO_2$ max** (maximum aerobic capacity).

> ⟳ **KEY POINT**
>
> $VO_2$ max (or maximum aerobic capacity) is the maximum amount of oxygen that can be transported and used by the working muscles during one minute of exercise.

We will look at $VO_2$ in more detail in chapter 2.

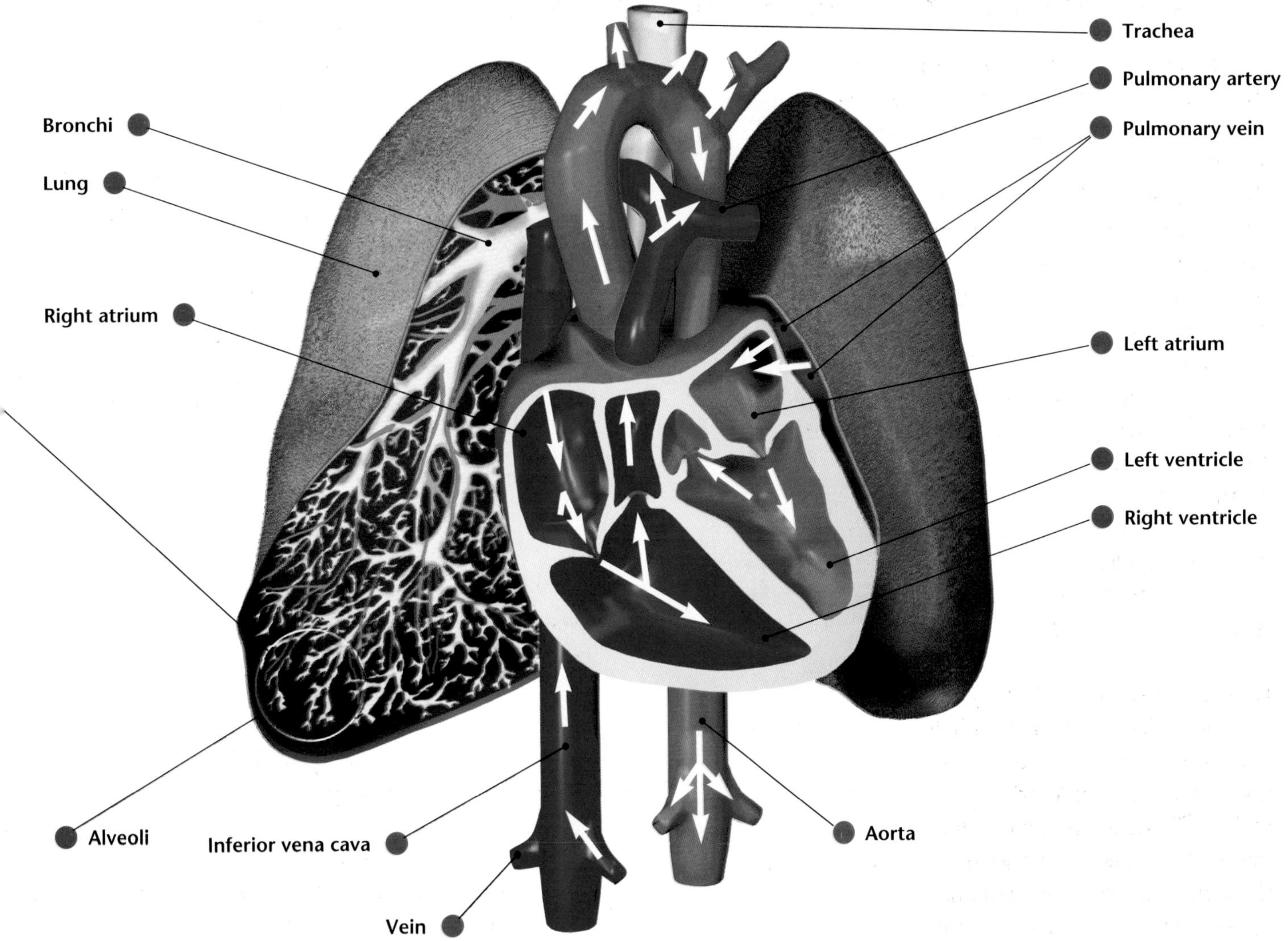

Trachea

Pulmonary artery

Pulmonary vein

Bronchi

Lung

Left atrium

Right atrium

Left ventricle

Right ventricle

Alveoli

Inferior vena cava

Aorta

Vein

# What happens to our respiratory system as we exercise?

When we exercise, more oxygen is needed by the working muscles and more carbon dioxide must be removed from the muscles. This can be done by:

- increasing the rate of breathing;
- increasing the depth of breathing, up to our vital capacity;
- increasing the blood flow through the lungs;
- increasing the oxygen taken up and used by the body.

Oxygen used during exercise can be up to 20 times a person's normal oxygen uptake. The maximum amount of oxygen a person can take up and use within a minute is called his $VO_2$ max. This may be, for example, 55 litres per minute.

When we exercise, we need more oxygen

## Spinal cord

Our spinal cord leaves the base of our brain through an opening in the skull. It is made up of nerve cells and fibres and it goes down the inside of our spinal column.

## Brain

Our brain is the control centre for every activity of our body. It is suspended in clear fluid and is surrounded by the skull which protects it.

**Our nervous system in action**

## Nerves

Nerves link the effector and receptor organs to the central nervous system.

# Our nervous system

Our nervous system continuously checks what is happening inside and outside our bodies. It then decides how to act. The nervous system acts by sending signals which are passed through interconnected nerve cells.

- our nervous system is made up of the brain, spinal cord, peripheral nerves and the sense organs;
- our **central nervous system** (CNS) analyses information, makes decisions and starts action;
- our **peripheral nervous system** collects information and takes the response signals to our muscles or any other organs which need to react. Some actions happen automatically, for example when we pull our hand away from being burned. For other actions we need to make conscious decisions;
- our **effector organs** are the muscles and glands which work when they receive information from our central nervous system. Our **receptor organs** get information from various sources (see Extension);
- **sensory nerves** carry information from receptor organs to our central nervous system;
- **motor nerves** carry information to the effector organs from our central nervous system;
- our spinal nerves carry information in both directions;
- our nerve fibres carry messages to and from nearly every part of our bodies. Bundles of nerve fibres enter our spinal cord and leave it again through gaps between our vertebrae.

⊃ EXTENSION

There are three different types of receptor organ. These are found in different places in our bodies. They are:

- **exteroceptors.** These receive information from outside our bodies, for example from our eyes and ears.
- **interoceptors.** These receive information from organs inside our bodies, for example from our lungs and digestive system.
- **proprioceptors.** These are found mainly in our muscles, tendons and joints. They tell our brain where our limbs are positioned. They help us to move our limbs with accuracy and speed.

## Our autonomic nervous system

Some of our bodily activities are completely automatic. These are controlled by our **autonomic nervous system**. Our autonomic nervous system is responsible for our involuntary muscles. It controls, for example, our breathing, our heartbeat and our digestive system.

Our reflex actions are extremely fast. In a reflex action, our whole bodies, or parts of our bodies, will react to a stimulus. Reflex actions help the body to protect itself from dangerous or harmful situations. Examples include blinking as a response to something touching the outside of our eye, and moving our hand away from something painful.

## What are conditioned reflexes?

We learn many complex skills during our lifetime. When we first learn to ride a bike we have to give it all of our attention. We have to think about how to keep our balance, travel in the way we want to go, keep pedalling and so on. As we become more skilful and confident, many of our movements will become almost automatic (we don't have to think about them). Skills which we have developed in this way are called conditioned reflexes.

**Conditioned reflexes** are reflexes which happen after a pattern of behaviour has been learned. They can cause problems if we try to change an incorrect sporting technique which we have used for a long time. For example, golfers who try to change their swing often find that when they lose concentration, their old poor swing returns. The conditioned reflex needs to be broken down and a new one established. This is often very difficult to do.

## Our nervous system in action

If we are skilled, the control of the skill is left to our proprioceptors. This leaves our exteroceptors to deal with other things. It helps to explain how a skilful badminton player can concentrate on exactly *where* to play the shot (taking into account the position of the opponent, the speed of the ball, the type of playing surface, etc.) and not have to worry about *how* to play her shot.

## What happens to our nervous system as we exercise?

Our nervous system plans, starts and coordinates all our movements. Blood flow to our brain is maintained during exercise.

**Our nervous system plans and coordinates all our movements**

# Our hormonal system

Our nervous system does not control coordination of all our body systems. Some coordination is controlled by chemicals produced by our hormonal system. This is also called our endocrine system.

Our nervous system acts quickly and has short term effects on specific body parts. Our hormonal system works more slowly and has longer lasting and more general effects.

Our endocrine system is made up of a number of glands which make hormones. Hormones are the chemical messengers of our bodies. These hormones are sent directly into the bloodstream, when they are needed. Each gland produces its own hormone which can affect particular organs of our bodies.

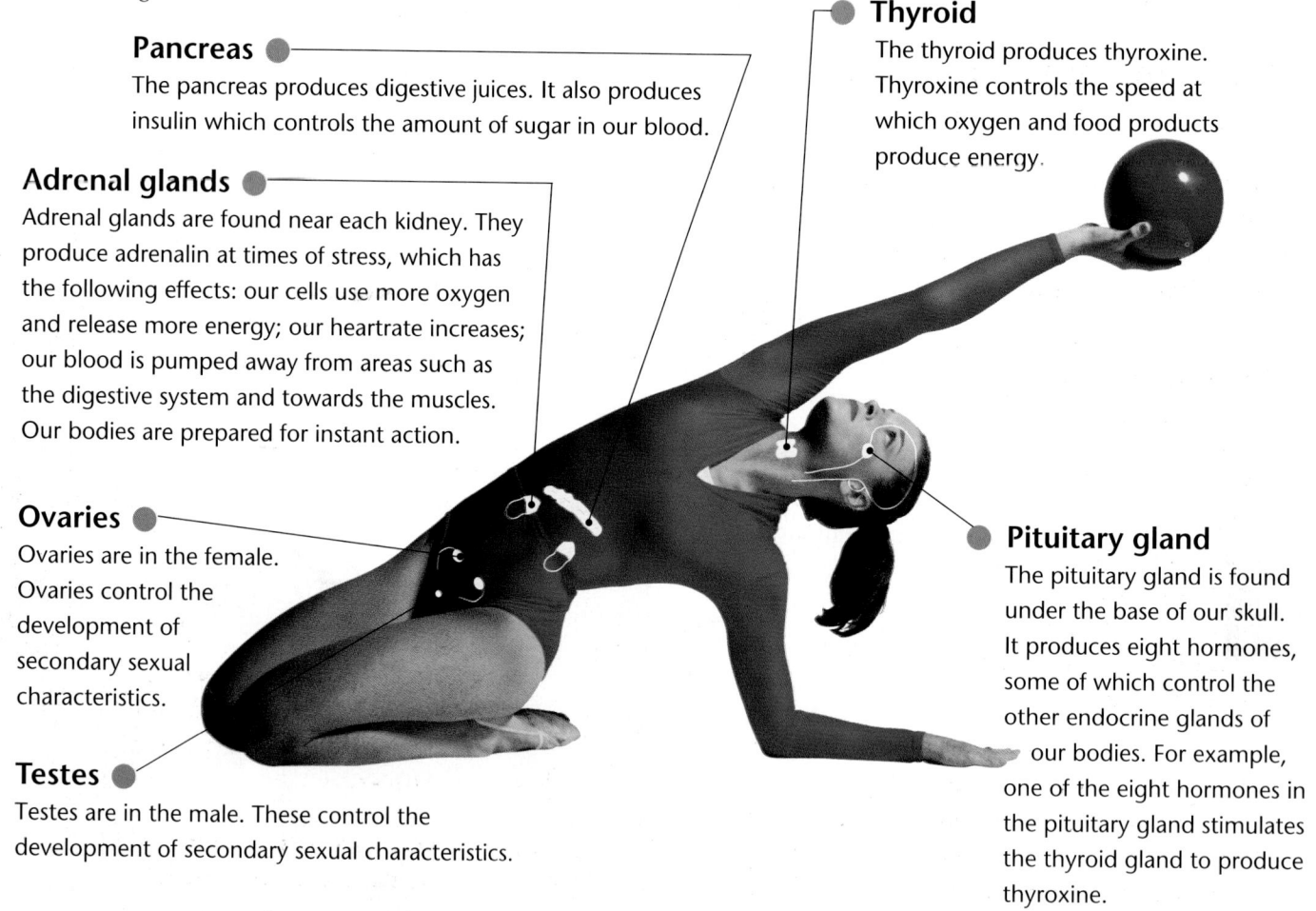

**Pancreas** ●
The pancreas produces digestive juices. It also produces insulin which controls the amount of sugar in our blood.

**Adrenal glands** ●
Adrenal glands are found near each kidney. They produce adrenalin at times of stress, which has the following effects: our cells use more oxygen and release more energy; our heartrate increases; our blood is pumped away from areas such as the digestive system and towards the muscles. Our bodies are prepared for instant action.

**Ovaries** ●
Ovaries are in the female. Ovaries control the development of secondary sexual characteristics.

**Testes** ●
Testes are in the male. These control the development of secondary sexual characteristics.

**Thyroid**
The thyroid produces thyroxine. Thyroxine controls the speed at which oxygen and food products produce energy.

**Pituitary gland**
The pituitary gland is found under the base of our skull. It produces eight hormones, some of which control the other endocrine glands of our bodies. For example, one of the eight hormones in the pituitary gland stimulates the thyroid gland to produce thyroxine.

## What happens to our hormonal system as we exercise?

We use many hormones when we take part in physical activity. These hormones have several effects, including the following:

- the rate and force of our heart contraction is increased;
- there is an increase in the breakdown of **glucose** in the muscles and the liver;
- there is an increase in the release of glucose into the blood;
- blood is redistributed to the skeletal muscles;
- blood pressure increases;
- respiration increases;
- fluid levels are controlled and **dehydration** is prevented.

# Our digestive and excretory systems

Our bodies need a constant supply of food so that they have the fuel to remain healthy and active. Our digestive system makes the food soluble. It breaks it down so that it is small enough to pass into the bloodstream and the lymph system. It also changes food into the basic nutrients which our bodies need for building new tissues, for repairing damaged tissues and for energy.

## What happens to our digestive system as we exercise?

As we exercise, blood flow to our digestive organs is reduced. This slows down the digestive process. As a result, food should not be eaten for at least two hours before we exercise.

- Digestion starts in the mouth where food is first ground upand mixed by the action of our **teeth**. This allows the food to be swallowed easily.

- The food is moistened by saliva from our **salivary glands**. Saliva contains an **enzyme** called ptyalin, which begins to turn starch into sugar.

- In the **stomach**, the food is churned about and mixed with gastric juices. These include enzymes and dilute acid. They break down the protein to form simple materials. Our stomach acts as a storage tank.

- The waste food passes into our **large intestine** (colon). It stays there for about 12 hours. Most of the water and any remaining nutrients are removed.

- In our **small intestine** (duodenum) alkaline enzymes are added to the food. They break it down into a mixture of simple amino acids, fatty acids and glycerol. Our digestion finishes in the **small intestine**. **Nutrients** are taken into the blood and lymph systems through the wall of our small intestine.

- The food is pushed down the **gullet** (oesophagus) by a wave like muscular movement called **peristalsis**.

- Food moves in small amounts into the first part of our small intestine, the duodenum. Food spends about four – six hours in our small intestine.

- The solidified remains leave the body through our **anus**. Waste fluids are taken to our kidneys. Here they are filtered and pass, as urine, through the ureters to the bladder. The urine then leaves the body through our urethra.

# What are the health benefits of exercise for our body systems?

We have seen how our body systems respond to exercise. When we exercise regularly our bodies adapt and our body systems become more efficient. Training for sport brings about specific changes in our body systems.

Exercise is good for us. Exercise is essential for all of us whatever our age, gender, race, religion or ability. The following are some of the benefits of regular exercise:

### Improved health

We have more energy for work, rest, play and emergencies. We also feel better.

### Improved heart-lung system

We can do more work before getting tired and we can recover more quickly. Our heart gets stronger and pumps more blood. Our lungs take in more air. We use oxygen more efficiently.

### Stronger muscles

Our muscles are stronger and keep working for longer. Our ligaments, tendons and joints will therefore be injured less often.

### More relaxed

Regular exercise helps us to relax and rest. We are less stressed and sleep better.

### Better social life

We have opportunities to meet people with similar interests and can develop friendships.

### Reduced risk of disease and ill health

With stronger, fitter bodies, we are less likely to have heart attacks, lung disease, diabetes, brittle bones and arthritis. Our blood pressure will be lower and we will build up less cholesterol.

### Better appearance

Exercise helps us to keep down fat levels, delays ageing and makes us happier about our bodies.

### Improved quality of life

We are likely to live a longer, healthier and more active life.

### Improved posture

Better muscle tone means that we can hold our bodies in position with less effort.

### Better flexibility

Our joints move more freely. This means that there is less chance of injury and that our skills improve.

# Questions

## Our Body Systems

### The circulatory, respiratory, nervous, hormonal and digestive systems

1  Name the parts of the heart described below.
   i  The two top chambers
   ii  The two bottom chambers
   iii  The vessel containing blood returning to the heart from the lungs
   iv  The vessel through which blood travels from the heart to the body

2  **a** How is oxygenated blood carried around the body?
   **b** Where is the oxygen taken to be used?

3  **a** What effect does exercise have on the respiratory system?
   **b** What effect does exercise have on the circulatory system?

4  Name the two circulatory systems. Explain the route of the blood in one of the systems.

5  Explain the following terms:
   **a** Stroke volume
   **b** Cardiac output

6  Describe the functions of the adrenal glands.

7  How does adrenaline affect performance?

8  "Do not eat immediately before exercising." Explain why this advice is given.

9  Explain the role of the central nervous system (CNS) during exercise.

10  Regular exercise benefits all of our body systems. List and describe four different benefits.

# 2 Energy in Action

Our bodies need energy for muscular contraction, growth and repair. Our bodies get energy from carbohydrates, fats and proteins in our food. Our bodies can store energy in a number of ways. They can only use energy when it is in the form of a chemical compound called adenosine triphosphate ATP. Muscles can only store small amounts of this energy, so our bodies have to keep making it. If our muscles use up energy faster than it is being made, we will get tired.

## Creatine phosphate system page 44

The three energy systems are different: the creatine phosphate system (immediate energy system) can provide you with energy more quickly than the others but this energy only lasts for a very short period of time.

There are three energy systems. These are called: the creatine phosphate system, the lactic acid system and the aerobic system. These systems work together to make sure our muscles are getting energy in the form of ATP.

## Aerobic system page 46

The aerobic system (long term energy system) is an energy system which can provide you with energy for long periods of time but it needs oxygen to work.

## Lactic acid system page 45

The lactic acid system (short term energy system) can also provide you with energy quickly but you will tire as painful waste products build up in your working muscles.

# Creatine phosphate system

**Our creatine phosphate system is very important when we need bursts of explosive speed**

The creatine phosphate **energy system** provides *immediate* energy.

Some energy is stored in our muscles. This means that it is available to us instantly, but it will not last long. The small stores of ATP energy in our muscles will provide enough energy for just five – eight seconds of hard work.

As the supplies of ATP energy in our muscles run out, more are created. Creatine phosphate is a high energy source which is stored in our muscles. Our bodies can break down the creatine phosphate to get more energy. The extra energy from the **creatine phosphate system** will give us about another 20 seconds of hard work.

Our creatine phosphate system is very important when we need bursts of explosive speed. Sprinters, throwers and many team players need to develop this system. After a burst of activity we will need to rest for several minutes to allow our bodies to refill their store of creatine phosphate.

## KEY POINT

Energy from the creatine phosphate system is available instantly, but it is also used up very quickly.

## EXTENSION

THE CREATINE PHOSPHATE SYSTEM

ATP → energy + ADP + P

ADP + CP (creatine phosphate) + energy → ATP + creatine

(ADP = adenosine di-phosphate; P = phosphate;

ATP = adenosine triphosphate)

# Lactic acid system

The **lactic acid system** provides *short term* energy.

When we start to work hard for longer than about ten seconds we breathe more quickly and deeply. This is because our muscles need more oxygen. It takes time for this extra oxygen to get into our bloodstream and to our working muscles. The energy supplies of ATP and creatine phosphate will be used up. We need to find another energy supply until enough oxygen arrives. We will now use **glycogen** to provide more ATP.

We produce glycogen from the breakdown of carbohydrates. We store it in the muscles as well as in the liver.

The breakdown of glycogen provides energy but lactic acid is also being formed. A build up of this lactic acid makes muscular contractions painful and causes tiredness. We cannot use the lactic acid system for very long.

The lactic acid system provides short term energy

## Oxygen debt

If we use the creatine phosphate or lactic acid system then we are creating an oxygen deficit. In other words, we need more oxygen than we can get. We take in the extra oxygen we need when we are resting, at the end of exercise. This makes up the oxygen deficit. The extra oxygen taken in at the end of exercise is called the **oxygen debt**. It allows us to:

- remove lactic acid;
- replace oxygen stores in our bodies;
- build up ATP and creatine phosphate supplies.

### ⬤ KEY POINT

The lactic acid system is very important when all out effort is continued for more than about ten seconds.

### ⬤ EXTENSION

THE LACTIC ACID SYSTEM

ATP → energy + ADP

ADP + glycogen → ATP + *Pyruvic acid
↓
(insufficient oxygen)
↓
Lactic acid

\* (If there is not enough oxygen, the pyruvic acid will change into lactic acid.)

# Aerobic system

The **aerobic system** provides *long term* energy.

We use the aerobic system in most of our daily activities. It gives us energy much more slowly than the creatine phosphate system, or the lactic acid system. It provides energy too slowly for intensive activity. However, the energy it provides is almost limitless.

The aerobic system is important for sports people who need to keep working over long periods of time.

When our muscles have enough oxygen, they are able to break down **carbohydrate** and **fat**, to get this energy. So, the aerobic system can only work when enough oxygen is being supplied to the muscles.

*The aerobic system is important for sports people who need to keep working over long periods of time*

## ⭢ KEY POINT

The aerobic system needs oxygen to work, provides energy slowly but enables us to keep working for long periods of time.

## ⭢ EXTENSION

THE AEROBIC SYSTEM

ATP → energy + ADP

ADP + glycogen → ATP + pyruvic acid

pyruvic acid + $O_2$ → $CO_2$ + $H_2O$

## Which muscle fibres will be contracting when we are working anaerobically?

It is our fast twitch muscle fibres which contract when we work anaerobically. They contract very quickly and are bigger and stronger than the slow twitch fibres. They do not have a good oxygen supply and get tired very quickly. Fast twitch fibres are only used in higher intensity exercise.

# Is one energy system more important than the others?

The answer is that it depends what we are doing. If we run a half marathon then 99% of the energy we use will come from the aerobic system. However, if we throw a javelin we will only make use of the CP (creatine phosphate) system for the actual throw. For most sporting events we will use all the energy systems. The amount we use each system will depend on the intensity of the activity (that is, how hard we have to work) as well as how long the activity lasts for.

We need to know the amount each of the different energy systems is used in our sport so that we can train appropriately. The aerobic and anaerobic energy requirements for each sport are shown right.

Sources of energy used for different sports

| % aerobic | Events | | Primary energy sources |
|---|---|---|---|
| 0 | weight lifting<br>200 metre | 100 metre dash | |
| 10 | wrestling<br>100m swim | basket ball<br>400m dash | Creatine phosphate and lactic acid system |
| 20 | tennis | | |
| 30 | | soccer | |
| 40 | | | |
| 50 | 800m<br>boxing | | Creatine phosphate, lactic acid and aerobic systems |
| 60 | rowing | | |
| 70 | | 1500m<br>800m swim | |
| 80 | 2 mile run | | Aerobic system |
| 90 | skating 10km | cross country running | |
| 100 | jogging | | |

# What do we need to know to focus our training precisely?

We need to know how hard to work so that our **training** is effective. If our training is too easy we will not improve our **aerobic fitness**. If it is too intense we will start to use our anaerobic system and will not be training our aerobic system at all.

The level of intensity we need in our training depends on our present level of fitness. We can work our fitness out by calculating the maximum amount of oxygen that we can take in and use during exercise. This is called our VO₂ max. VO₂ max (or maximal aerobic capacity) is the maximum amount of oxygen that we can transport, and our muscles can use in exercise. From this we can work out our individual **training threshold** (the level of intensity at which we should work) for both aerobic training and anaerobic training.

## Our aerobic threshold

Above the level of our **aerobic threshold**, continuous exercise will have a training effect on our aerobic fitness. In other words, we can push our limits to get more aerobically fit.

## Our anaerobic threshold

When we reach our **anaerobic threshold**, it means that we are working so hard that we cannot get enough oxygen to the muscles. Our muscles will have to get energy from the anaerobic energy system instead. Lactic acid will immediately start to build up. This causes pain, makes us tired and we will not be able to continue at the same intensity for very long. We will build up an oxygen deficit. We will also use up our limited supplies of oxygen.

# Can we use our heart rate to work out how hard to train?

To measure VO₂ max we need expensive equipment and specialist knowledge. Fortunately there is a very close link between our VO₂ max and our **maximum heart rate (MHR)**. By calculating our maximum heart rate we can work out the level at which we should work (our threshold).

Our maximum heart rate can be estimated in the following way:
Maximum heart rate = 220 minus our age. If you are 16, your MHR is 220-16 = 204 beats per minute.

## General guidelines

The exact percentage of MHR which is necessary to achieve different training effects varies from person to person. The percentage will also vary with our level of fitness. If we are very unfit, a level below 60% would improve our fitness at the beginning.

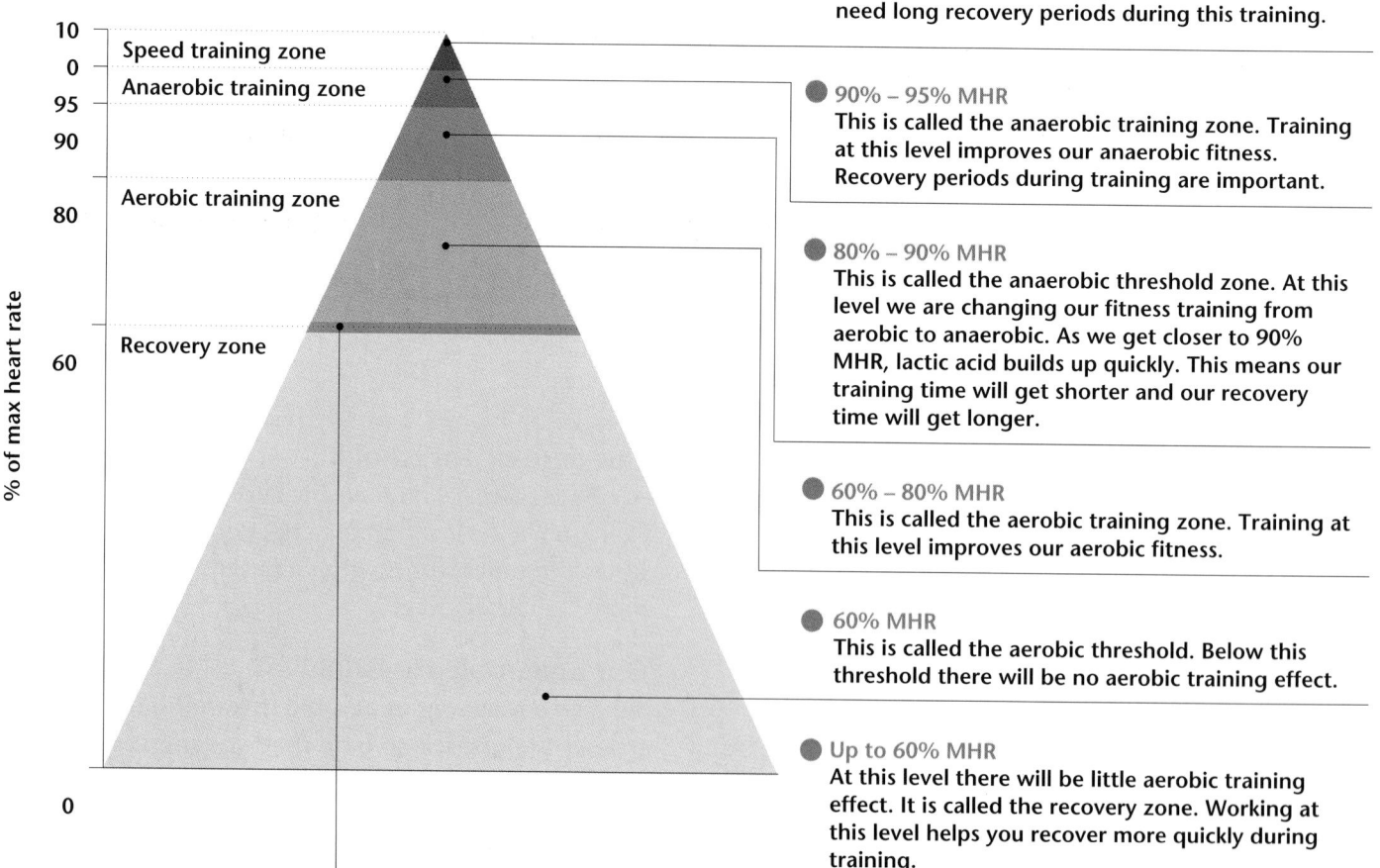

**Over 95% MHR**
This is called the speed **training zone**. This means training nearly flat out, which is necessary to improve our speed and our recovery time. We need long recovery periods during this training.

**90% – 95% MHR**
This is called the anaerobic training zone. Training at this level improves our anaerobic fitness. Recovery periods during training are important.

**80% – 90% MHR**
This is called the anaerobic threshold zone. At this level we are changing our fitness training from aerobic to anaerobic. As we get closer to 90% MHR, lactic acid builds up quickly. This means our training time will get shorter and our recovery time will get longer.

**60% – 80% MHR**
This is called the aerobic training zone. Training at this level improves our aerobic fitness.

**60% MHR**
This is called the aerobic threshold. Below this threshold there will be no aerobic training effect.

**Up to 60% MHR**
At this level there will be little aerobic training effect. It is called the recovery zone. Working at this level helps you recover more quickly during training.

# Questions

## Energy in Action

1  Describe the differences between anaerobic and aerobic exercise.

2  List four sporting activities that are mainly anaerobic.

3  List four mainly aerobic sporting activities.

4  What is meant by the term 'oxygen debt'?

5  Which muscle fibres are used when we work anaerobically.

6  In most sporting events we use all of the energy systems. What determines the amount that each system is used?

7  **a** What do you understand by the term 'VO$_2$ max'?
   **b** How can we easily estimate our VO$_2$ max?

8  What prevents athletes from training above the anaerobic threshold for long periods of time?

9  Name the substance used in the lactic acid system that is produced from carbohydrates.

10  What advice should a physically unfit person receive before taking up exercise?

# 3 Fitness for Health and Performance

## What is aerobic capacity? ●
**page 54**

The ability of our heart/lung system to cope with activity over a period of time.

**Health related fitness**

## What is flexibility?
**page 62**

The ability of our joints to move with a full range of movement.

## What is strength? ●
**page 56**

The ability of our muscles to carry out our daily tasks. This involves maximum strength, muscular power, and muscular endurance.

## ● What is body build?
**page 59**

Our ability to carry the correct amount of body fat and muscle.

Being fit is central to our health and to our sense of well being. Health and fitness mean so much more than just the absence of illness. If we are healthy and fit then the physical, mental and social and spiritual aspects of our lives are working well together.

Fitness is crucial to success in sport. It is essential for us to look at the particular demands of our sport and identity in what ways we need to develop our fitness.

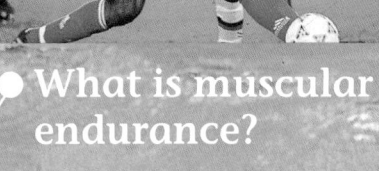

## What is muscular power? page 57

This is part of strength. Our ability to contract muscles with speed and force in an explosive act.

## What is muscular endurance? page 58

This is part of strength. Our ability to work our muscles very hard for a period of time.

### Sport related fitness

## What is speed? page 64

Our ability to move all or part of our body quickly.

## What is agility page 65

Our ability to change the direction of the body at speed.

## What is coordination? page 66

Our ability to perform complex movements with ease.

## What is reaction time? page 67

Our ability to react to a stimulus quickly.

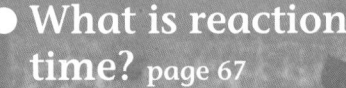

## What is balance? page 68

Our ability to retain our balance when stationary or moving.

# What is good health?

To be healthy means more than just the absence of illness. If we are in good **health** then the physical, mental, cultural, and social aspects of our lives are all working well together.

Our health is to some extent affected by heredity. This means the health records of our parents and grandparents are important. Problems such as high blood pressure and heart disease tend to run in families. If our parents and grandparents live a long and healthy life then we are likely to do so as well. However we cannot assume that this will be the case. We all need to work at keeping healthy. We can do a great deal to make sure that our health is as good as possible by following a sensible lifestyle. We should avoid the things which are known to damage our health.
We should:

• eat sensibly;
• take regular physical activity;
• get regular rest and sleep;
• limit our intake of alcohol;
• not smoke tobacco or take any other social drugs;
• improve our ability to cope with stress.

# What is physical fitness?

**Physical fitness** is the ability of our body to carry out everyday activities with little fatigue and with enough energy left for emergencies. Fitness means different things to different people. A man who is fit for his work as a taxi driver may be dangerously unfit for a game of squash. A marathon runner may be quite unfit for lifting weights. If you are asked the question, 'Are you fit?' you should always answer with another question 'Fit for what?'.

Fitness is a blend of a number of physical qualities. We all need these qualities to a greater or lesser extent. There is a minimal level of fitness which we all need, to have good health. We call this **health related fitness**.

To have enough fitness for good health we need:

Health means
more than just
the absence
of illness

### Aerobic capacity
This means that we need to be able to work for relatively long periods of time without becoming overtired.

### Strength
This means that we need to be strong enough to carry out all our daily tasks easily.

### Body build
This means that we need to carry the right amount of fat and muscle.

### Flexibility
This means that we need to be able to move our joints through their full range of movement. This helps us use our body in the way it was designed to be used.

# Fitness and exercise

Exercise helps to make us fit. It is good for our heart and it makes us feel good. Fitness and exercise go together. Fitness is an active state. It is achieved by movement and effort. We cannot get fit by reading about it, thinking about it or seeing examples of it on television.

Although we may be fit from a health related point of view we may not be fit for sport. There are many different kinds of sporting activities and each makes its own particular demands on our body. For example, the fitness required to be a jockey is totally different from the fitness needed to be an ice skater.

We need to have **sport related fitness**. To be successful in most sports it is important to be as fit as possible in a number of areas:

Jockeys need to be strong, light and have good muscular endurance

## Speed

**Speed** is our ability to move all or part of our bodies as quickly as possible.

## Muscular power

**Power** is our ability to contract muscles with speed and force in one explosive act.

## Agility

**Agility** is our ability to change the direction of our body at speed.

## Coordination

**Coordination** is our ability to perform complex movements with ease.

## Reaction time

**Reaction time** is our ability to react to a stimulus quickly.

 **KEY POINT**

Fitness is specific. In other words, if you are asked the question 'Are you fit?' you should always answer with another question, 'Fit *for what*?'

## Balance

**Balance** is our ability to retain balance when stationary or moving.

## Muscular endurance

This is part of strength. Our ability to work our muscles very hard for a period of time.

Ice skaters need very good agility, balance and coordination

We will now look at all the aspects of health related and sport related fitness to see what they involve, how they can be improved and how they can be measured.

# What is aerobic capacity?

Aerobic capacity is also known as cardio-respiratory endurance or stamina. This is the ability of our heart and lung systems to cope with activity over a period of time. We need to keep our active muscles supplied with energy and to get rid of waste products during prolonged periods of strenuous activity involving the whole body. This depends on the efficiency of our heart, lungs, and blood vessels The better our aerobic capacity the better we can keep going for long periods of time when, for example, swimming, running, cycling or rowing.

Our maximum aerobic capacity is called our **VO₂ max**. It is the maximum amount of oxygen that can be transported to, and used by, our working muscles during exercise. If we have a high $VO_2$ max we can use much more oxygen than other people. We can work our body at a higher rate for long periods and will suffer less fatigue than others with a lower $VO_2$ max.

## How do we improve our aerobic capacity?

We can improve our aerobic fitness by regularly taking part in continuous exercise involving our whole body. It does not matter whether we jog, run, cycle, swim or row, as long as the activity is continued for a long enough time. Our heart rate must be kept between 70-85% of our maximal heart rate (see page 48) so that our aerobic capacity will improve. We should at first exercise for a minimum of 12 minutes, although as we become fitter we can extend our training time up to at least 40 minutes. Serious endurance athletes regularly work in excess of an hour at least four sessions per week. If we wish to improve our aerobic capacity we should use continuous training (page 76) and interval training (page 77).

## How do we measure our aerobic capacity?

We need to work out our $VO_2$ max. There are complicated laboratory methods to do this but it is possible to estimate our $VO_2$ max by using a test such as the NCF Multistage fitness (or beep) test.

### Multistage fitness test

To measure our $VO_2$ max, we perform a number of 20 metre shuttle runs in time to beeps from a pre-recorded tape. After each minute the time interval between beeps gets shorter so our running speed has to increase. We keep going until we can no longer keep up with the speed set by the beeps. At this point we stop and record the level.

We can check our score with published tables and so work out our $VO_2$ max. The test is easy to use and motivating, particularly if it's done with a group of people. It is the most widely used of all fitness tests. You can compare your score and the average score of your group with the MSFT average levels obtained by British national squads as shown in the table.

Multistage fitness test

| National team scores on MSFT | | |
|---|---|---|
| Sport | Male | Female |
| Basketball | 11–5 | 9–6 |
| Hockey | 13–9 | 12–7 |
| Rugby league | 13–1 | |
| Netball | | 9–7 |
| Squash | 13–13 | |

## Harvard step test

There are a number of different versions of this test but this is the simplest one. Our resting pulse rate is taken before the test begins. We step on and off a 45cm high bench at the rate of 30 times a minute for a period of five minutes. We must start with the same foot each time and we must also fully extend our leg at the top of each step.

At the end of the five minutes our speed of recovery is recorded. This is done by taking our pulse for 30 seconds at three different time intervals: one minute after the end of the exercise; two minutes after the end of the exercise and three minutes after the end of the exercise.

The greater our aerobic capacity, the lower our pulse rate will be at the end of the exercise. Also it will return to normal more quickly. We can work out our fitness score using the following formula:

$$\text{Fitness score} = \frac{\text{Duration of exercise in seconds (5 x 60 = 300)}}{2 \text{ x (Pulse after one minute + pulse after two minutes + pulse after 3 minutes)}} \times 100$$

**Harvard step test classification**

|  | High score | Above average | Average | Below average | Low score |
|---|---|---|---|---|---|
| Males 15–16 years | above 90 | 90–80 | 79–65 | 64–55 | less than 55 |
| Females 15–16 years | above 86 | 86–76 | 75–61 | 60–50 | less than 50 |

## Cooper 12 minute run

In this test we run as far in 12 minutes as we can around a marked area. The total distance we run is recorded. We can check our aerobic capacity using this chart.

**Cooper 12 minute run**

|  | High score | Above average | Average | Below average | Low score |
|---|---|---|---|---|---|
| Males 15–16 years | above 2800 | 2799–2500 | 2499–2300 | 2299–2200 | below 2200 |
| Females 15–16 years | above 2300 | 2299–2000 | 1999–1900 | 1899–1800 | less than 50 |

**Distance in metres**

> ⭮ **KEY POINT**
>
> Our aerobic capacity is the ability of our heart and lungs to cope with activity. The better our aerobic capacity, the longer we can keep going for.

Harvard step test

# What is strength?

Strength can be defined as the ability of a muscle or muscle group to apply force and overcome resistance. Muscles work in a variety of ways. We will look at the three types of strength important for health related exercise *and* sport.

The three types of strength are:

- **maximum strength** – this is also called static strength;
- **muscular power** – this is also called explosive strength;
- **muscular endurance** – this is also called endurance strength.

## What is maximum strength?

Maximum strength, or static strength, is the maximum force than can be applied by a muscle group to an immovable object. Maximum strength can be of particular importance in activities such as scrummaging in rugby, wrestling and tug-of-war. In these activities we have to hold our body in a steady position against an opposing force.

## How do we improve our maximum strength?

We can improve our maximum strength by training with heavy weights (80–100% of our maximum) and a low number of repetitions. We must exercise through the full range of joint movement and work slowly when lifting (see page 79).

> **● KEY POINT**
>
> In, for example, tug-of-war, a force is applied to you to move you from your steady position. Your **maximum strength** is the amount of force which can be applied before you are moved.

## How do we measure our maximum strength?

We need to find out what is the maximum force which a muscle group can apply. We can use special dynamometers to measure our maximum strength at a range of speeds and angles and when our muscles are lengthening or shortening. The machines can be set to allow our limbs to be moved in the same way that they move when we are taking part in our particular sport.

### Hand grip dynamometer

In schools and colleges we can use a **hand grip dynamometer**. In this test we squeeze the handle as hard as possible with our hand. This will give us a reading of the strength of our hand grip.

**Hand grip strength test**

|  | High score | Above average | Average | Below average | Low score |
|---|---|---|---|---|---|
| Males 15–16 years | above 56 | 56–52 | 51–48 | 47–43 | less than 43 |
| Females 15–16 years | above 37 | 37–34 | 33–32 | 31–29 | less than 29 |

Score in kilograms

### One repetition max test

Maximum strength can also be found if we attempt a **one repetition max test** using free weights or multigym equipment. By adding weights gradually we will be able to work up to the maximum weight we can lift just once. This is called our **one repetition max**. We must allow at least two – three minutes between each lift, for recovery.

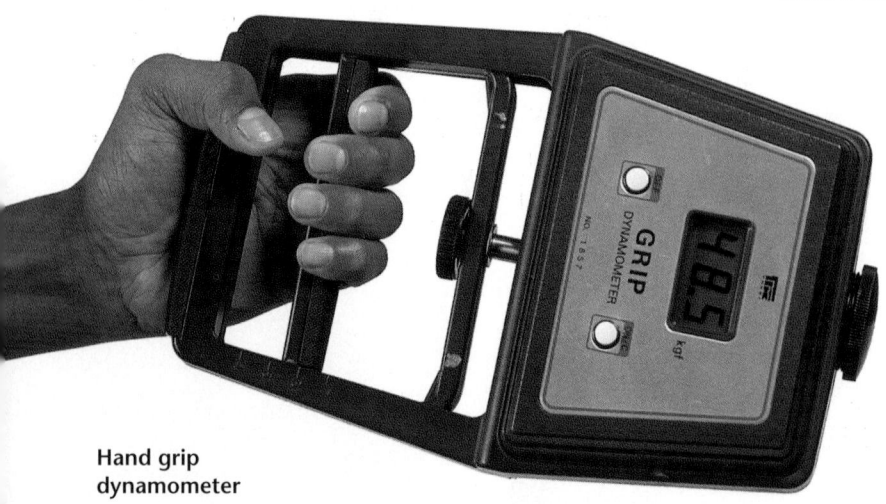

**Hand grip dynamometer**

# What is muscular power?

Muscular power, or explosive strength, is the combination of strength and speed of movement. It is shown clearly in activities such as throwing and jumping when we try to move ourselves or an object as far and as fast as possible. The energy for muscular power comes from the anaerobic system.

## How do we improve our muscular power?

We can improve muscular power by training with medium weights (60–80% of our maximum) and performing the repetitions at speed. Plyometrics training is also an excellent way of improving our power (see page 80). As power is a combination of strength and speed it is also important to train both of these areas of fitness.

## How do we measure our muscular power?

There are two simple ways to measure muscular power: the standing broad jump and the standing vertical jump.

### Standing broad jump

For this test we stand with our feet comfortably apart and our toes immediately behind the start line. We then bend our knees and jump forward as far as we can. The distance we score is measured from our rear heel back to the start line. We are allowed two attempts.

> **KEY POINT**
>
> Your **muscular power** is how far you can move yourself, or an object. For example, jumping and throwing require muscular power. Muscular power is essential.

### Standing vertical jump

In this test we stand next to a wall and reach up with our arm nearest to the wall. The highest point we can reach with the fingers of this arm is marked. Both feet must remain flat on the floor at this stage. We chalk our finger tips and leap upwards tapping our fingers against the wall at the highest point. The distance between the two marks gives a measure of how high we can leap from the ground from a stationary start. It takes into account our own height and so is a fairer test than the standing broad jump.

#### Standing vertical jump

| | High score | Above average | Average | Below average | Low score |
|---|---|---|---|---|---|
| Males 15–16 years | above 65 cm | 65–56 cm | 55–50 cm | 49–40 cm | less than 40 cm |
| Females 15–16 years | above 60 cm | 60–51 cm | 50–41 cm | 40–35 cm | less than 35 cm |

Distance in cms

#### Standing broad jump

| | High score | Above average | Average | Below average | Low score |
|---|---|---|---|---|---|
| Males 15–16 years | 2.10 2.01m | 2.00 1.86m | 1.85 1.76m | 1.75 1.65m | less than 1.65m |
| Females 15–16 years | 1.85 1.66m | 1.65 1.56m | 1.55 1.46m | 1.45 1.35m | less than 1.35m |

Distance in metres

# What is muscular endurance?

Muscular endurance or endurance strength is also called **anaerobic endurance**. It is the ability of a single muscle or muscle group to work very hard for a a period of time. It is the efficiency of our anaerobic system within our working muscles. This means high intensity, repetitive or even static exercise. For example, a sprint canoeist produces lots of force from a number of muscle groups over the short distance she races. Also in the tug-of-war our muscles are working hard but with little actual movement.

## Press up test

This test measures the muscular endurance of our chest and shoulder muscles. One way of carrying out this test is to complete as many press ups as possible in 60 seconds. We record our score. This can then be used as a target to beat as we become fitter.

### Abdominal curl test

|  | High score | Above average | Average | Below average | Low score |
|---|---|---|---|---|---|
| Males 15–16 years | above 27 | 26–25 | 24-23 | 22–21 | below 21 |
| Females 15–16 years | above 24 | 23–21 | 20-19 | 18–17 | below 17 |

Number in 30 seconds

## The NCF abdominal curl test

This test measures the muscular endurance of our abdominal muscles. We have to complete as many abdominal curls as possible within a time limit of 30 seconds. Our score is taken at the end of the 30 seconds. We must perform each curl properly. We start flat on our back and sit up to 90 degrees. Our arms must remain across our chest. Only light pressure is allowed to hold our feet in place.

## How do we improve and measure our muscular endurance?

We can improve our muscular endurance by training with light weights (40 – 60% of our one repetition maximum). We need to do the exercises at speed and with a high number of repetitions (20 – 30).

> ## ⊙ KEY POINT
>
> Our muscular endurance is being tested when our muscles are working hard for a period of time with very little actual movement.

# What is body build?

Our sporting success comes from a combination of ability and the appropriate body build. Usually we find that top high jumpers are tall and thin and gymnasts short and muscular. However, deciding what is the right body for each sport is complicated.

There are three main components of body build. These are:

- body type – muscularity, linearity, fatness;
- body size – height compared to weight;
- body composition – amount of fat.

There are three extremes of body types. These are called mesomorph, endomorph and ectomorph.

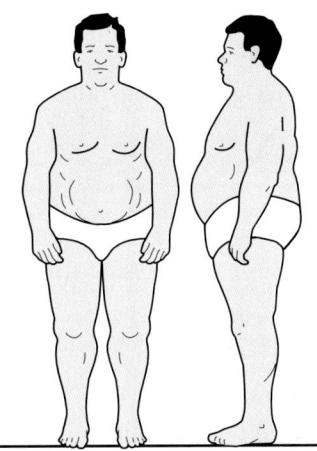

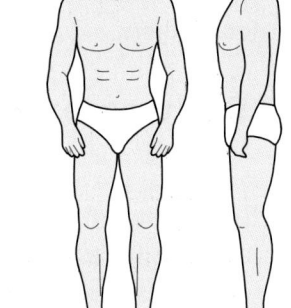

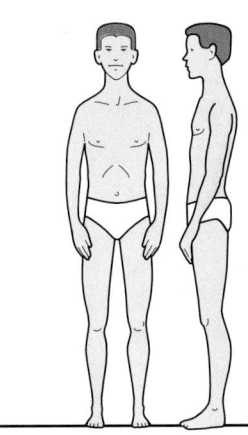

**Endomorph**

- a pear shaped body;
- wide hips and wide shoulders;
- a rounded head;
- a lot of fat on the body, upper arms and thighs.

They are wider front to back rather than side to side.

**Mesomorph**

- a wedge shaped body;
- wide shoulders and narrow hips;
- a massive cubical head;
- broad shoulders and heavily muscled arms and legs;
- a minimum amount of fat.

They are narrow from front to back.

**Ectomorph**

- narrow shoulders and hips;
- a narrow chest and abdomen;
- thin arms and legs;
- a high forehead and receding chin.

They have little muscle and little fat.

## Body type

There is a method of body typing called somatotyping. Three extremes of body types have been described. They are called endomorphs, mesomorphs and ectomorphs.

These extreme body types are rare. We are all part endomorph, part mesomorph and part ectomorph. We can all be given a score (from one – seven) for each of these basic body types. For example: two, six, three means: two (low endomorphy); six (high mesomorphy); three (low ectomorphy). In this way we can compare our body type with that of other people. Height is not important at all in working out our body type.

Most successful sportspeople are high in mesomorphy. They are suited to sport requiring explosive strength and power. Their muscular bulk also helps them in contact sports.

If we are high in endomorphy we could work to develop our strength and control our diet. Then we might be successful at sports needing power but with only a limited movement, such as weightlifting and wrestling.

If we are high in ectomorphy we could develop our endurance and might be successful at long distance events. By developing our muscular strength we might also succeed in events such as basketball and high jump.

Basketball players are at an advantage if they are tall. Jockeys need to be small

# Body size

Height and weight are important factors in **body size**. The ideal body size for sport depends on the needs of the individual sport or the position the person plays in the game. For example, a height of 1.90m would be short for a top basketball player but very tall for a gymnast. Long distance runners keep their weight down to reduce the load they have to carry. If we watch a game of rugby we can see a variety of heights and weights. Some sports such as wrestling, boxing and weight lifting have fixed weight categories. Controlled diets are essential for these athletes to prevent problems caused by rapid weight loss through crash diets.

# Body composition

Scientists are able to work out how much of our body is fat. The rest of our body weight is called 'fat free' and this includes our bones, muscles, organs and connective tissue.

In most sports, the higher the percentage of a participant's body fat, the poorer their performance. Therefore most sportspeople try to keep their body fat low and their fat-free weight (their muscle weight) high. However, this is not the case for long distance runners. They must keep both their fat and non fat weights as low as possible, as they have to carry all extra weight for the length of the race.

Standard height-weight tables give the correct range of weight for a particular height. They do not help sportspeople because they do not allow for body composition.

> ## ◯ KEY POINT
>
> Being overweight is not a problem for a sportsperson if the weight is composed of extra muscle. However, being overfat will reduce sporting performance.

We need to look at body
type, size and composition,
in different ways

# How do we improve our body build?

Our body type, body size and body composition
depend to a large extent on heredity. But we must
not think that we can do nothing about our body
build. Body composition can be changed a great deal.
Through careful diet and exercise, we can reduce the
amount of fat in our bodies and improve the
proportion of lean muscle. This will, of course, affect
our body size by changing our weight. Our height
will not change once we have reached physical
maturity. Any long term change in the amount of
fat and muscle in our bodies will affect our body type.
However, it is clear that we cannot change our basic
bone structure.

# How do we measure our body build?

To measure our **body build** we need to look at body
type, size and composition in different ways.

### Body type
**Somatotyping** is too lengthy and
complicated a procedure to do in college
and school. We can look at our athletics
team and put the athletes into
approximate **body types**. The throwers
are likely to be **endomorph**, the long
distance runners **ectomorph** and the
sprinters **mesomorph**.

### Body size
We can measure height and weight accurately.

### Body composition
It is very complicated to work out accurately how
much of our weight is fat and how much is fat free.
A good estimate of our **body composition** can be
made using skin-fold measurements.
A skinfold caliper is used to
measure the amount of fat
at five different places on
our bodies. These are at the
triceps, biceps, sub-scapular,
anterior suprailiac and the
medial calf. Using tables it
is possible to find a score
showing the percentage
of fat on our bodies.

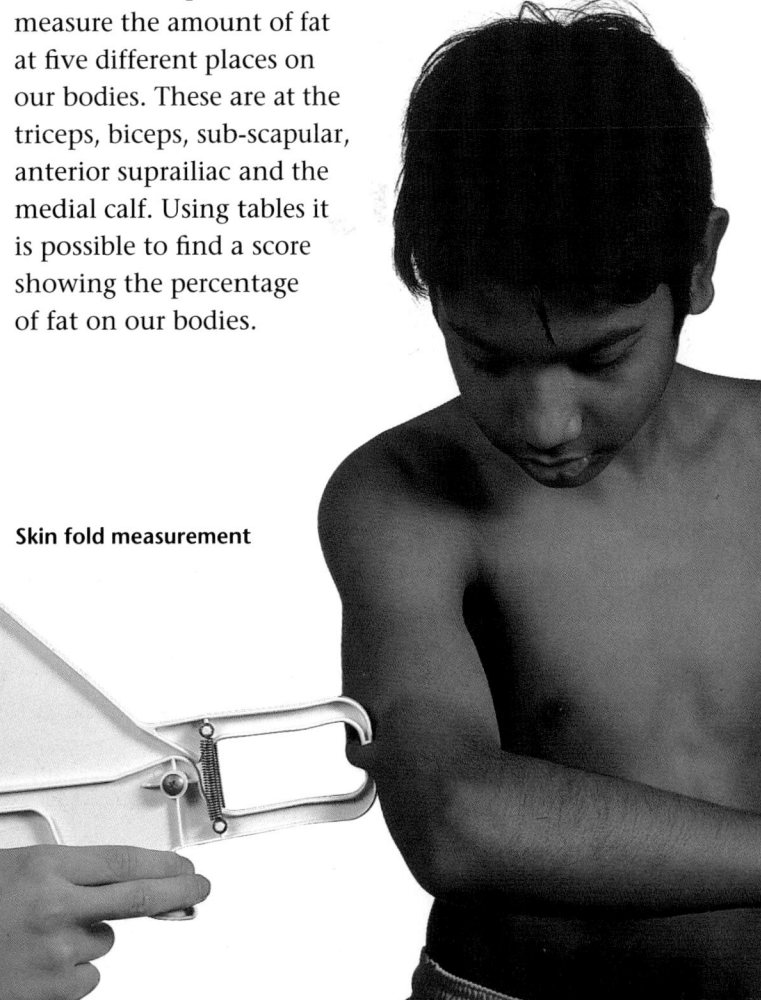

**Skin fold measurement**

# What is flexibility?

**Flexibility**, mobility and suppleness all mean the range of limb movement around joints. Some sports, such as gymnastics, require a great deal of overall body flexibility. Other sports, for example javelin, require flexibility in particular parts of the body.

Our flexibility can be improved by:

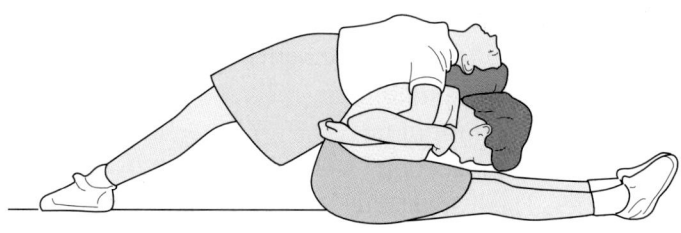

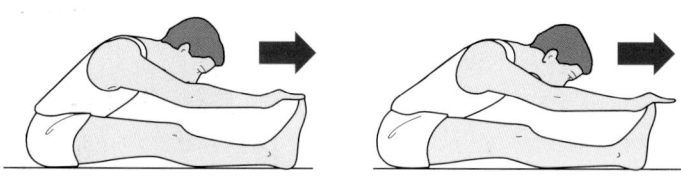

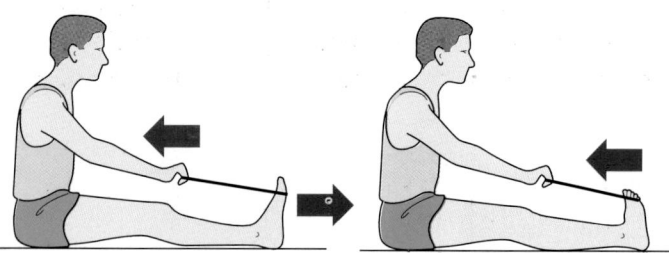

## Static stretching

In **static stretching** we extend our limb/limbs beyond their normal range. We hold the position for at least ten seconds. After a few seconds rest we repeat the stretch. We should continue this for at least five repetitions of ten seconds. We try to build up the time we hold the stretch.

## Passive stretching

In **passive stretching** we improve the flexibility of our joints by using a partner or coach to apply external force. They move the limb being exercised to its end position and keep it there for a few seconds. It is most important that this type of stretching is carried out carefully. If the force applied to us is too vigorous we may be badly injured.

## Active stretching

In **active** (or ballistic) **stretching** we extend a movement beyond our normal limitation. We repeat this rhythmically over a period of 20 seconds. It is very important that the muscles are warmed up before active stretching is started. Bouncing or bobbing methods were popular in the past. However, they can increase the risk of muscle damage. We should perform active stretches slowly at first.

## PNF stretching

**PNF stretches (or proprioceptive neuromuscular facilitation)** have grown from the knowledge that muscles are most relaxed (and therefore can most easily be stretched) immediately after contraction. In PNF stretching we first contract the muscle as hard as we can. It can be against a resistance such as a partner. We then stretch the muscle to the end of its range and hold the stretch for a few seconds. We then relax the muscle for a few seconds before we start again.

## How do we improve our flexibility?

Flexibility exercises, or stretching, are a part of most training programmes. Our flexibility does not depend on our shape. We can improve our flexibility by stretching our muscles and tendons and by extending the ligaments and supporting tissues beyond their normal range of movement. We should only overload our muscles whilst it feels comfortable. We must stretch the agonist and then the antagonist muscles (see page 22). This makes sure our muscles will recover and adapt in a balanced way.

**Gymnasts need to be very flexible.**

## How do we measure our flexibility?

The tests we use will depend upon the joints which we are measuring.

### Sit and reach test
We sit on the floor, legs straight, feet flat against the box, fingertips on the edge of the top plate. We bend the trunk and reach forward slowly and as far as possible, keeping our knees straight. We hold this position for two seconds. We then measure the distance from the edge of the plate to the position reached by the fingertips. (We can check our scores with those in the chart below.)

### The shoulder hyperextension test
This test measures our ability to stretch the muscles of our chest and shoulders. We lie face down on the floor with our arms stretched out in front of us. We hold a metre rule with our hands shoulder width apart. Keeping our chin on the ground at all times we raise our arms as high as possible, keeping the stick parallel to the floor. We hold our highest position for three seconds. The height reached is measured by a partner.

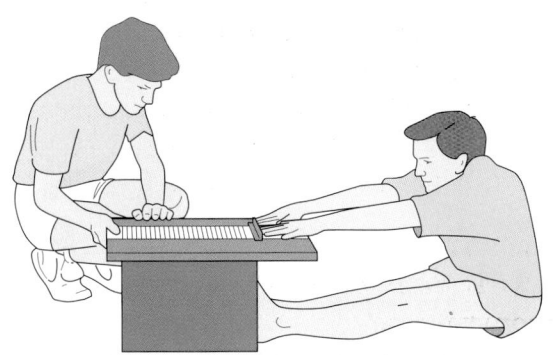

**Sit and reach test**

|  | High score | Above average | Average | Below average | Low score |
|---|---|---|---|---|---|
| Males 15–16 years | above 28 | 28–24 | 23–20 | 19–17 | below 17 |
| Females 15–16 years | above 35 | 35–32 | 31–30 | 29–25 | below 25 |

Distance in cm

# What is speed?

Speed is the ability to move all or part of the body quickly. Speed is important in sports which require a great deal of effort over a very short period of time. Sprinters, speed skaters and sprint cyclists all need to develop their speed. It is also important in many team games when a sudden change of pace and direction can bring success.

*Speed is important for sprint cyclists*

For our bodies to achieve speed, energy has to be supplied to the muscles very quickly. Muscles then have to contract in the shortest possible time. We will use our anaerobic energy supply system for speed work. If we have a high percentage of fast twitch fibres (see page 21) in our active muscles then we will have a natural advantage.

## How do we improve our speed?

Although we cannot increase the percentage of fast twitch fibres in our bodies, there are many other things we can do to improve our speed in sport. These include:

- increasing our strength through a programme of weight training and plyometrics (stronger muscles will give us more power and therefore more speed);
- improving our reaction time (see page 67);
- improving our ability to change speed and direction when moving quickly (see page 65);
- improving our ability to cope with lactic acid in our bodies (see page 45);
- improving the level of our skill in our sport, for example a more efficient swimming stroke will create less water resistance and lower our swim times.

*Speed skaters need to develop their speed*

## How do we measure our speed?

We can measure our speed simply by timing ourselves over a measured distance, for example 60 metres in eight seconds. Reaction time, speed off the mark, time taken to reach top speed and deceleration times can also be measured as part of a training programme.

# What is agility?

Agility is the ability to change the direction of the body at speed. It is a combination of speed, balance, power and coordination. Gymnasts, basketball players and skiers all need agility if they are to be successful. Only in static activities such as archery and shooting will agility be of no importance.

## How do we improve our agility?

We can improve our agility by training. We develop agility by rehearsing the movements made in our sport. This is done at full speed and under similar conditions to those in a competitive situation. We must also improve our speed, balance, power and coordination as all of these aspects of fitness affect our agility.

## How do we measure our agility?

The best way for somebody to assess our agility in a particular sport is to watch us playing it. We can assess our general agility using a test such as the following:

### Illinois agility run

A course is set up as shown on the diagram. We lie face down on the floor at the starting line. When told to start we leap to our feet and complete the course in the shortest possible time. We can then compare our time with those of others in our group.

**Agility is the ability to quickly change direction**

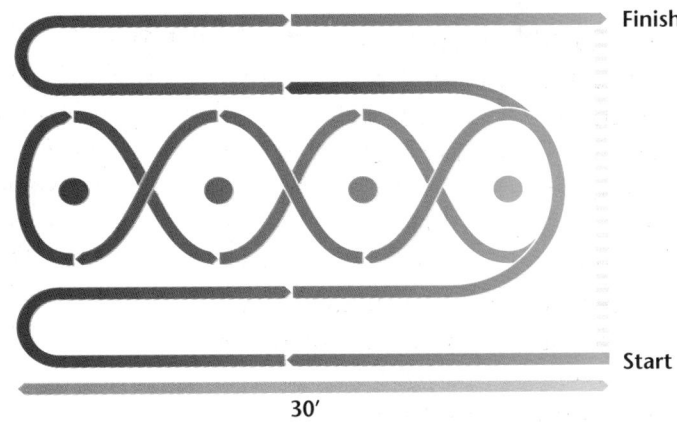

Illinois agility run

**Illinois agility run**

| | High score | Above average | Average | Below average | Low score |
|---|---|---|---|---|---|
| Males 15–16 years | faster than 15.9 secs | 15.9–16.7 | 16.8–18.6 | 18.7–18.8 | slower than 18.8 |
| Females 15–16 years | faster than 17.5 secs | 17.5–18.6 | 18.7–22.4 | 22.4–23.4 | slower than 23.4 |

Time in seconds

# What is coordination?

Coordination is the ability to carry out a series of movements smoothly and efficiently. Such movements happen as a result of the nervous system and muscular system working well together. Good coordination is essential for skilful performance. Sport is full of examples of good coordination, from triple somersaults to saving penalties. We are only too aware of poor coordination when we try to learn a new sporting skill from scratch.

## How do we improve our coordination?

Coordination improves with practice. Very many of the toys we played with when we were young helped to develop our whole body coordination as well as hand eye and foot eye coordination. Our P.E. lessons in primary school, in which we took part in gymnastics and played with balls, hoops and skipping ropes, will have further developed our coordination. As we learn the new skills necessary for a particular sport we go through a stage in which our coordination is not perfect. With good coaching (see chapter 4) and plenty of practice we soon become well coordinated.

## How do we measure our coordination?

The best way to measure our coordination in a particular sport is to play it. There are a number of ways of testing hand eye coordination. Two of these ways are described opposite.

## Alternate hand wall toss test

In this test we stand two metres away from a smooth wall. We throw a tennis ball with our right hand against the wall and catch it with our left hand. We then throw it with our left hand and catch it with our right. We do this as quickly as possible for 30 seconds. We can compare our results with the norms shown in the chart below.

Alternate wall toss test

|  | High score | Above average | Average | Below average | Low score |
|---|---|---|---|---|---|
| 15–16 years | above 35 | 35–30 | 29–25 | 24–20 | below 20 |

Number of catches

## Juggling test

An enjoyable way to test our coordination is to try juggling with first two and then three balls. In any group of people tested we will find that some will be able to achieve the three ball juggling much more quickly than others.

**Badminton requires great coordination**

# What is reaction time?

Our reaction time shows our ability to react to a stimulus quickly. A reaction can be simple, or it can involve choice. An example of simple reaction time is the time delay between the gun going off in a sprint race and our first movement. An example of **choice reaction time** is when we receive a ball from our opponent in a tennis match. In both of these cases we will have to react quickly. However, in the second case, we will have to decide where and how to hit the ball. These decisions will depend on where the ball is about to land, in which direction our opponent is moving and many other factors. We are involved in making choices. The more skilled and experienced a tennis player we are, the more likely we will be to make the right choice and the most appropriate type of return.

Choice reaction time is important for footballers

## How do we measure our reaction time?

We can use a number of computer reaction time programmes. They all ask us to respond as quickly as possible (usually by pressing a key) to a stimulus such as a sound or a visual cue. Some measure our simple reaction time by only asking for a single response to a single stimulus. Other programmes, to measure our choice reaction time, give us a variety of responses only one of which is correct.

## How do we improve our reaction time?

The speed of reaction to a single stimulus is determined to a large extent by the efficiency of the nervous system. If we are lucky, our sensory and motor nerves will be capable of transmitting messages very speedily. Therefore, our muscles will get the message from our brains to contract very quickly. If we have a high percentage of fast twitch fibres then we will be able to respond more quickly than those individuals with a high percentage of slow twitch fibres.

Research shows that it is not possible to improve our simple reaction time through training. Choice reaction time can be improved a great deal, however. In a team game such as soccer, we will be receiving stimuli from our eyes about the position of the ball, the opposition players, our own team players and the goal; we will be receiving stimuli from our ears, as we hear the sound of an opposing player coming in from behind, the call from a team player, the whistle from the referee; we will be receiving stimuli from our **kinaesthetic sense** about the position of our feet and whether they are in a position to pass, shoot at the goal etc. If we are skilled we are able to reduce our response time by knowing which information coming to us is important, and by anticipating the action of players and the ball. We only gain this skill through training and experience.

We can also improve our movement time by strengthening the power of our muscles.

> **◯ KEY POINT**
>
> We can improve our choice reaction time. We can make our reactions quicker and more appropriate.

# What is balance?

Balance is the body's ability to keep its **equilibrium** when stationary or moving. Keeping our equilibrium means keeping our centre of gravity over our area of support. If we do not keep our equilibrium we will fall over. Stationary, or static, balance is shown in activities such as gymnastics. Moving, or dynamic, balance is important in most sports. Snowboarders and surfers must have very good dynamic balance. They move very fast over uneven surfaces and must constantly readjust their positions. We maintain our balance through the coordinated actions of our eyes, our ears and the proprioceptive organs in our joints.

Snowboarders need good dynamic balance

## How do we improve our balance?

We can improve the balance needed in particular sports by developing the appropriate skills thoroughly. We can then put these skills to the test under the stress of competitive or team situations.

## How do we measure our balance?

Static balance can be measured in a number of ways. The stork stand described below is a test of static balance.

### The stork stand

In this test we stand comfortably on both feet and with our hands on our hips. We then lift one leg and place the toes of that foot against the knee of the other leg. On command, we raise the heel and stand on our toes, balancing for as long as possible without letting either the heel touch the floor or the other foot move away from the knee.

We can compare our results with the norms in the following chart:

**The stork stand**

|  | High score | Above average | Average | Below average | Low score |
|---|---|---|---|---|---|
| 15–16 years | 60–50 | 49–40 | 39–26 | 25–11 | below 10 |

Time in seconds

# Questions

## Fitness for Health and Performance

1   Name two tests of cardiovascular fitness.

2   Strength is one of the components of health related fitness. Name one other.

3   Describe and name the three body types and explain their suitability for physical activity.

4   Agility and coordination are sport related components of fitness. Define each component and give one example from sport to illustrate the importance of each to that sport.

5   Sportspeople need to train specifically for their event or activity. Name two components of fitness which a gymnast should work on and two components that a discus thrower should work on.

6   Muscular power is needed for explosive events.
    **a** What is the meaning of 'muscular power'?
    **b** Name one event in which muscular power is essential for success.

7   Explain why the heart rate is a reliable indicator of physical fitness.

8   Explain the importance of flexibility for everyday living.

9   Name the two areas of fitness that an attacking player in a team game should aim to improve.

10  Muscular endurance differs from cardiovascular endurance. Explain the difference and give examples of training methods to improve each of these types of fitness.

# 4 Training for Success

For sporting success, we need to ensure that our energy systems and sporting skills are at the highest level possible. We can reach these high levels by training. In this chapter we look at the principles of training, how to plan our training, training methods and their long term effects on the body.

## Principles of training page 72

**Specificity**

We must train for our own particular sport, for example surfers need to work with waves.

**Progression**

We must increase our training gradually, for example surfers must start with small waves.

**Overload**

We must work harder than normal, for example surfers must build up their whole body fitness.

**Reversibility**

We will lose fitness when inactive, for example surfers must keep in condition by staying on the waves.

**Tedium**

We must make our training interesting, for example surfers must look for new waves and new beaches.

## Planning a training programme page 74

**Frequency**

We must train regularly, for example trampolinists need to bounce daily.

**Intensity**

We must work hard in training, for example trampolinists will not reach the top without hard work.

**Time**

We must gradually increase our training time, for example trampolinists need more time in the air.

**Type**

We must know the demands of our sport, for example trampolinists must know which way to turn.

## Training programme – phases

page 74

### Warm up

We must get our bodies ready for action, for example water polo players need to warm up in the water.

### Fitness

We must work hard to improve fitness, for example water polo players need water fitness.

### Skill development

We must work hard to develop our techniques and skills, for example water polo players need ball handling and teamwork skills.

### Warm down

We must cool our bodies down gently, for example water polo players can relax in the pool.

## Training methods page 76

### Continuous training

We can develop aerobic fitness, for example lacrosse players can go for long runs.

### Fartlek training

We can develop the fitness we choose in the way that we like, for example lacrosse players can plan their running to suit their needs.

### Interval training

We can develop fitness in a short time, for example lacrosse players can work hard to gain fitness quickly.

## Long term effects of training

page 81

To train effectively, we need to know about:
The long term effects of aerobic training;
The long term effects of anaerobic training;
The long term effects of resistance training.

### Circuit training

We can develop fitness using a variety of different activities, for example lacrosse players can train together as a team.

### Weight training

We can develop different types of strength, for example lacrosse players can build up their strengths.

### Plyometrics

We can develop power, for example lacrosse players can become more powerful.

## Age and training page 83

## Gender and training page 84

# Principles of training

To become fitter we need to train. To train effectively we should follow the following principles:

- **S**pecificity
- **P**rogression
- **O**verload
- **R**eversibility
- **T**edium

Progressive training will strengthen our muscles

## What do we mean by Specificity?

The effects of training are very specific. If we wish to develop the **strength** of our upper arm muscles, exercising our legs will not help. We need to use a training programme which puts regular stress on the muscle groups we are concerned with. We must not assume that exercises used to improve flexibility will also improve strength.

Sprinters must include a large amount of speed work in their training. This ensures that their fast twitch muscle fibres are fully developed. Endurance athletes need to develop their slow twitch muscle fibres. They will use training which puts their bodies under prolonged steady stress. Sportspeople who need both speed and endurance must include both types of exercise in their training to develop both their fast and slow twitch muscle fibres.

## What do we mean by Progression?

When we increase the amount of exercise we do, we place added stress on our body systems. We must add this stress in a progressive (or, gradual) way. Too big an increase in stress can cause us to stop training, or suffer injury. An increase in stress which is not big enough can lead to staleness and boredom – we need a challenge.

It is not only our muscles which have to adapt to greater stresses being put on our bodies. Bones, ligaments and tendons also have to change. However, bones, ligaments and tendons may take longer to change and adapt than muscles. We need to understand about training thresholds so that we do not over-work or do too little training (See page 48).

We can tell whether we are working too hard, or not hard enough, by keeping a check on our heart rates during aerobic training (see page 48). If it rises too steeply following a change in training load, then we have probably increased our overload by too much.

**Our volleyball skills can be improved by specific training**

**We need variety in our training**

## What do we mean by Overload?

To improve the fitness of our various body systems we need to overload (or stress) them. This means we need to make them work harder than normal. Our bodies will gradually adapt in order to cope with this extra work and we will become fitter. We can improve our aerobic ability, strength and flexibility by gradually increasing the amount of overload which we put on our bodies.

If we have been training our aerobic systems by running five miles twice a week and at the same pace, we will have reached a certain level of fitness. To become fitter we must either increase the distances we run (eg. from five to six miles), complete the run in a shorter amount of time, or complete the run more times a week. Each one of these methods will overload the aerobic system. The aerobic system will gradually adapt in order to cope with the overload.

> ## ⊃ KEY POINT
>
> **S**pecificity **P**rogression **O**verload **R**eversibility **T**edium
> When training we must:
> * train for our own *particular* sport (the needs of other sports will be different);
> * increase our training *gradually*;
> * work *harder* than normal;
> * understand we'll *lose* our fitness when we're inactive;
> * make our training *interesting*.

## What do we mean by Reversibility?

Our bodies are able to adapt to more stress by becoming fitter. In the same way, our bodies will adapt to less stress. It takes only three to four weeks for our bodies to get out of condition. We can lose our aerobic fitness more easily than our anaerobic, as the muscles quickly lose much of their ability to use oxygen. Our anaerobic activities are affected less by lack of training. Our strength gains are lost at about one third of their rate of gain. If we have been training to improve our leg muscles three times a week for about four weeks and then stop, all of our strength gains will disappear after about 12 weeks. If our muscles are not used they atrophy, (or, waste away). We gradually lose both speed and strength.

## What do we mean by Tedium?

Tedium (or, boredom) should be avoided in all training programmes. By using a variety of training methods we will keep our enthusiasm and not become stale.

We can also avoid overuse injuries by varying the way we perform certain activities. For example, running on hard surfaces all the time can lead to shin splints. By running on grass for some of the time we will cut down the possibility of suffering from them. (See page 76 for examples of different training programmes.)

# Planning a training programme

When planning a fitness programme, we need to think about: frequency, intensity, time and type, or **F.I.T.T. principles.**

## Frequency

We should train at least three times a week. Our bodies will need time to recover between training sessions and so we should space these sessions out over the week.

## Intensity

We will not improve our fitness unless we work hard enough to make our body systems adapt. We must understand our training thresholds.

## Time

If we wish to improve our aerobic fitness then our training sessions must last longer and longer, gradually over time. We should also increase the heart rate level at which we work.

## Type

Our training programmes must include the type of activities which develop the fitness and skills we need. We should analyse the needs of our particular sport.

> **KEY POINT**
>
> **F**requency **I**ntensity **T**ime **T**ype
> When planning a fitness programme, we should arrange to:
> - train *frequently*;
> - work *harder*;
> - train for *longer*;
> - develop the *right fitness and skills*.

# Training programme – phases

Olympic sports people often have their training programmes planned out in advance with their sessions set out on a daily, weekly, monthly and even yearly basis. Dividing the training programme into different parts is called **periodisation.** Sports people design their training programmes so that they peak (or, perform at their best) at the times of major competitions. If we take part in competitive sport on a regular basis then we must also plan ahead.

## Planning a training programme for the year

**Off season.** The emphasis is on developing our muscular strength and aerobic fitness. We should also continue to develop the skills of our sport.

**Pre season.** (eight–ten weeks before the start of the season) The emphasis is on intense training, including muscular endurance work. We should develop the techniques, skills and strategies necessary for our sports.

**Early season.** The emphasis is on power and speed work. Our training should aim for us to peak on competition days. We should further develop our techniques, skills and strategies in competitive situations.

**Peak season.** The emphasis is on speed. We should develop our skills by practising them at high speed and in competitive situations. Extra fitness sessions may be necessary if competitions are not frequent enough to keep our fitness levels high.

# What should we put in our individual training sessions?

We should divide our training sessions into four phases: 'warm up', 'fitness', 'skill development' and 'warm down' (cool down).

## Warm up

Our warm up should include:

- a period of gentle exercise using the whole body, for example light jogging. This will gradually increase both heart rate and breathing, ensure that the blood flow to our muscles gradually increases, warm up our muscles and prepare us mentally for the hard work to follow;
- gentle stretching. We should work on the joints most likely to be stressed during our main training session;
- practising the various techniques and skills to be used in our training session. For example, a basketball player would perform some lay up shots, set shots, etc.

It is sensible to carry out flexibility exercises during a warm down period. This is because our muscles are thoroughly warmed and less likely to be overstretched and injured. These exercises also stop our muscles from losing heat too quickly and will prevent muscle soreness.

## Fitness

The fitness activities we use will depend on the demands of our sport. If we follow the warm up with a fitness session we must ensure that we are not too tired for the skill development session which will follow. Being too tired will prevent us from working well when practising our skills. It is often more sensible to include a harder fitness session at the end of the skill phase.

## Skill development phase

This is the time when we develop the skills necessary for our particular sport. If we are team players we will need to develop our individual techniques. We also need to develop our skills in small groups and whole team situations. This is also the time when we play small sided or modified competitive games. (For more details see page 98).

## Warm down

We should always finish a training session with a period of lighter exercise. This is a warm down (or, cool down). We should not go directly from hard exercise to rest. Light exercise shortens the recovery time necessary by helping to remove carbon dioxide, lactic acid and other waste products which have built up in our bodies. It also ensures that our blood continues to circulate well and does not pool in the skeletal muscles. Pooling can cause a rapid lowering in blood pressure and make us feel light-headed and dizzy.

# Training methods

There are many different training methods. They are all based on an understanding of how our body adapts to training. Different methods of training include: continuous training, fartlek (or, speed play) training; interval training; circuit training; weight training; plyometrics.

## Continuous training

For **continuous training** we exercise without rest intervals. There are two types of continuous training: **long, slow distance training** and **high intensity continuous training**.

For long, slow distance training, we run, swim, cycle, row, take part in aerobics or do any other whole body activity. We work at between 60–80% of our maximum heart rate. This type of training is ideal if we wish to be fit for health related reasons. It is also suitable for sportspeople in their off season. We should work for extended periods of time (30–60 minutes) for maximum benefit.

For high intensity continuous training, we work at between 85–95% of our maximum heart rate. The emphasis is on training at nearly competition pace. For example, if a 20 year old middle distance runner runs five miles at five minute mile pace, his heart rate will be approximately 180bpm (beats per minute). This is very hard work. It is high intensity training. It improves his leg speed, leg strength and muscular endurance. High intensity work should be only one part of any training programme as **fatigue** is high and injury always possible.

## Fartlek training

**Fartlek** is a Swedish word meaning 'speed play'. Fartlek training involves training over distances far greater than our actual competition distance. We vary the pace at which we walk, run, cycle, or ski and the type of country over which we travel. The emphasis is on the enjoyment of running fast yet within our ability. The way the activities are put together will produce aerobic or anaerobic effects. It is very good for games players as they are involved in short intense activities followed by brief periods of recovery.

Hard training
is necessary
for success in
competition

# Interval training

**Interval training** means alternating between strenuous exercise and rest. The rest periods give us time to recover from each period of exercise. We can train for longer periods of time. Interval training can be used to develop both anaerobic and aerobic fitness, depending on how we organise our training sessions.

We can vary the:
- time or distance of each period of exercise;
- amount of effort (intensity) we put into each period of exercise;
- length of time we rest between each period of exercise;
- type of activity we take part in during each period of rest;
- number of exercise and recovery periods in each training session;

- if we use interval training to increase our aerobic endurance, we have to exercise for long periods. In these periods we exercise at about 70% of our MHR (maximum heart rate).

- if we want to develop our anaerobic endurance we work for short periods. In these periods we exercise at 80–95% of our MHR;
- if we work on high quality speed training, the rest periods are at least two–three minutes long. This gives enough time for the the ATP and creatine phosphate stores in our muscles to develop again. Very short rest periods develop our ability to work when tired;
- we recover more quickly if we exercise lightly during our rest periods. This is especially important for games players as it reflects what happens in the game.

# Circuit training

In **circuit training** we perform selected exercises or activities in a given sequence. This is called a circuit. A circuit usually has between six and ten exercises or activities which take place at a 'station'.

Circuits can be designed to improve our aerobic or our anaerobic fitness. The type of activities included in the circuit, the time spent at each activity and the number of circuits completed will determine which type of fitness is improved.

Good circuits will have activities which are needed for our particular sport. If leg power is important in our sport then the circuit should include a number of exercises using leg power. We should make sure that they do not follow one another in the circuit so that our leg muscles have time to recover.

As our fitness improves we can make the circuit more difficult by increasing the:

- number of stations;
- time spent at each station;
- number of repetitions at each station;
- number of complete circuits.

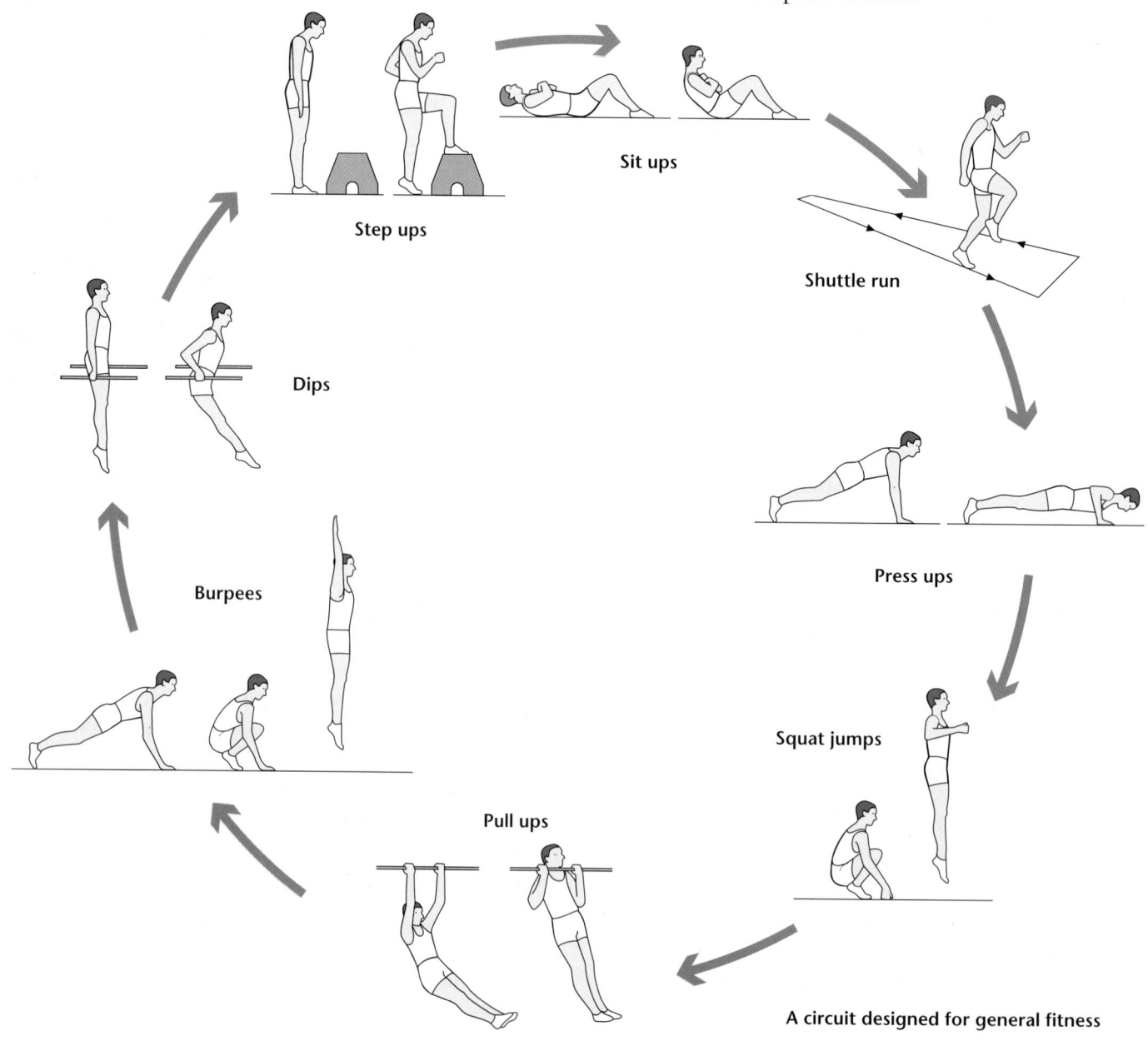

**Step ups**

**Sit ups**

**Shuttle run**

**Dips**

**Press ups**

**Burpees**

**Squat jumps**

**Pull ups**

**A circuit designed for general fitness**

# Weight training

In **weight training** we use either free weights or machine weights as a form of resistance training. Weights can be increased gradually. We can overload muscles in a safe manner over a sensible period of time. Our individual strength training programme can be designed for our particular sport. It can also take into account our current state of fitness.

When weight training, our muscles shorten as we lift the weights. These are called isotonic contractions. We can also use weights for concentric and eccentric contractions (see page 20). Many sports centres now have excellent weight training equipment which makes training safe, enjoyable and highly motivating.

We should use the S.P.O.R.T. training principles when designing a weight training programme.

The following guidelines will also help us:
* we should aim for at least three training sessions a week;
* we must warm up thoroughly before starting each session;
* we must breathe in when the weight is lifted and out as it is lowered. We must never hold our breath as this will increase our blood pressure and may cause us to faint;
* we must increase the weights as our muscles grow stronger;
* we should decide which are the important muscle groups in our sport and select exercises which develop them;
* maximum strength is developed by at least three sets of six repetitions at near maximum weight;
* muscular endurance is developed by at least three sets of 20–30 repetitions. A **set** is a number of exercises performed one after the other. The weight should be between 40–60% of our **repetition maximum** (the maximum weight we can lift a number of times) for example, 1 RM;

**Weight training**

* muscular power is developed by at least three sets of ten to 15 repetitions. These are carried out at speed using **resistance** of between 60–80% of our repetition maximum.

# Plyometrics

When we are running, our strong thigh muscles are slightly stretched before they contract to drive us forward. This stretch stores up elastic energy. When the muscle contracts, this elastic energy is released. This release makes the contraction more powerful. This extra power does not take up much extra energy. It provides more power without any extra effort. The same principle applies whenever a muscle is stretched before it contracts. Training methods that use this principle to develop power are known as plyometrics.

**Plyometrics** training has one key feature, which is the training of our nervous and muscular systems to allow faster and more powerful changes of direction. We do this when, for example, we move from down to up in jumping, or switch leg positions in running.

If we can reduce the time needed for this change in direction, our speed and power will increase. Ski jumpers, cross-country and downhill skiers, volleyball players, sprinters and high jumpers can all benefit from this type of training. In plyometric training we use bounds, hops, jumps, leaps, skips, ricochets, swings and twists.

When using plyometrics there is a lot of strain on muscles and joints. We should be well warmed up. Beginners, particularly, should take great care. It is better to start any training using this system on grass or, if in the gym, on mats.

**Plyometric exercises**

# Long term effects of training

A well planned, long term training programme brings about changes in the body. These changes will depend upon the type of training carried out. We will now look at the long term effects of aerobic training, anaerobic training and resistance training.

## What are the long term effects of aerobic training?

### On our heart
- our **heart** has larger chambers with thicker and stronger muscular walls;
- our heart empties its chambers more completely;
- our **stroke volume** (the amount of blood pumped out in each contraction) can be double that of an untrained person;
- our heart beats more slowly when at rest. It can cope with hard work better and will go back to its resting rate more quickly than an untrained heart.

### On our blood and arteries
- our arteries become larger and more elastic. There is less risk of our arteries hardening (arteriosclerosis); our **blood pressure** is reduced;
- the quantity and quality of our blood is increased;
- more oxygen is carried in our **haemoglobin** because we have more red blood cells. There are lower levels of fat in the blood;
- we can cope with more **lactic acid** during exercise.

### On our tendons, ligaments and bones
- our **tendons** become stronger;
- our ligaments become more flexible as a result of stretching;
- our **bones** become stronger as more calcium is produced.

### On our body fat
- Our body uses more fat and less carbohydrate as fuel for exercise. This is helpful because we have good supplies of fat.

### On the way we use oxygen
- we can breathe in much more air and continue to do so for a longer time;
- we will be able to work closer to our $VO_2$ max (the maximum amount of oxygen which we can take in and use in our bodies in one minute);
- we can increase our $VO_2$ max by as much as 20%;
- the number of alveoli in our lungs increases. This helps more oxygen get into the bloodstream and more carbon dioxide to get out. The muscles involved in breathing become stronger;
- our muscles are able to hold and use greater supplies of oxygen and nutrients. The increased blood vessel network can get more oxygen to the muscles. More of this oxygen can be stored ready for use in the muscles.

## What are the long term effects of anaerobic training?

A long term effect of anaerobic training is that our anaerobic threshold is increased. This means we are able to work much harder than before, and for longer periods of time, before becoming tired. Our recovery rate after exercise is also quicker.

Most of the long term training effects will take place in our muscles. This is because our muscles have to work without oxygen during anaerobic training. Actual changes include:

- our fast twitch muscle fibres increase in size. They are able to cope better with more lactic acid before becoming tired;
- our muscle cells will store greater amounts of ATP, creatine phosphate and glycogen;
- there is an increase in the quantity, speed and efficiency of the chemical reactions which produce and use energy in our muscles.

## What are the long term effects of resistance training?

- greater amounts of ATP, creatine phosphate and glycogen are stored in our muscle cells;
- our muscles **hypertrophy**, (become larger), and contract more quickly and more strongly;
- our fast twitch muscle fibres increase in size;
- our ligaments and tendons become stronger;
- our muscles decrease in size and strength (**atrophy**) when they become inactive, for example in injury.

## What are the long term effects of resistance training for different types of strength?

- our muscles adapt to the amount of work they have to do;
- if very heavy weights are lifted for just a few repetitions then our muscular strength (static strength) increases;
- if heavy weights are lifted with just a few fast repetitions then our muscular power (explosive strength) increases;
- if light weights are lifted with many repetitions then our muscular endurance (endurance strength) will be increased.

**Resistance training improves strength**

# Age and training

## Childhood and adolescence

We grow very quickly in the first two years of our lives. Our rate of growth then slows down until we reach puberty. We then grow very rapidly with girls reaching full height at about 16.5 years and boys reaching full height at about 18 years.

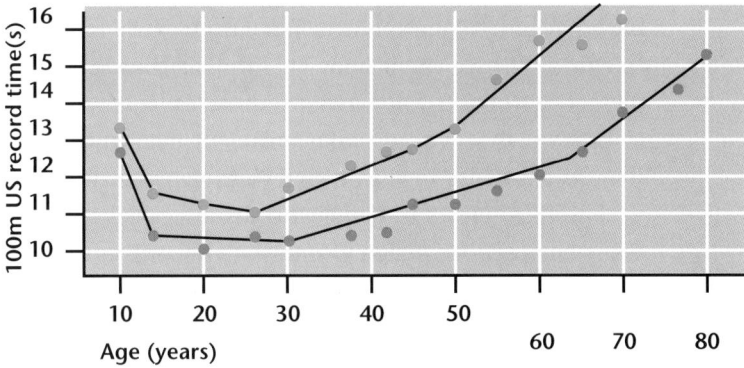

Our performance changes as we grow older

Regular physical exercise during childhood and adolescence establishes a healthy pattern of activity for the rest of our lives. Exercise also ensures our bones grow properly. Balance, agility and co-ordination increase as our nervous system grows.

Training programmes should be designed for specific age groups. During childhood, strength can be increased by careful resistance training. However, we must take care that we do not damage the growth areas at the end of our long bones by, for example, heavy weight training before our bones are fully formed. Training can improve the strength, aerobic capacity and anaerobic capacity of young sportspeople.

As their body systems develop, children have more control over their movements. Their ability to perform will increase as they approach physical maturity.

## Physical maturity and beyond

Sports records suggest we are in our prime during our late 20's and early 30's. After this age, our physical powers in both strength and endurance activities decline by about 1-2% a year.

From our mid twenties:

- our maximum heart rate decreases at about the rate of one beat per minute per year;
- our arteries gradually lose their elasticity. This increases our blood pressure and reduces the blood flow to our working muscles;
- our maximum stroke volume, heart output and vital capacity of our lungs steadily decreases. These changes mean that less oxygen is carried to the working muscles and our $VO_2$ max decreases;
- our maximum strength decreases steadily. This is due to a loss of muscle mass;
- our muscles change to slow twitch rather than fast twitch muscle fibres;
- we increase our body fat steadily over the years. This is due to our decreased physical activity, our increased food intake and our reduced ability to make use of fat for energy.

This steady decline in our physical ability is due largely to a reduction in the amount of endurance activity we undertake on a regular basis. If we continue to exercise on a regular basis, we can slow down the effects of ageing on our cardiovascular and muscular systems.

> **KEY POINT**
>
> Our physical ability declines as we grow older, but we can slow down these effects.

# Gender and training

One of the vital factors in deciding our sporting potential is whether we are male or female. For the first nine or ten years of our lives, boys and girls mature at about the same rate. We have similar body shapes and similar amounts of bone, muscle and fat. Sporting competition between the sexes is quite fair at this stage.

## Body size and shape

At puberty, the release of testosterone in boys leads to larger bones and a big increase in muscle size. Adolescent boys are larger and more muscular than girls.

The release of oestrogen in girls results in breast development, broadening of the hips as well as an increase in body fat. Women have more fat in the hips and lower body whilst men carry more fat in the abdomen and upper body. An average man between the ages of 18-24 has 13-16% fat whilst an average female of the same age has 20-25% fat. Male athletes range from 4-15% fat compared with 8-20% for females.

Women have narrower shoulders, broader hips, and smaller chest diameters. Women need wide hips for childbearing. As a result, their legs are in a less mechanically efficient position for running.

## Strength

Women are generally weaker than men. However, when their body size is taken into account, the differences are not at all significant. Men are much stronger in the upper body than women. When women train with weights, it is body tone which is increased rather than body size. With men, weight training helps their muscles become larger and stronger because of their high levels of testosterone.

## Aerobic power

Up to the age of ten, girls and boys have the same oxygen carrying capacity. Boys' capacity develops throughout puberty. Girls stop improving after about the age of 12. The best male competitors in endurance events are better than the best females by at least 30%. These differences are due to the smaller lungs and hearts in women, as well as a lower percentage of blood volume. Women also have up to 30% less haemoglobin in the blood. This means that less oxygen will get to the working muscles. It is important that women take sufficient iron in their diet, as they lose iron in blood during menstruation.

The differences in times and distances achieved in sport between men and women are becoming smaller. It is important that women have equal opportunity to take part in sporting activities and are given every encouragement to do so.

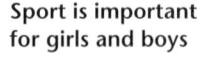

Sport is important for girls and boys

# Questions

## Training for Success

1  **a** Describe the benefits of circuit training.
   **b** Devise and describe a circuit of ten exercises. Explain the effects of each exercise.
   **c** State two reasons why the order in which the exercises are performed is important.

2  Name three of the principles of training.

3  Name three types of training likely to be used by middle distance athletes.

4  How does regular aerobic exercise affect the heart?

5  **a** Select a sport and describe one method of training specific to it.
   **b** Explain why you have chosen the type of training selected.
   **c** Describe, in detail, one training session.

6  Choose a sporting activity and describe an annual training programme. Explain how it should change throughout the year.

7  Explain each of the following in relation to training:
   **i** intensity
   **ii** duration
   **iii** frequency.

8  List three long term effects of
   **a** anaerobic training
   **b** resistance training.

9  Explain how resistance training can be adapted to improve:
   **i** maximum strength
   **ii** muscular power
   **iii** muscular endurance.

10 Volleyball players use plyometrics when training. Describe typical plyometric exercises and explain their effects.

# 5 Skill in Sport

## What is skill? page 88

We need a basic amount of natural ability in order to develop techniques and skills.

We also need adequate health related fitness together with our own sport related fitness.

Our ability to be skilful also depends on how efficient our brain is at processing information. We receive information from our senses. Our perception and memory help us to make sense of this information. We then make a decision. Our muscles respond with movement and our brain then gets feedback from our senses telling us whether or not we have been successful.

Other factors affecting our performances are our motivation, the goals we set ourselves and things to do with our personality.

## How do we learn skills? page 96

There are three phases of skill learning which we must pass through to become skilled. These are called cognitive, associative and autonomous. An understanding of these will help us to progress.

Certain things help us to learn skills. These are:
- guidance;
- practise;
- feedback;
- experience.

Training sessions are organised to include a warm up, time to practise skills, games, fitness training and a warm down.

We may be able to transfer experiences and skills from one sport, or activity, to another.

Major influences on our skill learning are our P.E. teachers at school, our coaches and the officials who control our competitions.

## Competitive sport and skill page 100

There are different types of competitive sport. They involve
using different sorts of strategies and tactics.

Team games are also concerned with teamwork, game plans,
formations, restarts and set plays.

Planning, performing and evaluating competitive
performances are valuable assets for everyone.

# What is skill?

When we watch top sportspeople in action, we see them perform their skills smoothly. They are exciting to watch because they seem to make difficult actions seem very easy. What we do not see are the hours of practice over many years which have enabled them to become highly skilful.

## What is the difference between a technique and a skill?

Skill refers to a standard of performance. It is essential to all sports performances. Sportspeople use their skill to achieve their objectives, for example scoring a goal, completing a trampoline routine or winning a race.

Techniques are the basic movements in sports, for example a volley in football is a technique, as is a smash in badminton or a handstand in gymnastics. In sport, we usually combine a number of different techniques into a pattern of movement. This is what we call skill.

Skill is our ability to choose and perform the right techniques at the right time, successfully, regularly and with a minimum of effort. For example, the skilled basketball player is able to put together the techniques of shooting, passing and dribbling at the right times in the game. He is usually successful in his play and always seems to have plenty of time.

We can think of skill in sport as being a combination of physical and mental qualities. The badminton player needs a variety of techniques, for example different strokes. She also needs to know what her opponent is doing now and what she is likely to do next. She must decide which stroke to use and where to hit the shuttlecock. Decision making is a very important part of skill. We are not born with skill. We have to learn to be skilful.

When we see top sportspeople in action, we do not see the hours of practice it took to make them skilful – Pinsent and Regrave winning gold in Atlanta

## What do we mean by ability?

Ability is our make up as a person. We inherit ability from our parents. If you are very tall, strong and well coordinated you may have a natural ability for basketball. This is inherited. By learning techniques and practising skills, you could use your ability and become a skilful basketball player.

Ability + Learning + Practise = Skill (A.L.P.S.)

> ### ⊙ KEY POINT
> Techniques are basic movements. We use techniques to build skill. Being skilful means using our techniques effectively, consistently and efficiently.

# What types of skill are there?

We all know that there are very many different sports and an amazing variety of different skills. Sports such as judo, archery and lacrosse seem to have little in common. However, we can classify skills in different ways, for example we can divide them into open and closed skills, and we can place them on a continuum.

## Open and closed skills

Dividing skills into open skills and closed skills is a way of looking at them (a system). In this system, we look at how the sporting environment affects the skills of the sport. The environment includes such things as weather, surfaces and players on both sides.

Open skills are games like lacrosse which take place outside with many players. This gives these games a lot of uncertainty. For example, each player must take account of his opponents, his own team players and such things as the speed of the ball, the surface of the pitch and the weather. In other words, where you can't control what will happen next you need open skills.

Closed skills take place in a fixed environment where the performer has the situation under control. For example, a vault in gymnastics, where the equipment is fixed and there are no influences from other people or the weather. In other words, where you can control what will happen next you use closed skills.

## A skill continuum

We can put skills on a line (called a continuum) which goes from 'open' at one end to 'closed' at the other. Judo is placed towards the 'open' end because the player must react to his opponent (in other words he can't control what happens next). However, the surface for competition is always the same and the weather has no effect (in other words he can control things more than people in sports which have to take account of, e.g. the weather). Archery is nearer to the 'closed' end because the whole action is learned and repeated for competition. However, wind strength and direction will affect the flight of the arrow, so it's not a completely closed skill. High jump could be put near the middle. The jump itself is a closed skill but the run up must take account of the weather, jumping surface and height of the bar.

In some open sports, closed skills will also be used. For example, squash and netball are open sports, but when players take a free serve or shot they are in control, so it is a closed skill.

Open  •  Judo  •  Lacrosse  •  High jump  •  Archery  •  Gymnastics  •  Closed

# How do we perform skills?

The information processing model is a theory about how we perform skills. In this theory the brain is a computer. Information comes to our brain from our senses. We use this information, together with our sporting experience, to help us make decisions. We then take action. Feedback is information which tells us whether or not we have been successful. We use it to guide our next movement.

## Receiving information

The first thing that happens is we receive information from our senses. This is called input. During this stage our brain gets information from our senses. The senses tell the brain what is going on. For example, in basketball our eyes tell our brain the positions of players and the ball. Our ears tell our brain what the coach is saying. Messages come from our joints and inner ear to tell our brain about our movements and body position. We add the information to our experience. The more experienced we are the easier it is to sort out this information.

## Selecting information

We must choose very quickly the pieces of information which are important. Quick reactions depend on selecting the right information, for example in sprint starts we must concentrate only on the gun. This process is called selective attention

In sport we get lots of information all at once. However, our brain can only deal with a limited amount of information at a time. This is called limited channel capacity. It must deal with the first piece before the second. This can cause overloading. That is why we must select the most important piece of information first.

If we are dealing with one piece of information and a second arrives, it is delayed. This delay can be seen in a fake shot. We move to block the fake shot because we are dealing with the first piece of information. We are then too late to deal with the actual movement.

### ⊙ KEY POINT

The information processing model consists of input, decision making, output and feedback.

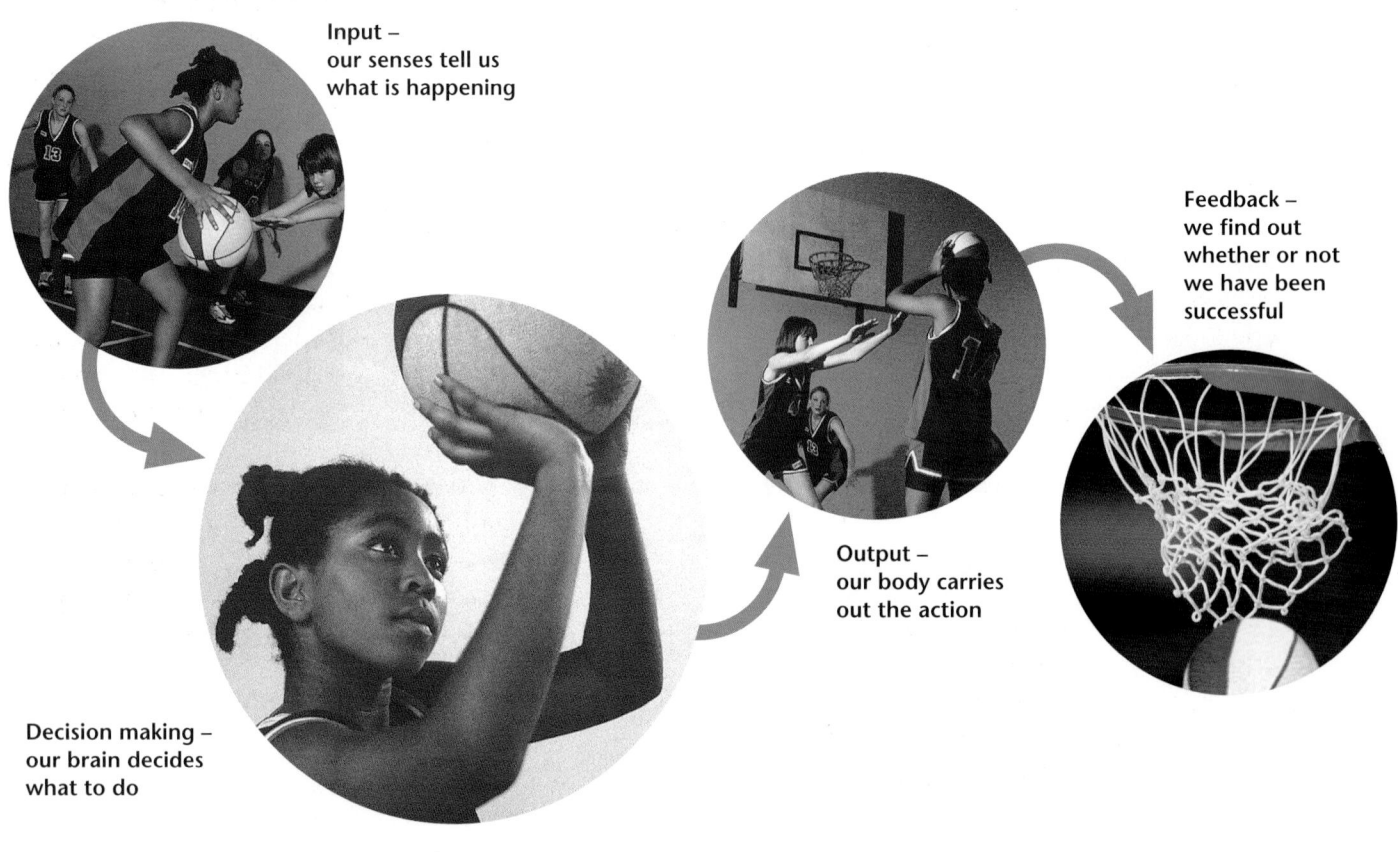

Input –
our senses tell us
what is happening

Decision making –
our brain decides
what to do

Output –
our body carries
out the action

Feedback –
we find out
whether or not
we have been
successful

**Linford Christie, focused on the starting gun**

## Decision making

At this stage, we must make sense of what is happening using our memory and perception. We can then decide on our action and form a plan for our next movement.

Our perception is the way we use our experience to sort out the information we receive. Skilled performers use their perception to anticipate what will happen next. For example, an experienced batsman can work out the sort of 'ball' to expect from the bowler's run up and delivery.

Our memory and experience help us make sense of the information we receive. They help us to decide what new action to take. Our memory has two parts, short and long term. When practising passing we keep our last attempt in our short term memory to help improve our next attempt. Anything important is transferred to our long term memory, for example some almost automatic movements, like cycling.

## Taking action

This is the stage when we react to the situation. Our central nervous system sends messages to our muscles which then contract. Movement is a complex process. Our muscles must work at the right time, in the correct order and with the right amount of force.

## Receiving feedback

We receive feedback as to whether our action has been successful. Feedback is vital information about our performances. By using feedback we are able to analyse and then improve our performances.

External feedback comes to us, for example, by watching ourselves on video, listening to our coach or being given our score.

Internal feedback comes to us from our senses. The proprioceptors in our joints tell us how the shot felt and our eyes tell us whether or not we were successful.

Two other forms of feedback are:

*   *knowledge of results.* These tell us the outcome of our performance. We know whether or not we scored the goal, how many points we were given or our position in the race;
*   *knowledge of performance.* This knowledge is about how well we performed rather than the result. Skilled ice dancers will know how good their performance felt. By talking to their coaches they can find out about the standard of their performance.

# Motivation and success

We all have different reasons for taking part in sport. Our reasons may change with our age and ability. Our motivation affects the standard of our performance. Highly motivated sportspeople will work very hard to improve their fitness and skill levels in training. In competition they will be determined to defeat their opponents.

## What are the different types of motivation?

Intrinsic motivation (also called self motivation) comes from our own inner drives. We may play for fun, for the satisfaction of performing well, for the pride in winning or for the enjoyment of taking part with others.

Extrinsic motivation comes from rewards and outside pressures. We may play to win trophies, to please other people who are important to us or to avoid letting our team down.

Most motivation is a mixture of both types. For example, we may play in the school team because we enjoy the sport (intrinsic motivation) and also because we want to win trophies (extrinsic motivation). Intrinsic motivation will keep us interested in sport when extrinsic rewards have gone.

## What is arousal in sport?

In a sporting situation the intensity of our motivation is called arousal. As we get ready to take part in sport our arousal level increases. When we do this deliberately it is called 'psyching up'. If our arousal gets too high we may become anxious and worried. This is called being 'stressed out' and causes our performance to become less effective.

The link between arousal and performance can be explained using the 'inverted U theory'. This theory suggests that our best performances come when we are moderately aroused. At both low and high levels of arousal our performance decreases.

Our motivation affects the standard of our performance

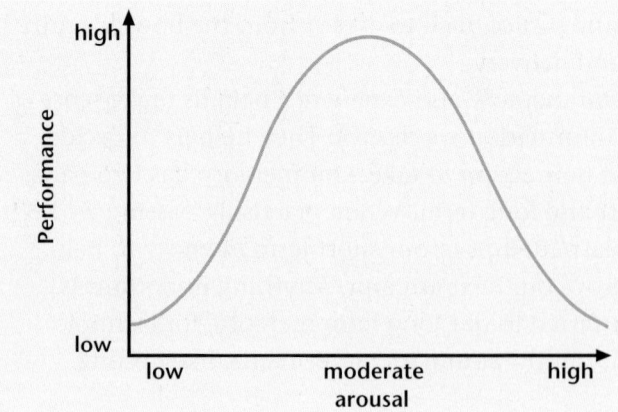

## KEY POINT

In sport, our motivation is caused by our own inner drives, by the rewards we hope to get, the pressures we feel and our arousal level (how 'psyched up' we are).

We cannot always win, but we can set our own goals – Roger Black was pleased with second

# Setting goals

Many of us have long term ambitions in sport. To achieve these we need short term goals along the way. These goals can help to motivate us. They can also give us confidence and help our performances.

The type of goals we choose and the way we set up our goals are important. We cannot win all the time in sport. It is important for us to focus on our achievements whatever happens when we compete.

There are two types of sporting goals:

1. outcome goals are linked to the result of a competition, for example winning a trophy or a league;

2. performance goals are concerned with the standard of our performance compared with previous ones, for example getting a better time for a race.

We have more control over our performance goals than over our outcome goals. We can, for example, improve our best time but still not win the race. It is better, therefore, for us to set performance goals as these give us a better chance of success. Success in turn can increase confidence and motivation.

The National Coaching Foundation has found a way to write performance goals.

| | |
|---|---|
| **S**pecific | • goals should be as specific as possible to focus attention; |
| **M**easurable | • they should assess progress against a standard; |
| **A**ccepted | • they should be accepted by both the performer and coach; |
| **R**ealistic | • they should be challenging but within the performer's capacity; |
| **T**ime phased | • there should be a specific date for completion; |
| **E**xciting | • they should be inspiring, challenging and rewarding to the performer; |
| **R**ecorded | • they should be written down by the performer and coach to evaluate progress, provide feedback and motivate performers. |

An example of a **S.M.A.R.T.E.R.** performance goal in volleyball is:

| | |
|---|---|
| **S**pecific | • to receive serve and make a controlled underarm pass to the setter; |
| **M**easurable | • ten repetitions; |
| **A**ccepted | • yes; |
| **R**ealistic | • 70% success rate; |
| **T**ime phased | • 31 December; |
| **E**xciting | • yes; |
| **R**ecorded | • performer and coach training diary. |

# How does our personality affect our sports performance?

Personality means the sort of person we are. Personality is to do with the qualities we have, such as character and temperament. We can talk about personality traits (features of our personality). It has been suggested that traits such as being friendly, easy going or determined are fixed. Our traits can influence our behaviour and therefore will affect how we prepare and perform in sport. Some traits are thought to make us suitable for particular sports.

Some researchers have described personalities called extroverts and introverts.

An extrovert – introvert continuum can be drawn. This is a line with these extreme personality types at the ends. Most of us would be somewhere in the middle of this continuum.

Extroverts are very confident and socially outgoing. They are often the centre of attention, they enjoy new situations and like to express their own views.

Introverts are less confident and quiet and shy in social situations. They prefer to keep themselves to themselves, do not enjoy new situations and are reluctant to express their own views.

Extroverts prefer team sports

Introverts prefer individual sports

## Extroverts and introverts in sport

Research suggests that extroverts and introverts prefer the following types of sports.

Extroverts prefer:
- team sports;
- activities involving the whole body;
- activities involving much movement;
- plenty of activity and uncertainty.

Introverts prefer:
- individual sports;
- activities involving fine physical skills;
- activities with limited movement;
- routine and repetitive sports.

Extroverts seem to need high arousal levels to perform well whilst introverts perform better at lower arousal levels. A quick look around at other sportspeople will suggest that the extrovert and introvert theory may well be true. However, a more detailed analysis will show that there are many exceptions to the rule.

It may be better to look at the way our personality traits react with the sporting environment. It is important to treat all sportspeople as individuals with different qualities.

> **◐ KEY POINT**
>
> Our personality may be linked to our success in different sports. However, successful sportspeople have a wide variety of different personalities.

# What types of aggression do we see in sport?

In sport we compete against opponents, standards of performance or the natural environment. The amount of aggression involved varies with the type and level of the sport.

We see both direct and indirect aggression in sport:

- direct physical aggression is a part of boxing, judo and rugby. We have to be very aggressive to be successful in these sports. However, we must compete within their strict rules;
- limited physical aggression is needed in some sports, even though body contact is generally avoided, for example in hockey. Players must be aggressive within the rules of limited physical contact.

We use indirect aggression in sports such as volleyball and tennis. We hit the ball towards our opponents, and the ball does the scoring rather than the player. In other words, the aggression is still aimed at the opponent but it is directed through the ball. (Aggressive players may find it difficult to mix both delicate and fierce shots.)

Sometimes spectators show aggressive behaviour

Object aggression is seen in some sports where an object, not the opponent, receives the aggression. For example, a golfer may hit a ball aggressively, but it does not guarantee success.

Some sports involve no aggression at all against opponents or objects. For example, in ice skating, trampolining, gymnastics, diving and archery there is no advantage in being aggressive.

LITTLE AGGRESSION

INDIRECT AGGRESSION

DIRECT AGGRESSION

Aggression in sport

# How do we learn skills?

Learning skills is a complex process. It involves putting together a number of different techniques. We can split skill learning into three different periods called phases: the cognitive phase, the associative phase, and the autonomous phase. They are not completely separate. However they do help us to understand how we learn skills.

## The cognitive phase

During this phase we are beginners. We need to understand what we have to do. We need a clear mental picture of the movements we need to make. We think carefully about technique and we may talk our way through it. We will often make major errors, for example missing the ball completely. We find it hard to correct our own actions. Our teachers need to give us clear demonstrations, simple instructions, short periods for practising and praise for the correct action. They must emphasise the technique not the outcome.

### ⬀ KEY POINT

- Cognitive phase – we get a clear understanding of the movement.
- Associative phase – we practise and get a feel for the skill.
- Autonomous phase – we perform the skill automatically.

## The associative phase

During this phase we concentrate on practising the skill, having learnt the technique already. Our performance improves a lot. We make fewer errors and begin to analyse our movements and make corrections. We start to use internal feedback from our senses as well as external feedback from our teacher. Some sportspeople do not move beyond this phase.

## The autonomous phase

We can now perform our techniques almost automatically. We can give more attention to decisions about strategies and tactics. In squash we can now focus on where to play the next shot, rather than the shot itself. We are skilled and use our techniques at the right time and in the right place. We can often detect and deal with our own errors. Our coach helps us with the fine detail of the skill, with tactics and with mental preparation.

# What helps us to learn skills?

We learn techniques and skills by practising. Our learning is affected by the:

- guidance given to us;
- type of practice we use;
- feedback we get;
- techniques we have already learned which can be transferred to the new skills.

## Guidance

Guidance is given to us in three ways:

1. *visual*. Demonstrations give us a good idea of what we hope to do;
2. *verbal*. Explanations must be brief and focus on the most important points;
3. *manual*. Support will keep us safe and give us confidence.

All guidance must be easily understood and linked to our phase of skill learning (whether cognitive, associative, or autonomous).

**We need guidance when learning skills**

## Practice

Skill can be taught as a whole or broken down into parts. This is called whole or part practice. If all the parts of the action take place at the same time we usually practise them as a whole, for example cycling. Skills which use a number of techniques following one another, such as a basketball lay up shot, are usually practised in parts at first.

Massed practice means using long active sessions without rests. For example, a gymnast spending an hour on one vault. Distributed practice means having rests between shorter practice periods. For example, a gymnast having three sessions of vaulting practice in an hour, with other activities in between. Long practice sessions can lead to tiredness and boredom, which may be dangerous for difficult activities.

## Feedback

Feedback is essential when learning skills. Full details are on page 91.

## Experience

We can learn new techniques more easily if we have learned similar techniques in the past. The basic movement patterns may have been built up. Teachers can help by pointing out the similarities to us. For example, if we have learned to play tennis, then we usually find some 'transfer' to squash when we first learn the game. However, the transfer is not effective for long, as the strokes are very different. Transfer can also interfere with learning a new skill.

# How is a training session organised?

The objective of every training session is to improve our performance. Each session needs to be well planned. The teacher or coach must guide us through techniques and into skills. We must also improve our fitness. Training must include: warm up and warm down, practising skills, games, and fitness activities.

## Warm up and warm down

These are essential parts of our training sessions. They must be linked closely to the sporting activity. Full details are given in chapter 4.

## Practising skills

Skills practices in P.E. are drills used to teach us techniques and skills. A drill is a movement or number of movements which are repeated until they can be performed easily. We may practise techniques individually but will practise skills in groups. They can vary in netball from a very simple movement such as a player catching the ball to a highly complicated attacking movement involving many players.

Practices can be used to improve individual or team weaknesses. They can gradually be built up to be more realistic by including more players and passive opposition.

Skill practices must be right for our ability level. They must also be challenging and demand concentration. They can make training both enjoyable and valuable by improving our performance.

## Games

We need to transfer our skills from the practice session into the game situation. Modified games give each player plenty of action and lots of time with the ball, for example five on five hockey. Conditioned games have rule changes which focus on a particular skill, for example one touch football. Games practice can be used to help find our weaknesses and make improvements.

## Fitness training

Players must take responsibility for their own personal fitness. Nevertheless fitness training should be part of all training sessions. It can be part of the skills practices but must not exhaust players so much that they cannot concentrate on their skills. Regular fitness testing provides valuable feedback.

Skills practices help us improve our performance

# Who influences our sports performance?

Many people may influence our sports performance. However, the most important influences are likely to be our P.E. teachers, our coaches and the officials who control our competitions.

## P.E. teachers

The P.E. teacher's central task is to educate all the pupils in his or her lesson using a variety of physical activities.

P.E. teachers:

- introduce children to the basic techniques of sport;
- develop skill in all their pupils during the lessons;
- coach and develop excellence in interested pupils after school;
- help young people move smoothly from school to sports clubs;
- try to develop competence in a range of physical activities;
- give knowledge and understanding about sporting performance;
- aim to develop a positive attitude towards an active lifestyle.

P.E. teachers motivate their pupils

## Coaches

The coach's central task is to improve the performance of the sportspeople in his or her group in the following ways:

- establishing techniques;
- developing skill;
- improving fitness;
- encouraging mental preparation.

The achievement of these aims will lead to improved performances, which in turn will lead to success and enjoyment. This will provide sportspeople with the motivation to continue to seek improvement. In addition, it is the role of the coach to:

- specialise in one sport;
- have a deep knowledge of their sport;
- work with beginners and internationals;
- know the best way to develop techniques, skills and fitness;
- understand the needs of sportspeople and motivate them;
- plan programmes and training sessions;
- be aware of the problems of competitive sport, such as drug misuse;
- analyse performance and check progress.

## Officials

The official's central task is to enable sportspeople to take part in sport fairly and safely. Administrators organise events, but officials control the sporting action.

Officials:

- have excellent knowledge of the sport and its rules;
- apply rules firmly and fairly;
- need to be patient, good with people (and have a sense of humour!);
- look after the safety of all those involved;
- may need to be in good physical condition.

# Competitive sport and skill

Different types of sport involve using different strategies and tactics. In order to develop our tactical skills, we need to understand the needs of our sport.

## What are strategies and tactics in sport?

Strategies are plans which we think out in advance of the sporting competition. They are methods of putting us in the best position to defeat our opponents.

Tactics are what we use to put our strategies into action. Tactics can also be worked out in advance of the sporting competition but they will often need to be adapted to the real situation during competition. Tactics involve planning and team work.

Strategies and tactics will be very different for different types of games. For example, an invasion game like rugby involves large numbers of players, a variety of set plays as well as an opportunity for individuals to respond to many different situations.

Football managers plan strategies, but they may also give instructions during the match!

It gives many choices to players such as kicking, passing or running with the ball. By contrast, in a judo competition there is only one opponent to concentrate upon and there are a limited number of attacking moves to make or defend.

Children at the associative phase of learning (see page 96) will not be able to cope with strategies. They will need only simple tactics such as 'Pass the ball to a player who is free'. It is the skilful players at the autonomous phase (see page 96) who are able to give time and attention to strategies and tactics.

**KEY POINT**

Strategies are the plans we produce in advance of sporting competitions.

Tactics enable us to put strategies into action in sporting competitions.

**National Curriculum – areas of activity**

- PHYSICAL EDUCATION ACTIVITIES
  - ATHLETIC ACTIVITIES
  - DANCE
  - GYMNASTIC ACTIVITIES
  - GAMES
    - INVASION GAMES
    - NET GAMES
    - STRIKING/FIELDING GAMES
  - SWIMMING
  - OUTDOOR AND ADVENTUROUS ACTIVITIES

# What sorts of strategies and tactics are used in sport?

Strategies and tactics become more important as the level of competition increases.

The important things are: teamwork, having a good game plan, using formations (positioning players strategically), and using set plays (moves planned in advance).

To develop strategies and tactics we need to know:
- the strengths and weaknesses of the opposition;
- our own strengths and weaknesses;
- our level of fitness;
- the importance of the competition;
- any important environmental factors.

For example, in a net game, such as tennis, our strategy might be to move our opponent around the court in order to get her tired and also out of position. This will then enable us to play a winning shot or to force an error. The tactic we use to achieve this might be to serve wide on both sides of the court and to come to the net quickly. In the game we might find that our tactics are not working because our opponent is returning our serve very well. In this case we will have to decide whether or not to continue with the same tactic or change it.

## Teamwork

A successful team will have good teamwork. This means that all members of the team will understand the agreed strategy. They will also put the tactics for each game into practice by working as a unit. Managers, coaches and captains have important roles to play in teamwork.

## Game plan

In some matches and competitions, players and teams talk of a 'game plan'. This is a set of tactics for use in one particular game. The game plan will be based on our own strengths and the weaknesses of the opposition.

## Formations

Teams can use different formations, that is the players can take up different positions on the field of play. Many sports have rules limiting where the players can move during the game. In some sports, like basketball, there are few restrictions on the position of players. In other games, like netball, the restrictions present the players with extra problems to solve.

## Restarts and set plays

All games have regular restarts, for example serves in racket sports and the ways of bringing the ball back into play used in invasion games. In football, restarts such as corners and free kicks can involve set plays. In other words, they give teams an opportunity to use moves planned in advance. The team has free possession of the ball and the opposition may not challenge for it.

**We plan our tactics for each game**

# Planning, performing and evaluating

Players, together with their coaches, spend a lot of time preparing for their next performance. They analyse past performances and plan strategies and tactics for the competition. However, all this preparation is wasted if the player does not play well.

## What happens when we play?

The National Curriculum for P.E. talks about sportspeople planning, performing and evaluating continuously whilst they are playing. Ruud Gullit, the football manager, coaches his professional players to play 'What if?' football. He is asking them to think about what is happening and also what might happen next. In other words, he wants them to be aware of the 'Plan, perform, and evaluate' process. We all use this process as we play competitive sport.

## What do we mean by planning, performing, and evaluating?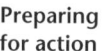

**Planning.** Each time a player does something in the game, for example makes a run off the ball in football, or a drop shot in badminton, he/she should know what he/she is trying to do. The player should also have an idea of what will happen as a result. This means he/she has a plan.

The next time this canoeist is in the same situation, he will have a chance to repeat his action more successfully or try something else

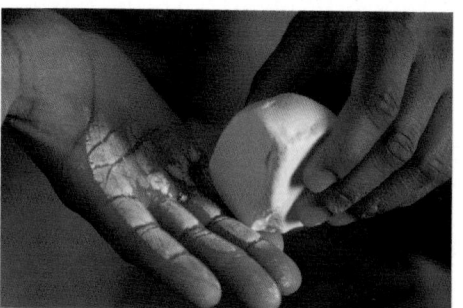

Preparing for action

**Performing.** The moment that he/she moves into action, he/she is performing. The performance may be successful or unsuccessful.

Planning our next shot

**Evaluating.** The next time he/she is in a similar situation in the game, there will be the chance to repeat the action.
- if it is successful he/she is likely to try it again;
- if it is unsuccessful, but he/she still thinks the plan was good, he/she might try to perform it better the next time;
- if it was unsuccessful and it was not a good plan, he/she should not repeat it.

This process is repeated over and over again during the match. The most skilful players can plan, perform, and evaluate very quickly. They will make many more good decisions than players who are less skilful.

The key to success in competitive sport is anticipating what your opponent is likely to do. You also need to be able to adapt to the new situations that arise.

Teachers and coaches analyse players' ability all the time. They are assessing their ability to plan, perform, and evaluate whilst playing.

# Questions

## Skill in Sport

1  **a** Choose one sport and name an individual skill and a group skill.
   **b** Describe a drill or practice that will improve either the individual or group skill that you have chosen.

2  Provide examples to explain how skills acquired in one game can help to improve your performance in another.

3  What is meant by the term 'extrinsic motivation'? How does it differ from intrinsic motivation?

4  What is 'knowledge of results'?

5  Define 'skill'.

6  Spectators play a vital role in sport. Explain how they can:
   **a** improve a performance;
   **b** hinder a performance.

7  Draw and label an information processing model.

8  Suggest two reasons why sports players become aggressive.

9  Explain the meaning of 'open' and 'closed' skills.

10 Performers receive information in a number of ways during a skill learning practice. Describe two of these ways.

# 6 Care of our Body

Our health is influenced by many factors, including what we inherit from our parents. Good health and a long life tend to run in families. However, this is not always the case. We must not neglect our bodies or abuse them by drinking unwise levels of alcohol. We must not expose them to the use of tobacco or non-prescribed drugs at all.

Taking regular exercise is a crucial way of maintaining our health. We also need to care for our bodies:

## Sensible eating page 106

We need to know about the food types and why they are important. We need to know about what makes a healthy diet. Food is energy and we need to know how we can use that energy for sporting success by looking at the effects of our eating before, during and after activity.

## The right lifestyle
### page 114

Sticking to certain rules of personal hygiene is an important part of caring for our bodies. These help us to keep our bodies healthy. We also need to give ourselves enough time to sleep and rest. This is especially important for sporting success.

We need to care for our bodies, to see that we stay in good health. If we have a healthy lifestyle when we are young, we will reduce the risk of an early death from disease and also slow down the ageing process. We can control many of the different factors which affect our health, such as lifestyle and diet. Good health is, therefore, mainly our own individual responsibility.

## Limiting alcohol

page 116

Drinking unwise levels of alcohol is harmful to our health. In addition, drinking alcohol affects our sporting performance.

## Don't smoke! page 117

Smoking is harmful to health and sporting performance.

## Don't misuse drugs! page 118

We need to know about the use of drugs in sport, including: why drugs are used by sportspeople (and why they are banned in the first place); how we test for drugs and which drugs are restricted and banned; who makes the rules about drugs and how.

# Sensible eating

To be healthy and successful in sport, we need to know about the food types, what makes a healthy diet and how food can provide us with the right energy.

## Why do we need food?

We need food for:
- energy;
- growth;
- repair;
- good health.

We get energy from food for our muscles to work. Food contains the basic materials needed for growth and repair. We need many different nutrients for good health and a balanced and varied diet will provide them. A balanced diet contains seven essential components – carbohydrates, fats, proteins, vitamins, minerals, fibre and water.

## What are carbohydrates?

Carbohydrates are broken down in the body into different sugars. There are two types of carbohydrate:

1. *sugars* (simple carbohydrates). We find sugars in fruits, honey, jam, sweets, biscuits, cakes, beer and table sugar. Highly processed food, such as sweets, will give us a quick supply of energy but no other nutrients. Biscuits and cakes often contain a lot of fat;

2. *starches* (complex carbohydrates). We find starches in vegetables, bread, rice, pasta and cereals. These foods also contain protein, minerals, vitamins and fibre. It is better to take most of our carbohydrates in the form of starches rather than sugars.

## Why are carbohydrates important?

Carbohydrates give us the energy we need for our working muscles. We can also get energy from fats and proteins, but not as quickly or as efficiently as we can from carbohydrates. Large amounts of carbohydrates are stored as glycogen in our liver and muscles. Small amounts are stored as glucose in our blood. Intense exercise quickly uses up these stores, so active sportspeople need plenty of carbohydrates in their diet. We store any extra carbohydrates as fat around our bodies.

> ### ● KEY POINT
>
> Carbohydrates give us energy.

We need carbohydrates and fat to give us energy for sport

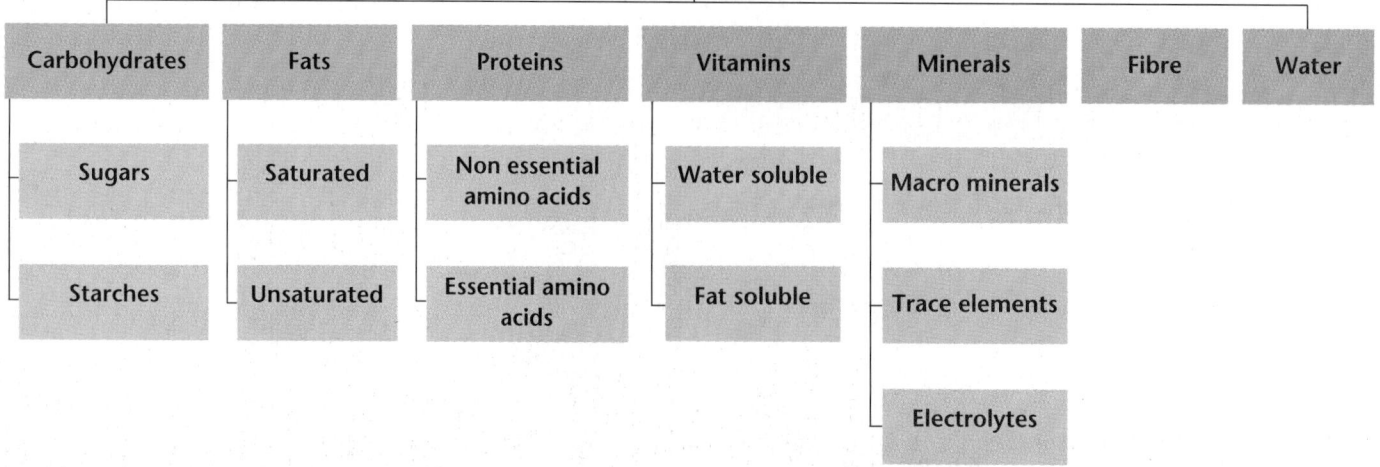

# What are fats?

Fats are broken down in the body into saturated and unsaturated fatty acids. There are two types of fats:

1. *saturated fats*. We find saturated fats in animal products such as milk, meat, cheese, cream and butter. They are also found in cakes, biscuits and chocolate. Saturated fats can raise our cholesterol levels;
2. *unsaturated fats*. We find unsaturated fats in fish and plant products such as corn, nuts and soya beans.

# Why are fats important?

Fats give us energy, although much more slowly than carbohydrates. Fats need extra oxygen supplies to provide energy. Fats are our main source of energy when we are resting or asleep. Fats keep the skin in good condition, help to keep us warm and protect our vital organs. Extra fat is stored just under the skin. This extra weight will not help sportspeople. Too much fat can lead to obesity and high cholesterol levels.

Cholesterol is a fat like substance found in our blood. It is present in some foods, especially fatty animal products. Cholesterol not needed by the body builds up on our artery walls. This may cause us circulatory and heart problems.

# What are proteins?

Proteins are broken down, in our bodies, into amino acids. There are two types of amino acids:

1. *non essential amino acids*. Amino acids are used by the body. We need 21 different amino acids. The body can only make 13 of these, which are called non essential;
2. *essential amino acids*. These are the eight amino acids which we need to take in from our food. We find them in both animal and plant foods.

We find proteins in fish, in animal products such as meat, poultry, eggs, cheese and milk, and plant products such as cereals, peas, beans and nuts. Proteins from animal products contain all the essential amino acids. However, plant proteins (apart from soya beans) lack some essential amino acids.

# Why are proteins important?

Much of our body tissue is made up of protein, including our skin, bones and muscles. Proteins are needed for the repair, growth and efficient working of our tissues. Protein is only rarely used as an energy source when no carbohydrate or fat is available. Excess proteins cannot be stored in the body.

> **⊙ KEY POINT**
>
> Fats are a reserve energy store.
> Proteins build our bodies.

Fats give us energy for sport more slowly than carbohydrates

# What are vitamins?

Our bodies cannot make vitamins. They must be supplied in our food. There are two types of vitamin:

1. *water soluble vitamins*. These are the vitamin B group and C vitamins. They cannot be stored in our bodies. Any excess is removed. We must therefore include them in our daily diet;
2. *fat soluble vitamins*. These are vitamins A, D, E, and K. They can be stored in our bodies.

We find vitamins in a wide variety of fresh fruit and vegetables. We need them in very small, regular amounts. Our balanced diet will contain all the vitamins we need. Many vitamins are destroyed when food is cooked or processed.

**We all need vitamins and minerals for healthy growth and development**

> ⬭ **KEY POINT**
>
> Vitamins and minerals keep our bodies working properly.

# Why are vitamins important?

Vitamins enable our bodies to work normally and efficiently. They regulate the chemical reactions of our bodies. They help in the growth and repair of our bodies' tissues, in the working of our muscles and nerves and in the release of energy from our food. They also help maintain our resistance to disease.

Vitamins all have their own functions, for example:

- vitamin A is needed for good sight and healthy tissue;
- vitamin C helps heal our wounds and fight viruses;
- vitamin D helps build bones and teeth.

# What are minerals?

Our bodies cannot make minerals. They must be supplied in our food. There are three types of minerals:

1. *macro minerals*. These are the minerals which we need in large amounts such as calcium;
2. *trace elements*. These are the minerals we need in extremely small amounts, such as zinc;
3. *electrolytes*. These are mineral salts found in our body fluids.

We find minerals in a wide variety of different foods, for example calcium in milk, iron in red meat and potassium in bananas. We need small but regular amounts of minerals and they can all be provided by our balanced diet. Too much of some minerals can be harmful, for example sodium in the form of salt can cause us increased blood pressure.

# Why are minerals important?

As with vitamins, minerals enable the body to work normally and efficiently. Minerals all have their own functions, for example:

- calcium is needed for our muscles to work, blood to clot and bones to be strong;
- iron is needed for red blood cells which carry oxygen to our muscles;
- iodine is made into thyroxine to control the workings of our bodies.

We must replace fluid lost when playing in the sun

## What is fibre?

Fibre is also called roughage or dietary fibre. Fibre is the part of a plant that we cannot digest. It does not contain any nutrients. Fibre is found on the outside of seeds, in vegetables, fruits and nuts.

## Why is fibre important?

Fibre adds bulk to our food. This helps us to move food through our digestive system and prevents constipation. Fibre is also involved in food absorption. It slows down the release of sugars from our food so that we get a more even release of energy.

Dietary fibre adds bulk without adding extra kilojoules. This can help us to lose weight if we need to. A high level of fibre helps to maintain good health.

## Why is water important?

Water is essential for living. It comes from the fluids and food we eat. We lose water in our sweat, urine, faeces and in the air we breathe out. About two thirds of our body weight is made up of water. Water is an important part of all our body tissues. It is the main component of blood and cells. As part of the blood it carries nutrients, blood cells and waste materials around the body.

Water in our blood also helps to control our body temperature by absorbing heat produced during exercise. This heat is then carried to our skin where it is lost to the air. Water as sweat helps to cool the body when it evaporates on the surface of our skin. Heat is also lost in the water vapour in our expired air.

During exercise we lose extra amounts of water in sweat and expired air. The amount of water we lose will depend on how hard we exercise, how long we exercise for and the weather conditions. This water must be replaced in order to prevent dehydration. In extremely hot conditions, dehydration can lead to heat exhaustion and heatstroke. Further details are on page 133.

**KEY POINT**

Fibre keeps our digestive system healthy. Water is necessary for all our systems.

# So what is a healthy diet?

How would you rate the following two meals?

**Meal A – chips, hamburger, eggs, parsley**
This meal is high in kilojoules and high in saturated fat because it has been fried. It contains some protein but very little fibre and few vitamins:

Potatoes are high in fibre and carbohydrate but chips have much higher fat levels and many more kilojoules. Hamburgers contain protein but are also packed with fats and other additives. Eggs contain protein but are also high in cholesterol. Parsley is the only fresh, uncooked vegetable.

**Meal B – grilled fish, salad, baked potato, lemon**
This meal gives us a variety of food, enough kilojoules and is low in fat:

A non-oily grilled fish is low in fat and low in kilojoules. Fresh, uncooked salad vegetables give us vitamins, minerals and fibre with no fat and few kilojoules. A baked potato is high in fibre and carbohydrate. Lemon gives the food extra taste without the fat and sugar of sauces.

# Do we eat a healthy diet?

In 1991, the Department of Health produced the Coma report. This looked in great detail at what we eat. The report found many problems with our national diet and gave a lot of advice for healthy eating. The report said that we should change our diets and follow these guidelines:
We should limit the amounts of each of the three components which supply energy by the following amounts.
1. carbohydrates (mainly as starch and natural sugars) 50 – 60%;
2. proteins (mainly from lean meat, fish, poultry and plants) 10 – 15%;
3. fat (mainly from unsaturated fat) 25 – 30%
We should decrease the amount of salt we eat.
We should increase the amounts we eat of:
• fibre;
• calcium;
• vitamin C.

Research shows that we have not followed this advice. There are links between our diet and health problems, for example; high sugar intake and tooth decay; low fibre diet and cancer of the digestive system; high fat intake and heart disease.

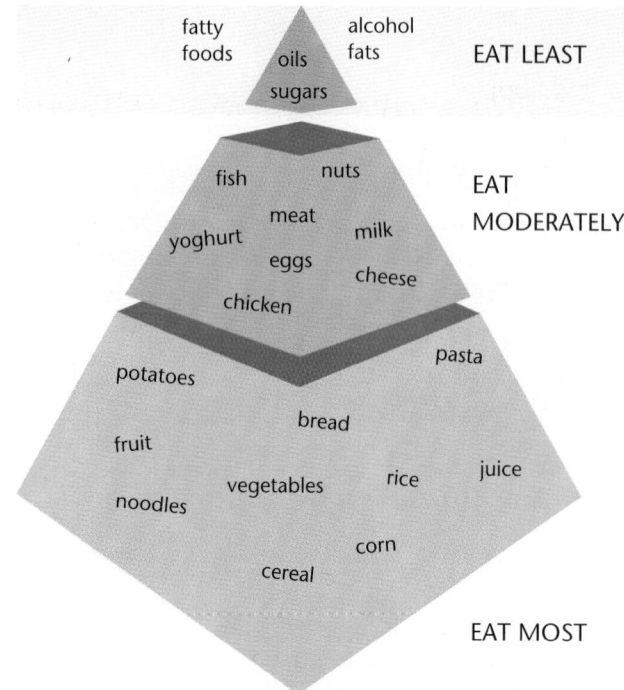

**The Food Pyramid**

# Why do we need energy?

We need energy to make our bodies work. There are two main purposes:
1. *energy to keep our body systems going.* Just keeping the body alive and healthy takes energy. This amount of energy is called our Basal Metabolic Rate (B.M.R.). Our age, sex and body size and composition affect our B.M.R.
2. *energy for our activities.* We use energy for all the everyday activities of walking, housework and gardening. If we take part in sport, we will use a lot more energy (depending on the type of sport and how much exercise is involved.) Our age, sex, work, health and lifestyle will all affect our physical activity level (P.A.L.).

We must remember that:
Our total energy needs = B.M.R. + P.A.L.

Energy is measured in kilocalories (kcal) or kilojoules (KJ). We can find energy charts to work out how much energy we use in our different activities.

# Diet, weight, energy – what are the links?

Our weight will stay the same if the amount of energy our body needs is the same as the energy provided by the food we eat.

We will lose weight if our body needs more energy than our diet is providing.

We will put on weight if our body needs less energy than our diet is providing.

**Kilojoules taken in each day = kilojoules burned up each day**

**Weight stays constant**
Kilojoules taken in each day equals kilojoules burned up each day

**Weight gained**
Kilojoules taken in each day is greater than kilojoules burned up each day

**Weight lost**
Kilojoules taken in each day is less than kilojoules burned up each day

# How much energy is there in our food?

The amount of energy in any food depends on how many carbohydrates, fats and proteins it contains. We can use charts to give us this information. For example:

| Food | Kilojoules per gram |
|---|---|
| Margarine | 32.2 |
| Milk chocolate | 24.2 |
| White sugar | 16.5 |
| Rice | 15.0 |
| White bread | 10.6 |
| Chips | 9.9 |
| Fresh eggs | 6.6 |
| Boiled potatoes | 3.3 |
| Milk | 2.7 |
| Apple | 1.9 |

| Activity | Energy used |
|---|---|
| Easy walking | 380 KJ |
| Golf | 560 KJ |
| Housework | 560 KJ |
| Badminton | 710 KJ |
| Heavy gardening | 880 KJ |
| Gymnastics | 880 KJ |
| Tennis | 1000 KJ |
| Rugby | 1130 KJ |
| Squash | 1254 KJ |
| Brisk jogging | 1320 KJ |
| Cycling | 1380 KJ |
| Swimming | 1500 KJ |

**⟳ KEY POINT**

Our weight is directly linked to our diet and level of activity.

# How do we get enough energy for sport?

When we work hard, the energy we use comes from stores of glycogen in our bodies. Glycogen is made from carbohydrates and also from fats. Our stores of glycogen are limited. We need to eat extra carbohydrates to have enough energy for endurance activities.

When we work aerobically, that is using oxygen, we can get energy from our fatty acids. Fatty acids are found in fat stores around our bodies. At low activity levels our bodies use a mixture of carbohydrates and fats. Endurance training teaches our bodies to use more fat during exercise. This helps our limited supplies of carbohydrates to last longer.

We use proteins as an energy supply only rarely, when we have no other energy sources.

# How should we gain and lose weight?

We should gain weight only as muscle, not as fat. We can do this by eating more carbohydrate and training harder.

We should lose weight slowly but permanently. We can do this by eating more starch, and less fat, as well as exercising.

### Extreme weight gain

We are obese if we are more than 20% over our standard weight for our height. Even being slightly overweight can increase our risk of heart, circulation and other health problems. Overweight sportspeople will find it difficult to perform at their best.

### Extreme weight loss

The eating disorders of anorexia and bulimia affect young women mainly, including sportswomen. Anorexia sufferers do not allow themselves to eat and they often think they are overweight. Bulimia sufferers eat a lot of food but then get rid of it by, for example, vomiting. Anorexia and bulimia are very serious conditions in which the sufferer becomes extremely thin and weak. Sufferers need urgent medical help.

> **⟴ KEY POINT**
>
> Under normal conditions, we get energy for all our activities from carbohydrates and fats.

We need to eat extra carbohydrates to have enough energy for endurance activities

# How should we eat for sport?

We need to look at how we eat before, during, and after exercise.

### Eating before exercise

We should:

- eat our main meal at least three to four hours and our snack meal at least one to two hours before exercise, to give us time for digestion;
- include starches such as bread, cereal and fruit, to give us a slow, steady release of energy;
- avoid simple sugars because they increase our insulin level which in turn reduces our blood glucose and make us feel tired;
- avoid foods high in fat and protein as they take longer to digest;
- include plenty of fluids to avoid dehydration.

## What is 'Carbohydrate loading'?

Carbohydrate loading increases the amount of carbohydrates, and therefore of glycogen, in our bodies. For at least three days before competition, we reduce our level of exercise and at the same time increase the amount of carbohydrate in our diet. This helps our bodies cope with long endurance events such as marathon races.

## What is 'Making the weight'?

In sports such as wrestling there are weight categories for different competitions. If a competitor tries to lose weight to get into a weight category, this is called 'Making the weight'. We should not try to compete in a weight category well below our natural weight. Our stores of glycogen and fluid will be reduced if we try to lose more than a kilogram in a week. As a result we will not be at our best. We should not take diuretic drugs to lose weight.

### Eating during exercise
We should:
- continue to drink fluids, not waiting until we feel thirsty but taking small sips regularly;
- drink liquid glucose to save our own limited stores of glycogen.

### Eating after exercise
We should :
- eat foods rich in carbohydrate within an hour of exercising, even if we do not feel hungry, to restore glycogen stores quickly;
- drink plenty of water to replace any lost fluid.

**There are weight categories in wrestling**

### ⊙ KEY POINT

Food plays an important part in our sporting performance.

# The right lifestyle

We can keep our bodies healthy by being hygienic and getting enough sleep and rest.

## What do we mean by hygiene?

Hygiene means the different ways we look after our bodies to keep them healthy.

### Skin

Our skin protects and maintains our bodies. If our skin is healthy, it can resist most infection. Soap and warm water removes any dirt and sweat which encourage bacteria. We know that we should wash our hands after going to the toilet, before meals, and whenever they are dirty.

We can keep our whole bodies clean by showering daily. We must wash or shower thoroughly after taking part in any physical activity. Most of us use deodorants and anti-perspirants, but they are only really effective if our bodies are clean.

Acne is a skin complaint which affects many teenagers. Glands in the skin which produce grease become particularly active at puberty. The openings of these glands can become blocked. Greasy material builds up under the skin if the blockage is not cleared. The skin becomes infected with bacteria. It helps to keep the skin very clean, to avoid make up and to get plenty of sunlight.

### Clothing

We should wash and change our clothes regularly. Our underwear, in particular, can become unhygienic very quickly. We should have a complete change of clothes for taking part in sporting activities. We should always remember our towel, soap and shampoo for the shower. Our sports clothing can become sweaty and dirty and so should be washed after each exercise session.

### Nails

Our nails should be kept clean and cut regularly. This will help to reduce injury in sport from scratches. Ingrowing toenails can be avoided by keeping our nails short and having footwear of the right size.

### Jewellery

Pierced ears and earrings should be cleaned carefully, to prevent earlobe infections. As much jewellery as possible should be removed during sport.

We must wash
after taking part
in sport!

> **◐ KEY POINT**
>
> Good hygiene helps to keep us healthy.

## Hair

Hair is found on nearly every part of our skin. We must wash our hair regularly to keep it clean and healthy. Long hair can be a hazard in some sports and it should be tied back.

## Teeth

Our teeth must be kept healthy and free from decay. We should avoid sugary foods. We must clean our teeth at least twice a day. Dental floss can be used to remove plaque. We can keep our gums healthy by eating food which needs chewing. Regular dental check-ups are essential.

## Feet

Our shoes and sports footwear must fit well. This will help to prevent painful feet, corns and other foot problems. We must wash our feet regularly and dry them carefully. If we also change our socks regularly this will help to avoid foot odour.

Athlete's foot is a fungal infection which affects our feet, especially between our toes. Our skin cracks open and it causes itching. We can treat it by drying our feet carefully and using anti-fungal creams and powders.

Verrucas are warts which can be found on our feet. They can be painful. We can treat them by applying a prescribed liquid.

# Does our pattern of sleep and rest affect our sports performance?

The answer is yes – how well we sleep and rest is very important to our performance in sport.

## Sleep

We will not be able to train or compete effectively without enough sleep. Most people need between seven and nine hours of sleep. If our patterns of sleep are disrupted, our sporting performance suffers. Our sleep patterns can be disrupted by drinking alcohol or caffeine, eating high protein meals or smoking.

## Rest

Rest is essential for our bodies to recover, both physically and mentally, from the activities of the day. It is especially important for sportspeople who exercise regularly and perform at a high level.

**Our shoes and sportswear must fit well**

> ### ⟳ KEY POINT
>
> Sportspeople must get enough sleep and rest to recover from their activities.

# Limiting alcohol

Moderate drinking of alcohol may not be harmful to our health. However, drinking alcohol before taking part in sport will certainly affect our performance. Alcohol is a depressant. This means it slows down the way our bodies work. It goes directly into our bloodstream and quickly affects our brain.

**Alcohol is a depressant**

## How does drinking alcohol affect our sporting performance?

The effects of alcohol on our sporting performance are:

### Reduced coordination, slower reaction time and poorer balance

These changes affect our movements and skills, especially where catching and balance is involved and in sports needing steadiness, such as archery, gymnastics and shooting.

### Dehydration

Alcohol is a diuretic and increases our urine production. This leads to water loss from the body. Dehydration seriously affects our performance in endurance events and all competition on hot days.

### Lower muscle glycogen levels and slower removal of lactic acid

Muscle glycogen is needed during endurance events. Lactic acid is produced during exercise and must be removed quickly. Therefore, drinking alcohol before any sport involving endurance will reduce our performance. It will also take us longer to recover.

### Rapid loss of heat

Alcohol causes the blood vessels in the skin to open up. We lose heat quickly through our skin, which reduces our body temperature. If we are already cold, hypothermia can develop.

### Longer injury recovery time

We use R.I.C.E. (see page 136) to reduce the blood going to an injured area. Alcohol will have the opposite effect. Our recovery time will be increased.

### Reduced size of arteries

Alcohol reduces the size of the arteries, so that less blood can flow along them. Our pulse and blood pressure both increase.

### Other effects

Alcohol also affects our:
- thinking, judgement, vision and hearing;
- stomach (and can cause vomiting);
- liver, as it takes a long time to process it;
- weight, as it is very high in energy.

> **◯ KEY POINT**
>
> Alcohol can affect our health, fitness and sporting performance.

# Don't smoke!

Cigarette smoking is always harmful to our health and therefore to our sporting performance. Cigarette smoke contains many harmful substances. In particular tar and nicotine have damaging effects on our body. Nicotine is a stimulant. This means it makes us more alert and better able to concentrate. It gets to our brain extremely quickly.

**Smoking is highly addictive**

## How does smoking cigarettes affect our sporting performance?

The effects of smoking on our sporting performance are:

### Reduced lung efficiency
The smoke damages the hairs lining our bronchial tubes. Dust is not removed from the air so our lungs become clogged and do not work efficiently. We need efficient lungs for all sport.

### Reduced oxygen carrying ability
Carbon monoxide is taken into our lungs in the smoke and passes to our blood. It reduces the amount of oxygen which we can carry in our blood. This affects our endurance activities.

### Reduced fitness level
Even if we train hard, our fitness level will be reduced because of the damage to our lungs and circulatory system.

### Lowered resistance to illness
Colds are caught more often and we take longer to recover from chest infections. Smoker's cough is a special hazard, as is bronchitis. Sportspeople need to keep well to train and compete.

### Raised blood pressure
Nicotine causes our brain to release hormones. These hormones make our heart beat more quickly and the blood vessels of our skin contract. This causes an increase in our blood pressure and a feeling of being cold.

### Other effects
Smoking is highly addictive. Smoking also affects our:
- life expectancy, as cancer and cardiovascular disease are a much greater risk amongst smokers;
- social standing, as we breathe harmful and unpleasant fumes on people around us. We also smell of stale tobacco;
- senses of taste and smell by reducing them;
- appetite, by reducing it.

### ⟳ KEY POINT

Smoking damages our health, prevents us becoming fit and lowers our sports performances.

# Don't misuse drugs!

Drugs are chemical substances which can affect our bodies. Medical drugs are made to fight illness and disease. Some can be used to improve sports performance. All drugs have side effects of some sort. Doping is the use of banned drugs in sport.

## Why do we use drugs?

We use drugs to feel better when we are unwell, or suffering from injury. Our doctors give us medicines to help us get well. We can also buy medicines directly from the chemist. Some of these medicines may contain drugs such as caffeine, ephedrine and codeine. These are banned by the International Olympic Committee (I.O.C.).

Many sportspeople take drugs legally. Legal drugs include alcohol, caffeine (in coffee and tea) and nicotine (in cigarettes).

Other so called recreational drugs are used by sportspeople. These include marijuana and cocaine, both of which are illegal. A number of sports have banned their players from using these drugs at any time.

Ben Johnson, who won the 100 metre Olympic title in 1992, was found to have taken drugs and was disqualified

## Why is doping not allowed?

The I.O.C. does not allow doping for three main reasons:
- to ensure that competition in sport is as fair as possible. Taking drugs to improve performance is a way of cheating;
- to protect the health of the sportspeople;
- to protect the wholesome image of sport.

### KEY POINT

Drugs which improve sports performance are banned because they are harmful to health, damage the image of sport and are a way of cheating.

## Why do sportspeople take drugs to improve their performance?

Individual sportspeople will have many different reasons for taking performance enhancing drugs, including:
- they want to be the best in the world at whatever cost;
- they hope their sporting success will make them rich;
- the media and the public put pressure on them to be successful;
- they believe that everybody else is doing it;
- their coach tells them to;
- they believe that they will not get caught;
- they are prepared to cheat in order to win.

## International Olympic Committee Medical Commission's list of doping classes and methods (1994)

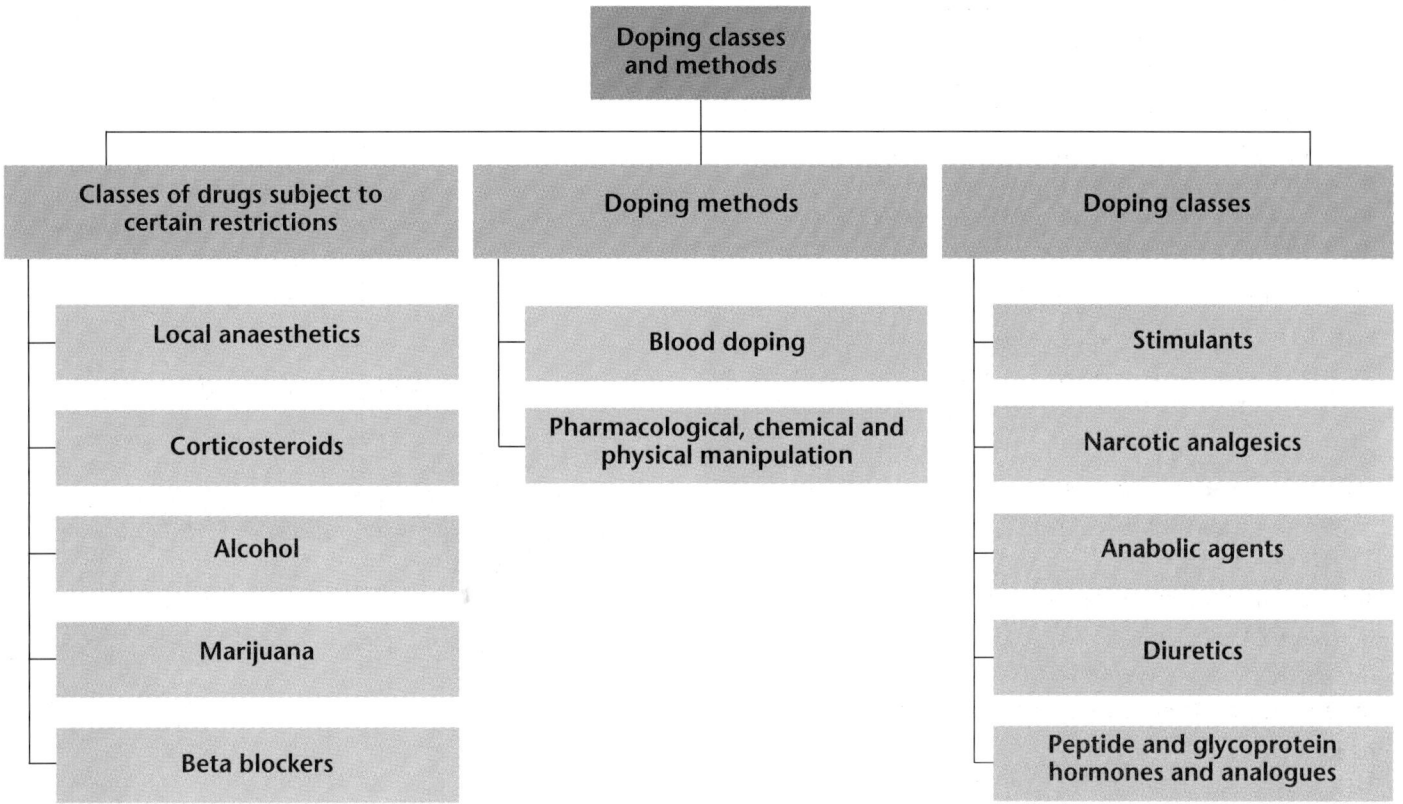

# Drugs subject to certain restrictions

The following are classes of drugs which are subject to certain restrictions by the I.O.C. medical commission (see chart above).

## Local anaesthetics
Local anaesthetics reduce pain but are allowed for medical reasons only. All details of treatment have to be given to the I.O.C. Medical Commission or the International Sports Federation (I.S.F.).

## Corticosteroids
Corticosteroids are used as analgesics, to reduce inflammation and for asthma treatment. They can be made in the body. Their use is now banned except for special cases. All details of treatment have to be given to the I.O.C. Medical Commission or the International Sports Federation (I.S.F.).

## Alcohol
Some sportspeople have used alcohol to reduce anxiety and shaking in events. Alcohol testing is carried out at the Olympic games in fencing and in the shooting aspect of the modern pentathlon.

## Marijuana
Marijuana can reduce worry and steady nerves. It can also result in lack of interest, poor judgement and personality changes. Its use is controlled in motor sport and some major team games.

## Beta blockers
Beta blockers are used to treat people with heart problems. They keep the heart rate and blood presure low even during periods of stress. The I.O.C. has banned them in archery, shooting, biathlon, modern pentathlon, bobsleigh, diving, luge, and ski-jumping.

# Doping classes

Diego Maradonna was found guilty of drug-taking

Diane Mohdahl successfully proved that she was innocent of drug-taking

The following are classes of drugs: stimulants, narcotic analgesics, anabolic agents, diuretics, peptide and glycoprotein hormones and analogues.

### Stimulants

Amphetamines and cocaine are examples of stimulants. The advantages of these are that they give us a lift, keep us awake and competitive. They speed up reflexes and reduce feelings of fatigue.

The disadvantages are that they increase heart rate and blood pressure, hide symptoms of fatigue and reduce feelings of pain. They are addictive and can cause acute anxiety and aggressiveness.

Many stimulants occur naturally. Caffeine is a stimulant found in coffee and tea. Nicotine is found in cigarettes. Many cold remedies and asthma inhalers contain stimulants such as ephedrine. These factors make stimulants difficult to test for.

### Narcotic analgesics

Examples of narcotic analgesics are methadone, heroin and codeine. The advantages of these are that they are pain killing drugs which mask injury or illness and reduce the feeling of pain.

The disadvantages are that injury can be made much worse and even permanent. They are also highly addictive.

Codeine is used in medicines. It cannot be distinguished from morphine when it is in the body.

Michelle Smith was tested for drugs more often than any other swimmer, but all tests were negative

### Peptide and glycoprotein hormones and analogues

Examples of peptide and glycoprotein hormones and analogues are corticotrophin, gonadotrophin, and erythrpoietin (EPO). The advantages of these are that they control pain, they are growth hormones, and they increase red blood cells, which helps endurance. The disadvantage of these drugs is that they may cause abnormal growth and increase the risk of a stroke.

## Doping methods

Doping methods include blood doping and pharmacological, chemical or physical manipulation.

### Blood doping

In the blood doping method, blood is injected into the body to increase the number of red blood cells (usually their own blood is injected, but it can come from another person). The advantage of blood doping is that the blood can carry more oxygen to the working muscles. This increases endurance (similar effects can be gained by training at altitude).

The dangers are that the circulatory system can be overloaded. In addition, kidney failure, A.I.D.S., or other diseases, can be caused by the injection of another person's blood.

The challenge in testing for blood doping is that it is difficult to distinguish between normal and abnormal amounts of red cells in the blood.

### Pharmacological, chemical or physical manipulation

This means sportspeople trying various methods to avoid testing positive for drugs. Some athletes have provided a 'clean' urine sample by deception. They have used urine from another person and hidden it on their body or put it into their bladder until they had to give a urine sample. Others have sent another athlete in their place when told that they have to be tested. It is against I.O.C. regulations to cheat in these ways. The testing procedures have been tightened up.

### Anabolic agents

Examples of anabolic agents are testosterone, stanozolol, and clenbuterol. The advantages of these are that they result in increased strength, weight, muscle growth, and endurance when combined with extra exercise. Clenbuterol is also used in asthma treatment.

For men, the particular disadvantages of these drugs are that they result in increased aggression, impotence, kidney damage, baldness and the development of breasts. The disadvantages for women are that they result in increased aggression, the development of male features, facial and body hair, and irregular periods.

The orally taken steroids work more quickly and are also removed from the body sooner than injected steroids. This makes testing for anabolic agents harder.

### Diuretics

Examples of diuretics are frusemide and probenecid. Advantages of these are that they result in rapid weight loss as fluid is removed from the body. They are used by competitors in sports which have weight categories. They are also taken to remove other drugs from the body. The disadvantages of these drugs are that they result in dehydration, cramps, dizziness, headaches and nausea.

# How are sportspeople tested for drugs?

**1. Competitors are chosen for testing**
Competition rules say who will be tested.
Competitors to be tested are told in writing.

**2. Competitors go to the Doping Control Centre**
An official goes with them.
All identity documents are checked.
The competitor may declare any medication used.

**3. Competitors produce a urine sample**
They are supervised the whole time.
Sealed drinks may be given to reduce dehydration.

**4. The sample is split and put into two separate, sealed containers**
The procedure is checked by the competitor.

**5. The containers are sent to the laboratory**
They are kept safe and secure under special conditions. Only I.O.C. agreed laboratories are used.

## The drug rules – who decides?

Each sport has its own international sports federation which controls its sport world wide. The international sports federations decide on their rules about doping. In the case of Olympic sport, the sport must also follow the drug code of the International Olympic Committee (I.O.C.). Each governing body in a country has the responsibility for testing sportspeople in and out of competition. In Britain, the UK Sports Council has taken on this responsibility. The sporting organisations have a constant problem trying to develop tests for new drugs.

## How is drug testing organised?

These guidelines are followed in competitions and are very similar in out of competition testing. Refusal to be tested is taken as a sign of guilt.

**6. Sample A tested** 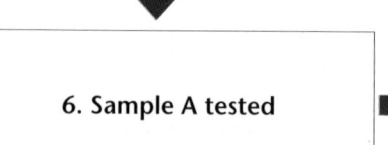 **Negative result**
No drugs found → **No further action**
Sample B is destroyed.
The governing body is told.
The competitor is told.

**7. Positive result**
Drugs are found.
The governing body is told.
The competitor is told and suspended.

**8. The governing body of the sport investigates**
The competitor is asked for an explanation.
Sample B is tested if this is requested.

**9. A governing body hearing is arranged**
The competitor presents his or her case.
If the competitor is found guilty he/she will be punished. The competitor may appeal.

 **KEY POINT**

The drug testers are always one step behind the sportspeople and their chemists.

# Questions

## Care of our Body

1  **a** How would you know that you had 'athlete's foot'?
   **b** How would you treat it?

2  Describe how you can maintain good hygiene in relation to:
   **i** personal cleanliness;
   **ii** disease prevention;
   **iii** clothing and equipment.

3  **a** Steroids are banned in sport. Name four other types of banned drugs.
   **b** List four side effects of continued use of anabolic steroids.

4  List the effects of smoking upon a sportsperson's performance.

5  Doping control involves regular drug testing.
   **a** Describe the drug testing procedures in the UK.
   **b** How might the fight against drug taking in sport be improved?

6  **a** Name one food that is rich in carbohydrates.
   **b** How does the body use carbohydrates?

7  Explain how eating a balanced diet and exercising regularly can improve a person's quality of life.

8  Explain the term 'energy balance'.

9  Give reasons why we should increase or decrease our intake of the following foods:
   **i** fibre;
   **ii** sugar;
   **iii** salt.

10 Explain the purpose of proteins and fats in a normal diet.

# 7 Safety in Sport

## Planning for safety page 126

When we organise sport for young people, we must ask:

- what does the law say?
- how must we prepare young people?
- how can we arrange fair competitions?
- how can we make sure that facilities and equipment are safe?
- what safety precautions can we take?
- what is the weather like?

Above all, we must be ready for emergencies.

## How can we make sure we are safe? page 128

As individuals taking part in sport, we need to prepare ourselves properly, prepare our dress and equipment properly and take part with the right attitude.

### Preparing ourselves properly
We need to look at our:
- health and fitness;
- techniques and skills;
- training;
- warm up.

### Preparing our dress and equipment properly
We need to make sure we have:
- the correct clothing and equipment;
- the right footwear;
- no jewellery.

Above all, our clothing needs to provide us with enough protection, and equipment needs to be safe.

### Taking part with the right attitude
We need to:
- obey the rules;
- respect our opponents and follow etiquette.

Keeping sport safe is a very important consideration for both the people who organise sport and those who take part. When we organise others to play sport, we need to plan for their safety. When playing sport ourselves, we are responsible for preparing ourselves properly and taking part with the right attitude. We also need to know about sports injuries – how to avoid them and how to deal with them when they occur.

## Emergency procedures page 132

We need to know about emergency procedures and when to use them:

- unconsciousness;
- concussion;
- shock;
- hypothermia;
- heat exhaustion;
- heatstroke;
- breathing stopped;
- no pulse;
- serious external bleeding.

## Sports injury page 130

We should know how to prevent, recognise, and deal with sports injuries. We need to use the following checklist when helping an injured person:

Danger
Response
Airway
Breathing
Circulation

## Soft and hard tissue injuries
### page 136

We need to know about soft and hard tissue injuries and the R.I.C.E. treatment:

Rest
Ice
Compression
Elevation

# Planning for safety

When planning for safety, there are some important questions we need to ask and answer.

## What does the law say?

The Health and Safety at Work Act, 1974, says that employers must ensure the safety of the people who work for them and all other people involved. This means that local authorities, governing bodies, managers of sports facilities and outdoor activity centres must look after their teachers, pupils, instructors and members of the public using their facilities.

## How must we prepare young people?

We must be sure that we have the right qualifications, knowledge and experience to teach, coach, train or instruct the young people in the activity.

If we are responsible for young people we must 'exercise a duty of care'. This means that we must take all reasonable precautions to see that they are safe. We must:

- prepare them properly;
- plan the activity carefully;
- check we have the right group size;
- make sure the facilities and equipment are safe;
- supervise them well;
- take safety precautions;
- have first aid ready;
- explain emergency procedures.

Competition should be fair and safe

## How can we arrange fair competitions?

If we organise a competition for young people we must ask ourselves:

- are they the same age?
- are they of the same physical development (weight and height)?
- are they of the same sex?
- do they have similar levels of skill?

The answers to these questions will help us decide whether or not the competition should go ahead.

## How can we make sure that facilities and equipment are safe?

Owners of sports facilities are responsible for the safe condition of their facilities.

The way we use and look after our outdoor playing surfaces will affect their condition. They are also affected a lot by the weather. If we fall over when pitches are hard and dry, we are likely to be injured. Equipment such as posts and nets must be in good condition. Synthetic surfaces can cause injuries to joints and ligaments because of the hardness of the surface, especially if we are not used to running on them.

Indoor facilities must be looked after just as carefully. Floors can be damaged by wear and tear. Dance and gymnastics need a very smooth surface and a sprung floor. Fixed equipment indoors must not be a hazard for other activities.

## Officials

All events need officials to organise and control the activities. They make sure that people play within the rules. This is for safety reasons as well as to ensure fair play. Organisers must ensure the safety of competitors and spectators.

# What is the weather like?

We can play most outdoor games safely in the rain and the wind, although it is usually not very enjoyable. However, when the surfaces are frozen, injuries are likely and it is too dangerous to play. Cold weather need not stop us playing, we just need to wear the correct clothing.

If we are taking part in outdoor activities the weather will affect what we do. Emergency procedures must be in place and explained to all. We must also consider the experience and ability of the group. It would be unsafe to take out inexperienced sailors in rough weather, whilst an advanced group might thoroughly enjoy the sail.

# What safety precautions can we take?

### Landing areas

Purpose built facilities for gymnastics have landing areas sunk into the floor to prevent injury during training. High jumpers and pole vaulters need special landing cushions. Mats used in gymnastics must absorb impact and be non slip.

### Changing rooms

Wet floors and broken tiles in changing rooms and showers can be dangerous.

### Large equipment

We all need to learn to use large pieces of equipment properly. Opening up trampolines, moving vaulting boxes and carrying goal posts are all dangerous activities if not done safely. Weight training equipment must be used carefully. We must take special care when using free weights not attached to a machine. We must lift, carry, place and use all equipment in a safe manner as we have been trained (see page 23).

### Water

All water can be dangerous. Swimming pools need lifeguards, depth signs and rules about behaviour to keep them safe. Outdoor water-based activities need lifejackets, correct clothing, careful training and safety precautions.

**We should always be prepared for emergencies**

### ● KEY POINT

All sport carries some risk of injury – we must always be prepared.

# How can we make sure we are safe?

We need to prepare ourselves properly for sport, we need to prepare our dress and equipment properly and we need to take part with the right attitude.

## Health and fitness

We must be in good health to take part in physical activities. We need health related fitness. We must also be sure that our body has been trained to cope with the demands of our sport. This means we need sport related fitness. Specific fitness for our sport will help prevent injuries. Tiredness and lack of sleep can reduce our skill which in turn can lead to injury.

We should check that our diet and fluid intake are sufficient for our activity. We need enough fuel for the activity to delay the start of fatigue. Eating should be completed two to three hours before the event so that our food is digested.

## Techniques and skills

We need the techniques and skills of our sport to perform well. We need to practise to perform difficult skills easily. Good skills mean we perform well, enjoy our sport and avoid injuries. For example, a hockey player who has not learned to tackle properly is likely to injure both herself and others. We need to know our ability and how far we can go. A fit, skilful player will have the confidence which helps to reduce injuries.

## Training

It is possible to train too hard. If we train very hard and often but do not give our bodies enough time to recover we might find we are not improving. The signs include such things as continuous tiredness and a loss of interest in the sport. The best way to deal with this problem is to rest for some time and then restart training when the body has recovered.

## Warm up and warm down

These are essential to prevent injury. They need to be closely related to the sport (see page 71).

Good techniques and skills make for safe sport

> **KEY POINT**
>
> When fatigue sets in, skill goes out of the window. Poor skills open the door for injury.

We must protect ourselves
from the sun's harmful rays

## The right footwear

All sport shoes must support and
protect the feet as well as be
comfortable. Shoes must also grip
the surface for which they are used
and absorb impact when we are
running and landing. This will
reduce injury. Sport shoes are
specially designed for different
types of sport.

## No jewellery

As much jewellery as possible should be removed
during sport. The risk of accidents due to jewellery
will vary with the sport. Rings on fingers will be
a much greater problem in judo than in shooting.
No jewellery at all should be worn in contact or
combat sports.

## The correct clothing and equipment

We should wear the correct clothing for the activity.
We should check our clothing and equipment
regularly to see that everything is in good order. Some
sports have rules to make sure protective equipment is
worn, for example fencing. For many sports, there are
few rules about clothing but players take sensible
precautions.

Protective equipment must:

- properly protect the sportsperson;
- allow freedom of movement;
- permit air to flow around the body;
- be comfortable;
- be safe and reliable.

In very sunny conditions today, players wear
protection against harmful ultra violet rays. This
includes sunglasses, hats, long sleeved shirts and
skin protecting products.

## Obey the rules

We need to know and understand the rules of our
activity. Rules encourage good sporting behaviour,
help games to flow and protect players from injury.
Rules must be followed and players punished if they
are broken. Injury causes pain and stops us from
playing. In high risk collision sports, injuries will be
part of the game. However, players who break rules
and harm opponents must be dealt with severely. In
recent years some deliberate foul play causing serious
injury has come before the courts.

## Respect opponents and follow etiquette

Etiquette means the special ways we are expected
to behave in our sport. They are not rules but have
become part of the sport over a long period, for
example shaking hands with your opponent after
a game of tennis. They usually involve ideas about
fairplay, sportsmanship, sporting spirit and respect
for your opponents. They can help reduce violence
in sport.

> **◯ KEY POINT**
>
> During the activity:
> - obey the rules;
> - remember the etiquette;
> - play with the right spirit;
> - follow the safety precautions.

# Sports injury

In order to avoid sports injuries, we need to know what they are and why they happen. We need to know what to do in an emergency.

When we say sports injury, we mean any damage to a sportsperson in action. This will include such things as hypothermia brought on by weather conditions, as well as broken bones and pulled muscles.

We are more likely to be injured when boxing than when taking part in archery. Some sports have a greater risk of injury than others.

There is a high risk of injury in boxing

## Accidental injuries

Accidental injuries can be due to forces from inside or outside of the body.

Forces *inside* our bodies (or, internal forces) are to do with the way our bodies work during exercise. Sometimes they are unable to cope with a sudden stretch or twist. The extra strain on the muscles, ligaments or tendons causes damage. These injuries may be caused by forgetting to warm up, by very sudden movements or lack of skill. For example, sprinters can tear hamstrings in a race and gymnasts can damage their ankles on landing.

Forces *outside* our bodies (or, external forces) are to do with violence or the environment.

## Violence

Injuries caused by violence are due to direct contact between players or equipment. Many sports have violent contact between opponents. Collisions may result in fractures, dislocations, sprains and bruises. They may also be caused by being hit by equipment such as balls, sticks or rackets. Breaking the rules can lead to violent injury.

## The environment

The environment can lead to injury in two different ways. An injury may be due to the facilities. For example, you might trip on the playing surface or collide with equipment such as posts. Alternatively, an injury may be due to weather conditions. Extreme heat may cause dehydration, heat exhaustion and later heatstroke. Extreme cold may lead to hypothermia.

## Over-use injuries

Over-use injuries are caused by using a part of the body again and again over a long period of time. Over-use injuries produce pain and inflammation.

Internal forces in the body can result in the following: Tennis players can get an inflamed elbow joint (called tennis elbow), rowers can suffer from sore wrist tendons and long distance runners may get pain on the front of the shins (shin splints). These are all injuries caused by over-use. They are sometimes due to incorrect actions.

External forces can produce over-use injuries such as blisters and calluses. They can be caused by gripping a piece of equipment very tightly during the activity.

## Chronic injuries

All injuries must be treated at once. We need to give them time to heal. If we put them under stress before they are healed they will get worse. If this continues to happen we will develop a chronic injury which is difficult to heal.

# What do we do when someone collapses ?

We must have a plan of action for any emergency. We need to know what to do first. Remember **D.R.A.B.C.** It tells us what to do in the right order.

> **⊙ KEY POINT**
>
> We must not move an injured sportsperson if we are at all worried about a spinal injury. We must wait for medical help. In an emergency we must:
> - assess the situation;
> - make everyone safe;
> - send for medical help;
> - give emergency aid.

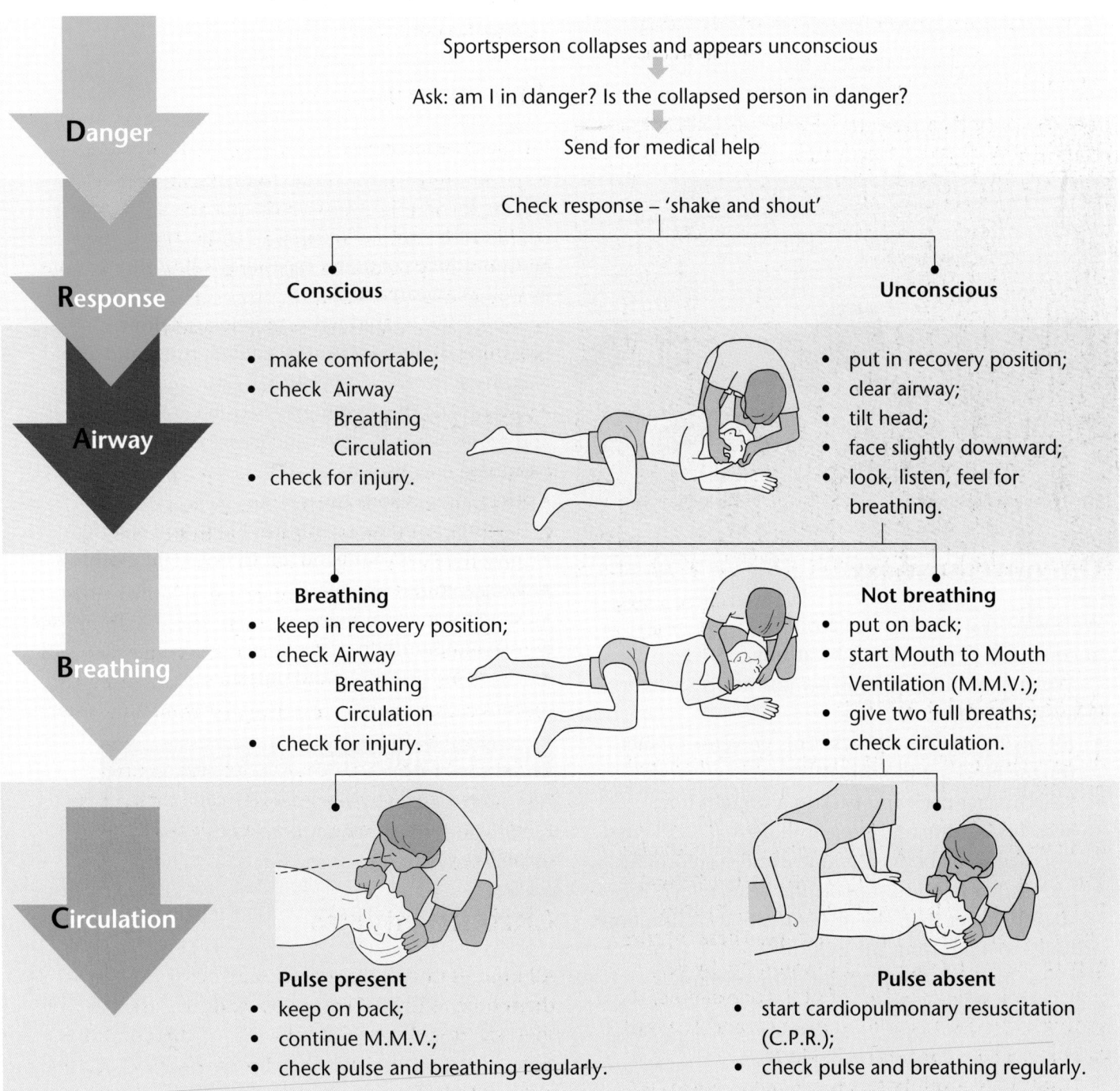

**Danger**

Sportsperson collapses and appears unconscious

Ask: am I in danger? Is the collapsed person in danger?

Send for medical help

Check response – 'shake and shout'

**Response**

**Conscious**

**Unconscious**

**Airway**

Conscious
- make comfortable;
- check  Airway
  Breathing
  Circulation
- check for injury.

Unconscious
- put in recovery position;
- clear airway;
- tilt head;
- face slightly downward;
- look, listen, feel for breathing.

**Breathing**

**Breathing**
- keep in recovery position;
- check Airway
  Breathing
  Circulation
- check for injury.

**Not breathing**
- put on back;
- start Mouth to Mouth Ventilation (M.M.V.);
- give two full breaths;
- check circulation.

**Circulation**

**Pulse present**
- keep on back;
- continue M.M.V.;
- check pulse and breathing regularly.

**Pulse absent**
- start cardiopulmonary resuscitation (C.P.R.);
- check pulse and breathing regularly.

# Emergency procedures

All of the following conditions require emergency procedures: unconsciousness, concussion, shock, hypothermia, heat exhaustion, heat stroke, breathing stopped, no pulse, and serious external bleeding. Faced with another person who is in any one of these situations, we need to know what (if anything) to check for, and how to act.

> **⟳ KEY POINT**
>
> We should be qualified to give first aid. We must keep the person safe and stable until medical help arrives. We may be able to provide life saving help in an emergency.

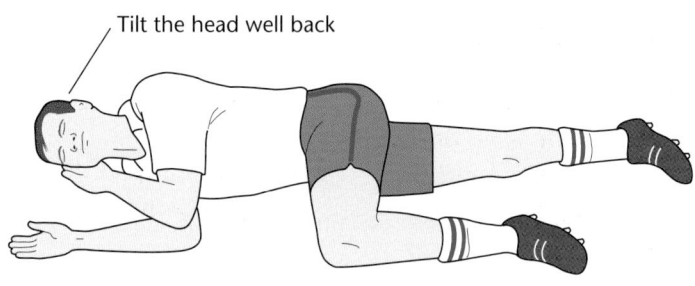

Tilt the head well back

**The recovery position**

## Unconsciousness

We always use the recovery position for an unconscious person who is breathing.

We may need to alter his/her position slightly if he/she has injuries.
- tilt his/her head well back. This prevents his/her tongue blocking the throat;
- keep his/her neck and back in a straight line;
- keep his/her hip and knee both bent at 90 degrees. This keeps the body safe, stable and comfortable;
- use his/her hand to support the head, which is slightly lower than the rest of the body. This allows fluids to drain from the mouth;
- check his/her breathing and pulse regularly;
- send for medical help.

## Concussion

We may lose consciousness after a violent blow to the head.

Check for: dizziness or sickness when he/she recovers. He/she may have a headache. He/she may not remember what has happened.
- put him/her in the recovery position until he/she becomes conscious again;
- check his/her breathing and pulse.

Sometimes there is a delay between the injury and losing consciousness.

## Shock

Serious injuries of many types may cause shock, as well as a heart attack.

Check for: a rapid pulse, paleness, shallow breathing, light headedness, nausea, thirst and a cold, clammy skin.

Eventually the person may become restless, anxious and aggressive, may yawn and gasp for air before becoming unconscious.
- treat any obvious cause;
- lay him/her down, with head low, and feet high;
- give him/her room and air, loosen tight clothing;
- keep him/her warm;
- send for medical help;
- reassure him/her;
- check for breathing and pulse.

> **⟳ KEY POINT**
>
> Any sportsperson who is knocked unconscious must not continue with their activity until after he or she has had medical advice.

# Hypothermia

Hypothermia can be caused by being outdoors in the cold and wind or being in very cold water. Our internal body temperature becomes dangerously low. Check for: shivering, cold, pale, dry skin, feeling confused, lacking energy; losing consciousness, slow, shallow breathing, slow weakening pulse.

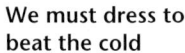

If someone is suffering from hypothermia:
* insulate him/her with extra clothing and cover his/her head;
* move him/her to a sheltered place;
* protect him/her from the ground and weather;
* use a survival bag if you have one;
* send for help;
* check his/her breathing and pulse;
* if he/she is conscious, give him/her hot drinks.

There are three methods of prevention of hypothermia during outdoor expeditions:
1. careful planning and proper training;
2. having equipment for emergencies, including spare clothes, survival bag, high energy food and drinks;
3. dressing to beat the cold, with layers of clothes and a wind and waterproof outer layer.

**We must dress to beat the cold**

# Heat exhaustion

Heat exhaustion develops during activity in hot conditions. It is caused by dehydration, that is loss of fluid and salt from the body due to excessive sweating.

Check for: headaches, lightheadedness, feeling sick, sweating, pale clammy skin, muscle cramps, rapid weakening pulse and breathing.
In the case of heat exhaustion, you need to:
* lay him/her down in a cool place;
* raise and support his/her legs;
* if he/she is conscious, ensure he/she sips plenty of weak, salt water;
* if he/she is unconscious, put him/her in the recovery position;
* send for medical help.

**Exercising in extreme heat can be dangerous**

# Heatstroke

The body becomes dangerously over heated due to being in the heat for a long time.
Check for: headache, dizziness, restlessness and confusion, hot, flushed, dry skin, very high body temperature.
In the case of heatstroke you need to:
* move him/her to a cool place;
* remove outer clothing;
* send for medical help;
* cool his/her body with wet towels;
* if he/she loses consciousness, put him/her in the recovery position;
* be ready to resuscitate him/her;
* if he/she is conscious, give him/her water to sip.

There are ways to prevent heat exhaustion and heatstroke:
1. careful planning and proper training;
2. taking plenty of fluid before and during the activity;
3. dressing to beat the heat with ventilation in headgear and light, quick drying clothing.

**🡆 KEY POINT**

Sportspeople must be prepared for extreme weather conditions.

# Breathing stopped

If the person has stopped breathing use Mouth to Mouth Ventilation (M.M.V.) to get him/her breathing again. Send for medical help. Take the following seven actions:

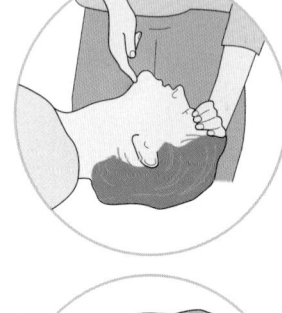
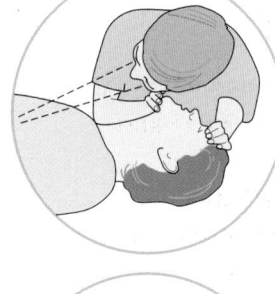
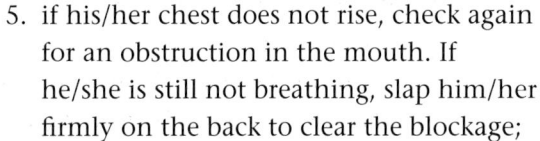

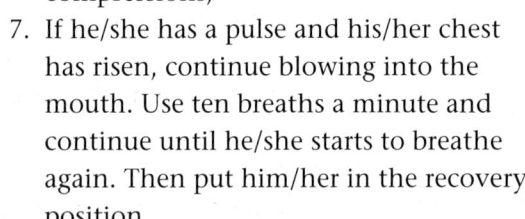
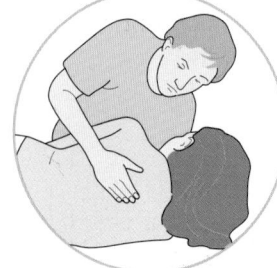

1. clear his/her mouth and throat of any obstruction;
2. open his/her airway by lifting the jaw and tilting the head well back;
3. check for breathing with your face close to his/her mouth. Look for chest movement. Listen for sounds of breathing. Feel his/her breath on your cheek;
4. if he/she is not breathing, pinch the nose. Take a deep breath. Seal your lips around his/her mouth. Blow into his/her mouth, and watch the chest rise. Take your mouth away and watch his/her chest fall back;
5. if his/her chest does not rise, check again for an obstruction in the mouth. If he/she is still not breathing, slap him/her firmly on the back to clear the blockage;
6. check his/her pulse before continuing. If there is no pulse, start chest compressions;
7. If he/she has a pulse and his/her chest has risen, continue blowing into the mouth. Use ten breaths a minute and continue until he/she starts to breathe again. Then put him/her in the recovery position.

> **◐ KEY POINT**
>
> The person will die quickly if oxygen does not get to the brain. We must breathe for him or her and get his or her own breathing and heart going as soon as possible.

# No pulse

If you are certain that the person has no pulse, use chest compressions to get his/her heart beating again. Send for medical help. Take the following six actions:

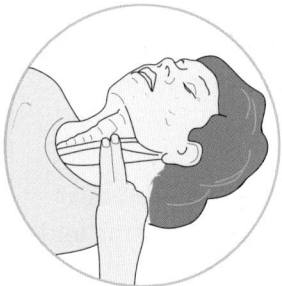

1. check for a pulse. If the heart has stopped, you will not be able to feel a pulse. His/her skin will be pale, the lips blue and arms and legs limp;

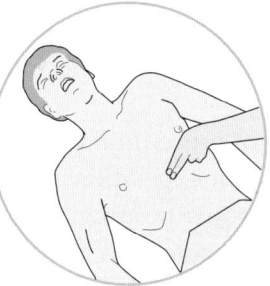

2. with him/her lying on his/her back, use your fingers to find the point where the ribs meet at the breastbone. Put your middle finger over this point and your index finger higher up on the breastbone;
3. put the heel of your other hand on the breastbone, just above your index finger. Apply pressure here;
4. place the heel of your first hand over the top of the other hand. Interlock your fingers;
5. lean over him/her, with your arms straight, press down firmly to press in the breastbone about 4/5 cm. Then rock backwards to release the pressure. Keep your hands in place. Repeat at a rate of about 80 compressions a minute;
6. check his/her pulse rate regularly. Stop compressions as soon as his/her pulse returns.

If we are certain that the person has no pulse then we need to start cardio pulmonary respiration (C.P.R.) at once. We can do it on our own or with help. We must call for medical help before we start.

If you are alone, you need to take the following five actions:

1. open his/her airway. Give two breaths using mouth to mouth ventilation (M.M.V.).
2. give 15 chest compressions;
3. give two more breaths (M.M.V.);
4. give 15 chest compressions;
5. continue until help arrives.

We should only stop to check for his/her pulse if we see signs of it returning; if his/her pulse does return, stop C.P.R. and check his/her breathing. Continue with M.M.V. and check his/her pulse every ten breaths. If breathing also returns, put him/her in the recovery position.

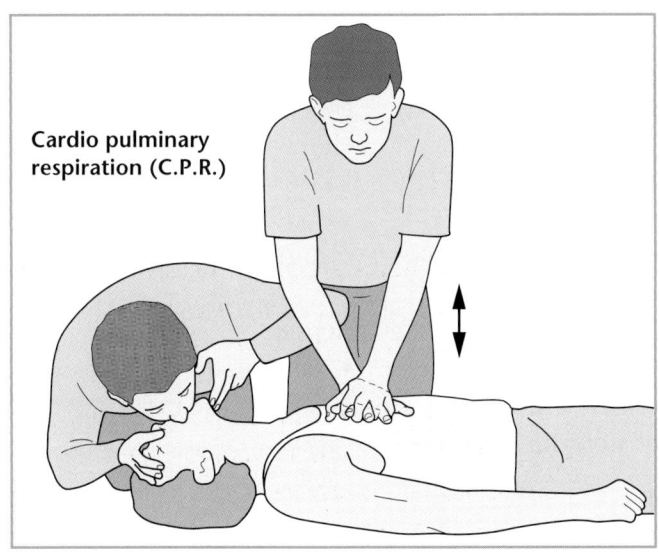

Cardio pulminary respiration (C.P.R.)

If we are not alone, but have some help available, we need to do one of the following:

1. we can do both the M.M.V. and the chest compressions alone for a period of time. This gives the other person a complete rest. We can then change over;
2. we can do chest compressions and our helper can do the M.M.V. This means that the work is not so hard as we work alternately.

We must check for the return of his/her pulse and breathing as explained above.

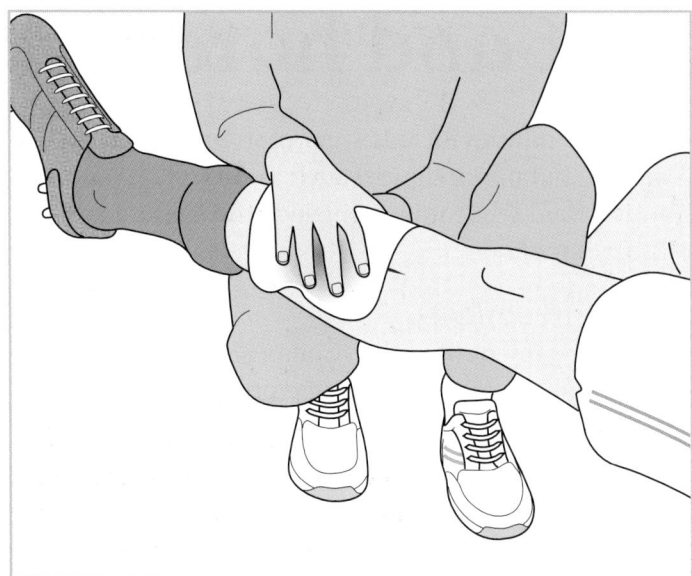

## Serious external bleeding

Massive bleeding is frightening. Remember D.R.A.B.C. Send for medical help. Aim to control bleeding and prevent shock:

* cover his/her wound with a clean pad and apply pressure with your hand or squeeze the sides of his/her wound together with your fingers;
* lay him/her down;
* raise his/her leg above his/her heart level, taking care in case there is a fracture. If the wound continues to bleed, add extra pads and bandage over his/her wound. Provide reassurance.

If bleeding continues, find a pressure point and apply pressure. Pressure points are found where an artery is close to the bone, for example in the groin and under the biceps.

**TAKE CARE! You must release the pressure within ten minutes to prevent permanent damage. You must not use a tourniquet.**

# Soft and hard tissue injuries

Soft tissue injuries include sprains, strains, cartilage damage, and minor injuries such as cuts, grazes, and bruises. Hard tissue injuries include the fracture and dislocation of bones.

## R.I.C.E. treatment

R.I.C.E. treatment (Rest, Ice, Compression, Elevation) is a checklist to follow in the case of soft tissue injury.

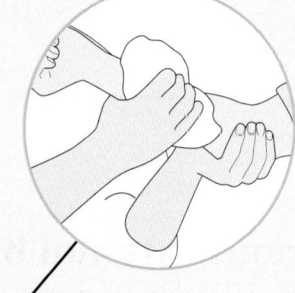

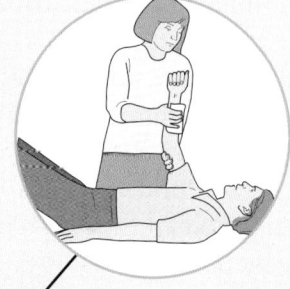

### Rest
**Rest the injured part**

Reason
- reduces bleeding;
- prevents further injury.

Action
- stop your activity. Support the injury in a comfortable position.

### Ice
**Apply Ice or a cold compress**

Reason
- reduces blood flow, pain and swelling.

Action
- put an ice pack or cold compress on the injury, for 20 minutes every hour.

### Compression
**Compress the injury**

Reason
- reduces bleeding and swelling.

Action
- wrap a bandage firmly over the injured area. Do not stop the blood flow.

### Elevation
**Elevate the injured part**

Reason
- reduces bleeding, swelling and throbbing.

Action
- raise the injury above the level of the heart.

## Add a P and a D to make P.R.I.C.E.D. treatment

**P for prevention**
- many injuries can be reduced by warming up, being fit and skilful;

**D for diagnosis**
- see a doctor or physiotherapist to understand what exactly has happened and what treatment should be followed.

## Remember H.A.R.M. – things to be avoided

**Heat**
- do not use heat for 48 hours because it increases bleeding;

**Alcohol**
- do not drink alcohol because it increases the swelling;

**Running**
- do not run because the weight and impact causes further injury;

**Massage**
- do not massage for 48 hours because it increases bleeding.

**Preventing, recognising, and dealing with injury**

# Soft tissue injuries

Soft tissue injuries include damage to muscles, ligaments, and tendons, as well as damage to cartilage.

When soft tissues are injured they become inflamed. Treatment aims to reduce the swelling, prevent further damage and ease the pain.

A sprain happens when we over stretch or tear a ligament. This can be caused by a twist or sudden wrench, for example a sprained ankle. In this case we must use the R.I.C.E. treatment. If the injury is severe we should treat it as a fracture.

A strain happens when we stretch or tear a muscle or tendon. This can be caused by a sudden stretch or extra muscular effort, for example a pulled muscle. In this case, we must use the R.I.C.E. treatment.

The two cartilages act as shock absorbers between the bones of our knee joint. They can be torn when the joint is twisted or pulled in an unusual way, for example when we are tackled in football. In this case, we would need medical advice.

# Soft tissue injuries: minor problems

We should deal with minor problems quickly and carefully. If we ignore them they may become more serious in the future.

### Skin damage

Cuts: Clean the cut with running water. Dab dry and cover using a dressing. Clean and dry the skin around the cut. Use an adhesive plaster over the dressing.

Grazes (called abrasions): The top layer of skin has been scraped off because of friction with a rough surface. Treat it as a cut. Be careful to check that the wound is clean.

Blisters: Damage to the skin by heat or friction can cause a bubble to form to protect the skin. Do not break the blister. Only treat it if it breaks or is likely to break. Cover it with a dry dressing.

### Other conditions

Bruises: These are the result of damaged capillaries bleeding under the skin. Bruises are caused by a blow. There can be pain, swelling and a change in skin colour. Treat by raising and supporting the bruised part. Put a cold compress (that is a pad soaked in cold water or an ice pack in a cloth) on the bruised part.

Cramp: A sudden painful muscle contraction. It can be caused by strenuous exercise or loss of fluid and salt through sweating. Treat by drinking fluid, stretching and massaging the muscle.

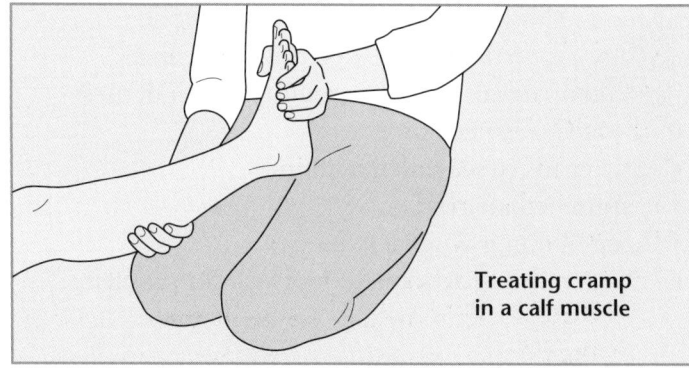

**Treating cramp in a calf muscle**

Stitch: Pain in the abdominal muscles due to over-use. These muscles keep us upright when we walk or run. Treat by sitting down and resting.

# Hard tissue injuries

Hard tissue injuries are injuries to bones and include fractures and dislocations.

## Fractures

A fracture is a break in a bone. There are two types:

1. a simple (closed) fracture – the bone stays under the skin;
2. a compound (open) fracture – the bone breaks through the skin.

Complicated fractures involve damage also to nerves and muscles. All fractures are serious and need urgent medical treatment.

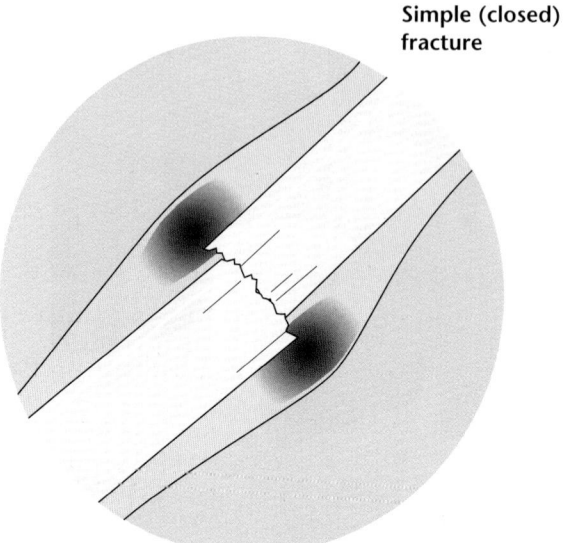

**Simple (closed) fracture**

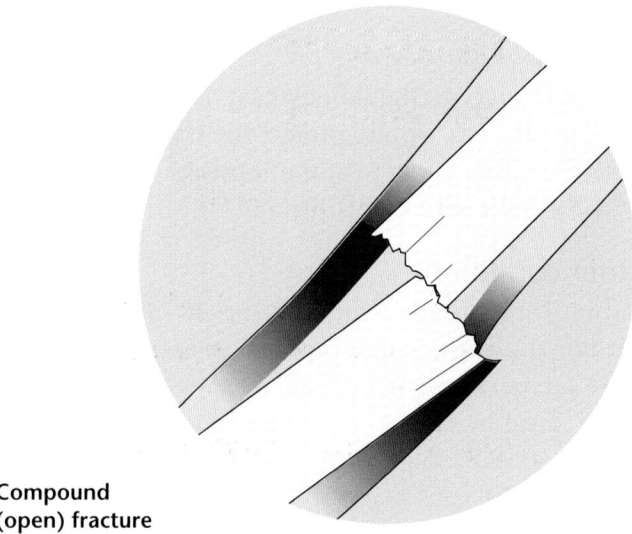

**Compound (open) fracture**

## Stress fractures

These are small cracks in a bone. They are often an overuse injury. They can be caused, for example, by too much running on hard surfaces.

Check for pain gradually getting worse in a particular part of the limb, swelling and tenderness in the area. We need to:

- use ice to reduce inflammation;
- get immediate rest;
- keep fit doing other activities;
- check running action and footwear for problems.

## Dislocations

A dislocation means that a bone at a joint is forced out of its normal position. The ligaments around the joint may be damaged also. The cause may have been a strong force wrenching the bone, for example a rugby tackle. Treat all dislocations as if they are fractures.

## Bone and joint injuries

**Recognition**
- a recent blow or fall;
- snapping sound of breaking bone or torn ligament;
- difficulty in moving the limb normally;
- pain made worse by movement;
- severe 'sickening' pain (dislocation);
- tenderness at the site (fracture);
- deformity, that is the limb has an unusual shape;
- swelling, bruising;
- signs of shock.

**Action**
- keep him/her still, steady and comfortable;
- support injured part;
- bandage injured part to his/her body or limb;
- reassure him/her;
- send for medical help.

# Questions

## Safety in Sport

1   List two sporting incidents which might damage ankle ligaments.

2   Describe the first aid treatment for ligament damage.

3   **a** Give two reasons for warming up before physical activity.
    **b** Give two examples of activities that might be included in a warm up.

4   Give four examples of safe practice in physical activity.

5   **a** What does R.I.C.E. stand for?
    **b** Give one example of an injury requiring this kind of treatment.

6   Your squash partner collapses. She is not breathing and has no pulse. Explain in detail the action you would take.

7   Name two environmental conditions that affect performance and can lead to injury.

8   What is a stress fracture? Explain how it is caused and how it should be treated.

9   The use of 'spotters' in trampolining is one example of an accepted safety rule. Describe two accepted safety rules for other activities.

10  Select one sport or activity and list the safety equipment worn by a performer.

# 8 The Changing Face of Sport

The link between society and sport is very important. To look at the history of sport is to look at the history of a society. Sport reflects the society in which it is found.

## The changing Olympics

**page 146**

The Atlanta Olympics showed how much the Olympics have changed since the first modern Games in Athens in 1896. Thousands of competitors and officials are now involved in an entertainment extravaganza on a world wide stage. The Games have survived one hundred years, two World Wars, boycotts, killings, demonstrations and other near disasters. The Games of Seoul and Barcelona seemed to have brought in a new era of sporting peace. This was shattered by the Atlanta bomb. Sydney will offer the opportunity once again to fulfil the Olympic aim of international goodwill and friendship through sport.

In the Olympic arenas of the past the champions competed for the glory of winning. They performed before the people of Greece and the Greek empire. Poems were written in honour of their victories. They inspired others to follow in their footsteps for a thousand years.

The contrast with today could not be greater. Yet sport has survived the centuries. To survive it has had to change as society has changed.

## Developments in British sport

**page 142**

Before 1700, sports took place in the villages on feast days. These were local events, loosely organised and with simple rules passed down through the generations. The Industrial Revolution moved people into the cities leaving behind their traditional sports and games. The public schools in Victorian times developed new highly organised sports.

These were taken up by the masses first as spectators then as enthusiastic players. This century, improving standards of living and physical education in schools combined to boost sport. Today 'Sport for All' is a reality for many.

Sport today is a world wide phenomenon of great importance. Through television, sport reaches every corner of the world. Our screens are filled with the images of the stars. We share their successes and their failures as they happen. We dream our own sporting dreams.

## The role of the performer
### page 154

The 'Gentlemen amateurs' of the last century would be amazed at today's highly paid stars, instantly recognisable as they jet around the world! They would also, no doubt, look in amazement at the thousands of runners of all shapes and sizes completing the London Marathon. The rewards for the elite professional sportspeople are very great indeed. They are, however, the top of a pyramid whose base is made up of all the ordinary amateurs throughout the country who play just for fun.

## New technology page 160

The search for success in sport is never ending. Sportspeople have always looked to technology to improve their own ability. Dramatic changes such as those seen in the design of modern Olympic racing bikes have been in the news. Other changes in materials, clothing, surfaces, buildings and equipment do not always get as much publicity but are equally important. They have raised sporting performances everywhere.

# Developments in British sport

## The early days of sport

Before 1700, sport in Britain was a local affair. The games and competitions took place on feast days. They were organised by the people of the village and followed traditional patterns. Travel around the country was difficult and most people taking part were from the local area.

## Patronage

At this time, social position was fixed and a system of **patronage** existed. This meant that wealthy people were able to support talented people who were poor. Patronage helped many sports develop. For example, the Duke of Cumberland was patron to Jack Broughton, the prize fighter. Prize fighting led to modern boxing.

## Gambling and the rules of sport

Gambling was closely linked to most sports. It encouraged cheating and the involvement of criminals because the results were so important. Prize fighting, cricket and horse racing all introduced rules to see that both the competition and the gambling were fair.

## Industrialisation

During **industrialisation** (the industrial revolution) large numbers of people moved to the towns and cities to work in the factories. They left behind their traditional games and sporting activities. Sports like mob football were often banned. People were worried about the lack of control and the damage to property.

## Violence

Society was used to physical violence and brutality. Many sports were based on cruelty to animals, for example bear baiting and cock fighting. Bare knuckle prize fights were only won when one fighter was unconscious. The first law to prevent cruelty to animals was not passed until 1822.

> ### ⊙ KEY POINT
>
> Sport after 1700 became more important throughout the country. It was influenced by patronage, gambling, rules, industrialisation and violence.

Many sports were based on gambling, and cruelty to animals

# Sport in Victorian times

The foundations of modern sport were laid during **Victorian times**. At this time sport became important nationally. This was due to changing social conditions, the influence of the **public schools** and a better transport system.

## Changing social conditions

For most working people life was hard. Large numbers of people worked in the industrialised cities. Work occupied six days a week with Saturday a full working day. There was a great need for physical recreation. People attended sporting events whenever they could. By the 1870s most workers only worked until lunch time on Saturday. This gave a great boost to both playing and watching sport.

## The public schools

In the early nineteenth century, the public schools tried to stop the pupils taking part in their traditional sporting activities. Teachers were worried about the drinking and bad behaviour that went with the pupils' sport.

However, this attitude changed with the coming of a new form of sport. Dr Arnold, the headmaster of Rugby School, is often given credit for this development. Sport was encouraged as a form of physical religion, called 'Muscular Christianity'. Team games, like cricket, rugby and football, were played to develop such qualities as concern for others, unselfishness and leadership. Above all, these games were believed to prepare the young men for their future careers.

The new games of football and rugby were developed by the public schools. In the early days, many schools had different rules. They found it difficult to compete against each other until the Football Association in 1863 set out the rules of football and the Rugby Football Union followed in 1871.

The first university boat race, between Oxford and Cambridge, took place in 1829. The interest shown by the public helped make rowing popular.

For most children outside the public school system, education was very different. The **state schools** did

**Large crowds attended sporting events**

not have the facilities, equipment or staff to provide a wide range of physical activities. Only exercises and **drill** were included at first, for disciplinary and health reasons. Later, **Swedish gymnastics** were introduced.

## The transport revolution

Better roads helped spectators to travel to sporting events. The railways allowed sports to develop nationally, for example horses could be moved quickly around the country for racing. Cricket teams toured the country. Football spectators and players travelled by rail to compete in the national Football League started in 1888.

International sport was also helped by easier and safer transport. The first England versus Scotland soccer match was played in 1872. The cricketers had started earlier with a tour of North America in 1859.

> **◗ KEY POINT**
>
> During Victorian times, sport changed so that it had to be:
> - between two matched teams or competitors;
> - governed by rules;
> - for the honour of winning only;
> - played in a spirit of fairplay;
> - without any gambling.

## British sport in the early twentieth century

In the early part of the century, working conditions continued to improve. This left working people with more time and energy to take part in **sport**. Thousands regularly watched professional football games and attended horse racing, cricket and rugby league. For people with money there were now many more sports to play. Tennis, golf and cycling became popular. At this time, most women still did not take part in sport at all.

After the first world war, sport became part of the entertainment industry. There was still great interest in the major sports like cricket, football and horse racing. New sports such as speedway, greyhound racing, ice hockey and motorcycle racing started up. Wealthy people were able to take part in polo, sailing, skiing and motor racing.

In the thirties there was a boom in outdoor activities including cycling, walking, camping and rambling. The Central Council of Recreative Physical Training (now the C.C.P.R.) was formed in 1935 to encourage sport and **recreation**.

In **physical education** at this time, drill had been replaced by exercises and games. In 1936 there were changes based on the development of a healthy, efficient body. There was also a gradual move towards the idea of physical training for recreation.

## British sport since 1945

The Second World War lasted from 1939–1945. Most people in Britain suffered a long period of hardship after 1945. Rebuilding the country was the first priority and therefore sport was slow to develop again. Changes in sport since the war have been due to:

- social changes;
- commercialisation;
- the media;
- government involvement;
- education.

**British sport in the early twentieth century was helped by improved working conditions**

## Social changes

The standard of living of most people has greatly improved since 1945. Most people have had more money to spend on leisure time activities. Basic working hours have been reduced giving people more time for leisure. More recently, the rise in unemployment, part-time working and early retirement have all led to more leisure time. Work and housework have both become less demanding physically. The general health of the population has improved. The importance of a healthy life style and the popularity of the fitness image have encouraged physical recreation. Facilities for sport and recreation have greatly improved through the efforts of the Sports Council and the local authorities.

## Commercialisation

**Commercialisation** means that a whole leisure industry has grown up around sport. This includes builders of specialist facilities, sports centre workers, equipment and clothing manufacturers and retailers. Today, sport is an important part of the economy.

All sports try to develop their commercial potential. **Sponsorship** is very important for them. Sponsorship helps sport to reward its top performers, pay for its events and to improve the sport itself.

## The media

**The media** (radio, newspapers and television) have greatly increased interest in sport. The arrival of colour television, for example, made snooker into a very popular sport. Sponsorship deals give sport much needed money, especially when the sport is seen on television. Sponsorship, television and sport are today closely linked. The media can make stars overnight and ruin those who are seen to fail. Sport in the media usually means male sport.

The media have increased public interest in sport

## The Government

After 1945, the Government became more involved in sport and physical recreation. The work of the C.C.P.R. was taken over by the Sports Council. In 1972 the Sports Council was given a royal charter and an annual grant from the Government.

Government money has been put into sports facilities in run down city areas to enable them to try to reduce their social problems. More recently, the National Lottery was set up and the Government's own ideas on sport, called 'Raising the Game', were published.

In international sport, the Government had a number of issues to deal with at this time. These included whether to have sporting links with South Africa during the apartheid period and the right of the British team to take part in the Moscow Olympics.

## Education

Education is also an area of Government involvement. There were many changes after 1945 in physical education in state schools. For example, local authorities had to provide facilities for physical education and **games**. Most importantly physical education as a subject was accepted as being a vital part of all pupils' education.

Much more recently a number of changes have affected physical education:

- surplus school playing fields were sold off;
- many primary schools abandoned competitive sport;
- the number of out of school sporting activities declined;
- health-related fitness programmes have been developed;
- physical education was included in the National Curriculum.

P.E. is a foundation subject in the National Curriculum

# The changing Olympics

In many ways, the changing face of the Olympics is an example of how sport changes over time to reflect changes in society.

The earliest known Olympic Games were held at Olympia in Greece in 776 BC. From this date they were held every fourth year, without a break, for over a thousand years. This is remarkable because the Greek city states were often at war. However, during the period of the Games there was a sacred truce.

The Games were not just athletics meetings. They were religious festivals of great importance. The Olympic Games were always held in honour of the god, Zeus. The Olympic Games were one of four famous Crown Games, so called because crowns or wreaths were awarded to the winners.

## How were the ancient Olympic Games organised?

Originally the Games only lasted one day, but this was gradually extended to five. This allowed time for making sacrifices, registering the athletes, taking the oath and prize giving. People also came to see special works of art produced for the Games. Only Greeks and citizens of Greek colonies were allowed to take part. At first all competitions were for men, but later boys took part. They usually competed naked. Women and slaves were not even allowed to watch the Games.

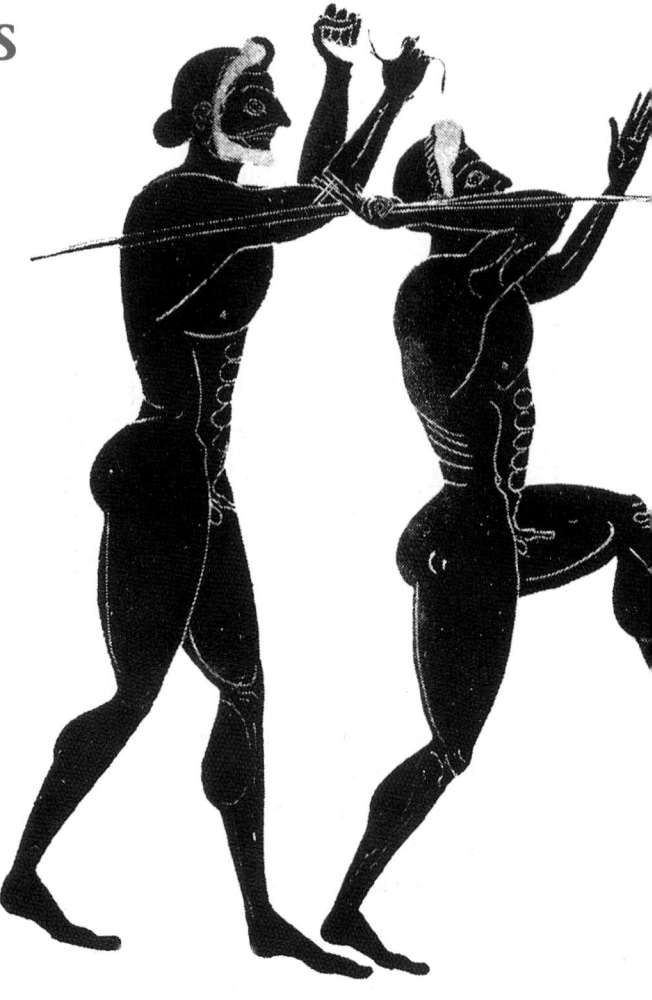

**The ancient Olympics**

## Which events took place at the ancient Olympics?

Athletic events, fighting events, and chariot racing took place at the ancient Olympics.

### Athletic Events
The three main running events were:
- *short sprint*, one length of the stadium (200 m);
- *double sprint*, two lengths of the stadium (400 m);
- *long distance race*, many lengths (about 4800 m).

These events formed the basic programme.
Other events were included at different times:
- *the pentathlon* included five events – the long jump, discus, javelin, short sprint and wrestling. Three wins were needed for victory;

- *the long jump*. In the long jump, strange weights called 'Halteres' were carried in each hand. They helped the performer gain extra distance;
- *the discus*. The discus was larger and flatter, and was thrown in a way similar to that used today;
- *the javelin*. A leather thong held in the hand was wound around the shaft of the javelin to increase the distance thrown.

The marathon race was not held at the ancient Olympic Games. It was first included in the Olympics of 1896.

## Fighting events

The three main fighting events were boxing, wrestling and the pankration.

- boxers wore no gloves, but they bound leather thongs around their hands. They fought until one gave in or was knocked out;

**Wrestling**

- wrestling, like the event today, continued until one wrestler forced his opponent's shoulder blades against the ground;
- in the pankration, competitors could punch, grapple, kick or throw. A submission or knockout decided the winner.

## Chariot racing

Chariot racing was held on a separate track, called a 'Hippodrome'. Races were very exciting and usually dangerous, especially at the turning posts at the ends of the stadium.

**Chariot racing**

# What do we know about the ancient Olympic Games?

About a hundred years ago, excavations at Olympia uncovered the ruins of a large sporting and religious complex. The stadium was close by and contained a rectangular track, about 200m by 30m.

In the early Olympic Games, competition was friendly and fair. As they became more important, so did the winning. Athletes found trainers and specialised in one event. They trained very hard, even following special diets. Many cities offered valuable prizes to the winners.

# Why did the Olympic Games stop?

The decline of the Olympic Games was gradual. The importance of winning and the large rewards given to winners changed the Olympic Games. There was bribery and corruption. The Romans conquered Greece in the second century BC. Although they kept the Olympic Games going they did not understand the Olympic spirit. Cruel events were introduced, eventually leading to contests between gladiators and fights with animals. In AD 393, the Christian Emperor Theodosius stopped the Olympic Games. He claimed they were a Pagan festival. The sacred site of Olympia was very soon destroyed. First there were invaders, then an earthquake, and then a flood which buried the remains under mud and water. It remained lost for many centuries. It was not until 1896 that De Coubertin was able to bring the Olympic spirit to life again (see page 148).

### ⟳ KEY POINT

The ancient Olympic Games were important to the people of the time. They were religious as well as sporting occasions. There was great honour in being a champion. They took place every four years for over one thousand years.

# The modern Olympics

The modern Olympic Games originated with Baron Pierre de Coubertin, a French aristocrat who became interested in sport and education. He visited England and was impressed by the sport he saw in the public schools. He organised a conference in 1894 with 79 members from 12 countries. They agreed to restore the Olympic Games. He wanted sport to help improve international understanding and promote world peace.

The following is a list of the venues, or **host cities**, at which the Olympics was held.

**Baron Pierre de Coubertin**

## 1912 Stockholm

This was a very well organised event. Nearly double the competitors took part as had done previously. Women took part in swimming. There were no incidents or protests.

## 1896 Athens

The Greek Government was unable to pay for the Games. They were saved by a wealthy businessman and 13 countries took part – Australia, Austria, Britain, Bulgaria, Chile, Denmark, France, Germany, Hungary, Sweden, Switzerland, USA, and Greece.

Most competitors made their own way at their own expense. There were nine sports and 311 male competitors.

## 1900 Paris

This was held at the same time as the Paris Universal Exhibition. It was a near disaster, poorly organised and largely ignored, although 13 new sports were added. Women competed in golf and tennis.

## 1904 St. Louis

This was held at the same time as the World Fair. It was a side show to the main event. Only 12 countries took part. Most of the competitors were American.

## 1908 London

Some pride returned to the Olympic Games when proper rules were used. However, there were arguments between the teams concerning the fact that all the judges were British.

## 1914–18
The First World War put a stop to these Olympics.

## 1920 Antwerp
Belgium had only just recovered from the First World War at this time and 29 countries took part although Germany, Austria, Hungary, Bulgaria and Turkey were not allowed to compete. Many competitors had suffered in the war.

## 1924 Paris
There was a large increase in the countries taking part (there were 44). There were also more competitors (3092 altogether). Germany was still absent. The Winter Games started in Chamonix, France.

## 1928 Amsterdam
48 countries took part. Women took part in athletics and gymnastics. Several women collapsed at the end of the 800m.

## 1932 Los Angeles
Travelling costs reduced the number of competitors. There were high spectator attendances and 100,000 attended the opening ceremony. First Olympic village to accommodate competitors.

## 1936 Berlin
Hitler's Nazi party was in power in Germany at this time. Persecution of Jews and other groups had begun. The International Olympic Committee (I.O.C.) insisted that the Olympic Games should take place. Hitler used the Games for propaganda purposes. He wanted to show the superiority of the German people. The black American Jesse Owens defeated Hitler's aim by winning four gold medals. Hitler congratulated the German winners but not Jesse Owens.

**Black American Jesse Owens won four gold medals, and defeated Hitler's aim**

## 1939–45
The Second World War put a stop to these Olympics.

## 1948 London
This was held in a blitzed city by an exhausted nation after the war. 59 countries and 4500 competitors took part. Germany, Japan, and the Soviet Union were absent.

## 1952 Helsinki
This was known as the 'Friendly Games'. Germany was still absent. The Soviet Union took part again after 40 years. This Olympic Games pointed to the beginnings of East–West rivalry.

A black power demonstration at the 1972 Olympics

## 1956 Melbourne

Equestrian events were held in Sweden because of Australia's quarantine laws. East and West Germany combined into one team. Spain and Holland withdrew because the Soviet Union invaded Hungary. The Peoples' Republic of China withdrew because Taiwan took part. Egypt and the Lebanon withdrew because of fighting over the Suez Canal.

### ➡ EXTENSION

THE TWO CHINAS

The island of Taiwan lies close to mainland China. The Peoples' Republic of China (P.R.C.) believes the island of Taiwan to be part of China. At Melbourne the P.R.C. refused to take part with Taiwan in attendance. After 1956, the P.R.C. withdrew from most world sport. Taiwan continued to represent China during this period. In 1976, at the Montreal Olympics, Taiwan withdrew because it could not compete as the P.R.C. In 1984, at the Los Angeles Olympics, both the P.R.C. and Taiwan (under the name Taipei) took a full part.

## 1960 Rome

There were no political problems at this event. Television showed the events world wide. A Danish cyclist died after using drugs. An all-white team represented South Africa.

## 1964 Tokyo

South Africa was banned from the Olympic Games at this time because of apartheid. Indonesia and North Korea were banned for taking part in an unofficial competition. The event was very successful in spite of its size, with 94 countries taking part altogether. The event was very expensive.

### ➡ EXTENSION

APARTHEID IN SOUTH AFRICA

Apartheid is a political system. The white minority in South Africa held power over the black majority. This resulted in discrimination against black people. In sport this meant that black people had inferior facilities and fewer opportunities, spectators were segregated and there were separate teams for different races. As a result, South Africa was expelled from the Olympic and other international sports organisations. In spite of many strong protests, some non-Olympic sporting contact continued, for example rugby union tours. Arguments over sporting contacts led to **boycotts** of the 1976 Montreal Olympics and the 1986 Edinburgh Commonwealth Games. In 1990, Nelson Mandela was released from prison and the apartheid system was removed. South Africa rejoined the Olympic movement in time for the 1992 Barcelona Olympics.

⊙ **EXTENSION**

BLACK POWER

Tommie Smith and John Carlos, black American athletes, were first and second in the 200m in 1968. At the medal ceremony, they raised black gloved arms. This was a protest against the way black people were treated as second class citizens in the USA. Members of the winning black American relay team also gave the **black power** salute. All the athletes were sent home.

## 1968 Mexico City

There was a demonstration against poverty and the cost of the Olympic Games. The demonstration was brutally broken up with many people killed. East and West Germany entered as separate teams. Mexico's high altitude caused problems for distance athletes. There were drug tests for the first time. During the medal ceremonies, black American athletes staged a protest at inequality and injustice in the treatment of black people in the USA. South Africa was not allowed to take part.

## 1972 Munich

This Olympic Games was technically brilliant, but there were many serious problems. Rhodesia was sent home because of claims they had been racist in selecting their (all white) team. Black American athletes again protested during the medal ceremonies. Palestinian terrorists killed Israeli athletes and officials. Some teams and individual competitors decided to go home.

⊙ **EXTENSION**

TERRORIST MASSACRE

In 1948, the state of Israel was founded in the land of the former Palestine. Since then there have been wars between Israel and her Arab neighbours. There have also been terrorist attacks against Israeli targets. The massacre in Munich in 1972 was intended to bring publicity to the Arabs' cause. The Israeli athletes were to have been used as hostages for the release of Arab prisoners in Israel. However, all the hostages were killed in a failed police trap. The Olympic Games were allowed to continue after a memorial service.

## 1976 Montreal

These Olympic Games were enormously costly and there was heavy security. French Canadians were angry at the Queen opening these Olympic Games. Taiwan was forced to withdraw as Canada only recognised the Peoples' Republic of China. There was a boycott by black African countries.

⊙ **EXTENSION**

BLACK AFRICAN COUNTRIES' BOYCOTT

All sporting contacts with South Africa had been discouraged because of apartheid. Before the Montreal Olympics, a New Zealand rugby team had played in South Africa. Black African countries demanded that New Zealand be banned from the Olympic Games as a result. The I.O.C. refused because rugby was not an Olympic sport. New Zealand said it was opposed to apartheid but did not have the right to ban the tour. Most Black African countries went home.

**The Olympic spectacle**

## 1980 Moscow

This event was successfully organised. There was high security. 81 countries took part altogether. There was a boycott by Western countries, led by the USA.

### ⊙ EXTENSION

WESTERN COUNTRIES' BOYCOTT
Before the Games there were worries about the Soviet Union's human rights record at home. Then, in 1979, Soviet troops went into Afghanistan. Many Western countries called for their withdrawal. When this did not happen the USA, Canada, Japan, West Germany and other countries decided to boycott the Olympic Games. The British Government also wished to boycott the Olympic Games. However it was not willing to withdraw passports. Individual sports and their members were left to make up their own minds about attending. A large British team decided to compete.

## 1984 Los Angeles

This was highly commercialised through marketing and sponsorship and indicated Hollywood showmanship. There was a huge financial profit from these Olympic Games. 140 countries took part altogether. Libya withdrew after two of its journalists were refused entry. The Soviet Union, Cuba and most East European countries withdrew.

### ⊙ EXTENSION

SOVIET UNION BOYCOTT
Following the boycott of the Moscow Games, it was no surprise that the Soviet Union boycotted the Los Angeles Games. Some American anti-Soviet groups had threatened violence before the Olympic Games. The Soviet Union said that the safety of their teams could not be guaranteed. They also complained that the commercial nature of the Olympic Games went against Olympic principles. The Soviet Union withdrew at the last moment along with Cuba and other East European allies, with the exception of Rumania.

## 1988 Seoul

This was superbly organised with a high profit. South Korea had no diplomatic links with communist countries. It was in a state of war with North Korea. There were no boycotts or disruptions at this event. Ben Johnson was disqualified for using drugs. Professional tennis players took part.

The sporting success of East Germany

Ben Johnson disqualified 1988, Seoul

## 1996 Atlanta

Nearly all countries took part, 197 in all. Competitors numbered 10,788. The Soviet Union was replaced by the Russian Federation and a number of former Soviet Union regions were now competing as independent countries.
Full professionals competed. A bomb shattered the peace in spite of the high security.

## 1992 Barcelona

This was a peaceful Olympic Games without incident. South Africa took part again. Germany took part as one country again. The Soviet Union was replaced by a 'Unified' team and some independent countries. Yugoslavians competed for Croatia or as independent competitors. The professional USA 'Dream team' took part in basketball.

### ⊙ EXTENSION

CHOOSING THE HOST CITY
The I.O.C. chooses the host city through its members' votes. Cities (not countries) put their names forward. They must convince the I.O.C. that they can run the Games successfully, efficiently and make them a commercial success. People are worried that cities buy votes by showering the I.O.C. members with gifts and hospitality.

ADVANTAGES FOR THE HOST CITY
All summer Olympics since 1984 have made a healthy profit. There is status and publicity for both the city and the country. They must improve their facilities as well as roads, transport systems, guest accommodation and tourist attractions. Holding the Olympics provides other commercial opportunities because of the large influx of competitors and spectators during the Olympic Games.

### ⊙ EXTENSION

GERMANY
After the Second World War Germany was split into two countries, East and West Germany. Until the 1964 Olympics a combined team represented Germany. From 1968, in Mexico City, the countries competed separately. In 1990 the country was unified. In Barcelona in 1992 Germany competed as one nation again.

EAST GERMANY – A SUCCESS STORY ?
The sporting success of East Germany was quite remarkable during the 1970s and 80s. East German women, in particular, dominated world athletics and swimming. The state sports system was very efficient. Talented youngsters attended sports schools. They trained full time as state supported athletes. After Germany was reunited it was discovered that drugs were given regularly to improve performance. The whole sports system was then disbanded.

## 2000 Sydney

Can they learn from the lessons of Atlanta? Will the security be good enough to prevent bombs? Can they solve the transport problem? Will there be Aboriginal protests? Can the disabled be integrated into these Olympic Games?

# The role of the performer

Between ancient times and the modern day, the role of the performer in sport has changed beyond recognition.

Organised sport developed in the public schools

## The status of players in the past

In the early days of sport in Britain, rewards and prizes were often given. Competitors accepted prizes if they won. There was also a lot of betting on the result, even between the competitors themselves. Making money out of sport, in whatever way, was not seen as a problem for organisers or those taking part.

In Victorian times, organised sport developed in the public schools. Boys from the middle and upper classes attended these schools. The boys came from families with money and they were prepared for well paid careers. Because they had no worries about money they were able to spend time playing sport. They were also able to afford the costs of playing sport such as equipment, clothing and fees for joining clubs. These sportsmen were called '**Gentlemen amateurs'**. This referred to their place in society. They were able to play sport as well as earn a living. They did not need to be paid for playing sport in order to earn a living. Rewards and prizes were not the reason for playing. These could be accepted if they wished. In fact, W.G. Grace, the famous cricketer, received a great deal of money from playing cricket. As he was a doctor by profession, he took part in cricket as a Gentleman amateur.

It was not so easy for the working class to play sport. They needed to work very hard to provide a living for themselves. They had little leisure time and little money to pay for sport. Some talented sportsmen did play sport professionally. There were professional cricketers from the earliest times. Although they played in the same teams as the amateurs they were kept quite separate, even having different changing rooms.

The problem for working class sportsmen at the highest level was that they soon found that their sport stopped them earning a living in a normal job. They therefore needed to be paid to play sport.

## ⊙ KEY POINT

The Victorians invented the idea of amateurs and professionals. This brought the class divisions of society into sport as amateurs were 'gentlemen' and **professionals** were from the working class. **Amateurs** could afford not to be paid.

## ⊙ EXTENSION

At the ancient Olympics, the winners received only a wreath of wild olives. No prizes were given. The glory and fame were enough. However, the athletes received support and rewards away from the Olympic Games. Talented boys were supported by their home city while they trained full time. Public gymnasiums were built for the athletes to use. Money was provided to pay for special diets and for people to oversee their training. Winning brought credit to the city. If they won at Olympia or any of the other Games, the athletes would receive prizes such as money, pensions or jars of olive oil. There was no distinction between the athletes apart from their ability and success.

**W.G.Grace, a Gentleman amateur**

As more people from all classes started to play sport, the rules about competitors changed. By the 1880s you were no longer an amateur if you accepted prize money or worked for a living at sport. However, not all sports were yet ready to accept professionalism. Payments and rewards needed controls. Business interests were growing. People running sport were worried that professionalism would bring major problems such as:

- unfair practices – professional sportsmen and teams would need to win to survive. They might be tempted to cheat in various ways;
- unfair competition – full time sportsmen would soon outclass amateurs. Amateur sport might then just fade away;
- a loss of traditional values – these values came from public schools. Some people were afraid that players who did not have this background might not play the game in the same spirit.

In practice, these problems did not get out of control. Rules were introduced to prevent unfair practice and to protect fairplay, whilst amateur sport became very popular.

Governing bodies of different sports then made their own rules about the place of professionals in their sport:

## Football

The Football Association decided to split the sport into amateurs and professionals, but to keep control of both the games.

## Rugby

The Rugby Union made the decision to have nothing at all to do with professionals. Those clubs willing to make payments to their players formed themselves into the professional Rugby League.

## Cricket

The clear distinction between the amateurs (known as the gentlemen) and the professionals (the players) was kept. They both continued to play together under the rules of the MCC.

## Golf

Amateurs and professionals continued to play in separate competitions and together in open competitions. They all played under the rules of the Royal and Ancient Golf Club.

## Other sports

For other sports, such as athletics, tennis and rowing, strict amateur rules were used. The small group of professionals involved in coaching were excluded from competition.

# The status of performers in the twentieth century

Labelling sportspeople as amateurs and professionals has continued for most of this century.

The Olympic Games were based on the ideal of the amateur sportsman. The I.O.C. wanted only true amateurs to take part and made strict rules to define an amateur. The I.O.C. did not believe that sportspeople should make a living from sport or receive any financial reward. They saw the Olympics as competition between part-time sportspeople, who played just for enjoyment. The problem was that governing bodies in different countries could not agree about what was an amateur.

 **EXTENSION**

At the Stockholm Olympics in 1912, Jim Thorpe from the USA, won both the pentathlon and the decathlon. He was told by the King of Sweden that he was the greatest athlete in the world. Later it was discovered that he had been paid a small amount for playing baseball a few years earlier. He was immediately declared a professional and his medals taken away.

As international competition became more serious standards of performance rose. In the period after 1945, the traditional amateurs training just in their spare time found it increasingly difficult to reach a high enough standard to compete. A number of different ways were then found to get around the amateur rules.

## College scholarships

In the USA, sport is highly competitive and big business. Colleges are always keen to have good sportspeople studying and playing sport. Outstanding sportspeople are offered **scholarships** to join the college. This means that not only are fees for study paid, but the college provides very good facilities and coaching, together with top competition. These sportspeople can then train full time but remain amateurs because they do not get paid.

As international competition became more serious, standards of performance rose

## State sportspeople

In the Soviet Union, sport was an official activity. Success in sport was seen as a way of showing the superiority of their political system. There were no professional sportspeople. Instead, the state allowed people to stay in the armed forces or at college for the length of their sporting careers. They were given all the time they needed to train together with first class facilities, coaching and competition. As students and soldiers they remained amateurs.

## Trust funds and sponsorship

The UK had neither the college nor the state system available and it did not want to be left behind in international sport. The first move to help top sportspeople came with the Sports Aid Foundation (S.A.F.). The S.A.F. collected sponsorship from business. It passed this on to our top sportspeople who were able to reduce or stop working in order to train more. The sponsorship paid for living, training and competition expenses.

In 1981, athletics set up **trust funds** and was quickly followed by many other amateur sports. The arrangement was to put all sponsorship and prize money into trust funds for the athletes. During their sporting career they were able to use this money for their expenses. On retirement, the balance of the money went to the athletes. It was a form of delayed payment to allow them to remain amateur.

Today athletes do not need to use trust funds. Money is paid directly to the athletes.

The 'Dream team'

## The situation today

At international level, it gradually became obvious that ideas about amateurism belonged to the past. The I.O.C. changed its rules on **eligibility**, that is the qualification needed to take part. The I.O.C. decided that the International Sports Federation for each sport should decide on eligibility. The word 'Amateur' was removed from the rules and no reference is now made to any rewards or payment. This resulted in open Olympics. The fully professional American basketball 'Dream team' won gold in Barcelona, in 1992.

In Britain, a number of universities offer scholarships to outstanding sportspeople who have the academic qualifications to study. They are helped financially by the universities and may extend their period of study. Other students can apply for bursaries, which are grants to help with the cost of their sport.

Modern rugby

## Rugby in the 90s

For more than 100 years the two rugby games of union and league took place entirely separately from one another. Recently, the whole situation has changed. The pressure came from the union players who wanted the rewards of top class international sportsmen. Rugby union became fully professional in 1995. This has allowed players from both games to play both codes. Matches under both union and league rules have been played between the champions of both codes, Bath and Wigan.

# Amateurs and professionals today

Throughout the country, thousands of people take part in sport in the traditional amateur way. At the same time, there is a small group of professional sportspeople who earn their living by playing sport. In between these two extremes are many people who get help in playing sport or receive rewards for playing sport. This group includes part time professionals, who are paid for playing but still earn a living outside sport. Sponsorship of all kinds helps both professional and amateur sportspeople.

Most sports today are called 'Open', meaning that distinctions between amateurs and professionals have gone. A few sports maintain the traditional differences. For example, in boxing, there are the Amateur Boxing Association and the Boxing Board of Control for professionals. In the case of boxing, the two parts of the sport take place quite separately and operate under different rules.

Amateur footballers

## Amateurs

Amateurs take part in sport because of the enjoyment and satisfaction they get from the activity. Taking part is more important than the result of the game or competition. They train and compete in their own time, usually after work or at the weekends. They are not paid. Above all, amateurs make their own decisions about sport. They choose to play. No one can force them to take part. Sport is quite separate from their work. It is a **leisure time** activity.

## Professionals

Professionals are paid to compete in sport. Winning is all important. The more successful they are, the more money they earn. They usually train full time and devote themselves to their sport. Sport is their work. They sign contracts and must take part in competitions.

**Professional footballers**

# What are the advantages and disadvantages of being a professional sportsperson?

For most of us, sport is a very attractive career. The idea of spending all day taking part in sport and getting paid seems an ideal life. Other advantages might include high earnings, the attention of the media, popularity with the general public, opportunities for travel around the world and eventual retirement to a life of comfort!

However, this is not a typical lifestyle for most professionals. Most earn a living out of the limelight. They may have failed to get to the top for a number of reasons:

- failure to fulfil early promise;
- the effect of serious illness or injury;
- personal problems reducing performance;
- pressure from younger players;
- difficulties in handling the media;
- lack of determination in training;
- pressure to win leading to cheating, for example taking drugs;
- age may have overtaken them.

Even those at the top will have to look for a new career when they are only half way through their working lives. For those who achieve star status, it is often short lived.

**Women have a high profile in professional golf**

# Opportunities in professional sport

There are a limited number of sports in Britain where professional players can earn a living. Most of these are male dominated. Only in tennis and golf do women professionals have a high profile, even though their rewards are much less than for men.

The following are the most common professional sports with approximate numbers of full time professionals shown in brackets:
basketball (70), boxing (30-40), cricket (450), cycling (70), darts (20), horse racing (600), football (2500), golf (3000), motor racing (20), rugby (figures changing), snooker (128), tennis (60).

In other sports which are still technically amateur, for example athletics, it is possible to earn a living through prize money and sponsorship.

# New technology

Technology continues to change sport. This happens in two ways.

Improved performances in sport and the improved communication of sport .

New technologies which have revolutionised sport

# Improved performances in sport

Sportspeople are always looking for new **technology** to help them make the most of their ability, in order to improve their performances. Scientific advance happens all the time. Sports scientists watch the latest developments to apply the new ideas to sport. Commercial companies need new markets and also know that being involved with sport helps business. Governing bodies try to see that the changes are safe and within the rules. Sometimes the rules need to be changed.

## Machines

Racing cars, motor bikes and power boats are so powerful now that rules have been introduced to keep top speeds down. In cycling, at the Olympics, frame design has revolutionised the sport. Modern materials keep racing bikes, hang gliders and sail boards both light and strong.

The speed of movement in some sports means that the officials need help. The 'Cyclops' machine checks if a tennis serve is in or out. Extra officials use television replays to decide run outs in cricket and tries in rugby league.

In athletics, precision is essential because winning can be by the smallest amounts. Gauges are used to measure wind speed and markers to record distances automatically. For sprinting, the timing is electronically controlled. The gun and starting blocks are linked to register false starts.

## Equipment

Players hit with greater power when using rackets with larger heads, frames of graphite and strings tightly strung. Many years ago, the introduction of the flexible glass fibre pole completely changed pole vaulting. With it came the need for better landing areas as heights increased. Recently the highly aerodynamic javelins were limited to reduce the distances they could be thrown and maintain safety for spectators. Changes to design and materials for skis, bobsleighs and luges have increased both speed and control.

## Clothing

Improved materials make clothes light and give them different qualities:

*   rain and windproof, for adventurous activities;
*   heat retaining, for sub-aqua sport;
*   heat removing, for distance athletes;
*   aerodynamic, for speed events.

Shoes can be designed for each specific sport to improve performance, safety and comfort. Skiers need boots for the skis, distance runners need shock absorbing qualities and tennis players need grip for the different court surfaces.

The use of light, impact absorbing materials helps cricketers get protection and keep their mobility.

At Atlanta, the Australian team used a new cooling jacket filled with ice. It helped sportspeople keep their body temperatures down before competing in the extreme heat.

## Facilities

All weather **artificial surfaces** have helped many sports. Top level athletics would be unthinkable today on any other surface. Hockey benefits from the speed and even bounce. League football experimented with artificial pitches. However, they changed the game too much and were returned to grass. Cricket is also a sport which needs a natural surface for the complete game. Only Wimbledon of the top four championships still uses grass. Most tennis at all levels is now played on a variety of synthetic surfaces.

Improvements in the design of specialist facilities have helped some sports. For example, gymnastics training has been made much safer by the use of landing areas placed below floor level.

Fitness clubs have the latest electronic machines. Personal programmes can be set up by putting in your personal details and requirements. During the exercise a constant stream of information, including heart rate and calories used, helps with motivation.

Modern all glass squash courts have been built to make the game suitable for television. Improved ball visibility and scoring changes have also been tried.

## Training and coaching

Detailed scientific research has resulted in a greater understanding of how the body responds to exercise. Coaches and trainers are able to use computer simulations which show the likely results of different types of training.

Computers can also analyse the movement of a sportsperson in great detail. Specialists in sports mechanics can then suggest improvements to the performer's action. Individuals can also have instant video replays of their action during training. This helps them to change their action. Modern watches can also check pulse rates and blood pressure during training.

**The referee must make a decision instantly, without the benefit of replays**

# Communications

Technology involved in communication is improving at an incredible speed. Through developments in satellite and cable television it is now possible to watch a great variety of sports around the world as they happen. This gives sport a bigger audience and also allows less well known sports to be seen for the first time.

No corner of sport can remain hidden anymore. Miniature cameras are placed in cricket stumps, in snooker pockets and on the top of racing cars. This gives the spectator almost the same view as those taking part in the sport. Ultra sensitive microphones pick up every grunt and groan and lots more besides! Cameras can record the action from almost any angle and replay it instantly in slow motion. Whilst this can record cheating and other unacceptable behaviour it can also enable the officials' decisions to be questioned. A football referee does not have the benefit of replays and views of the action from different positions. He must make his decision instantly on the basis of what he alone sees.

World wide communication using computers and the internet can also help pass information about sport quickly around the world. At present, this is mainly of help to those involved in research. However, it will not be long before we are all able to communicate in this way. We already have interactive CD Roms which allow us to move around inside the human body, and computer games which allow us to play sport in our own homes.

# Questions

## The Changing Face of Sport

1 Name and describe two technological improvements in sport in each of the following areas:

> **i** materials;
>
> **ii** equipment;
>
> **iii** facilities.

2 Many competitions and activities are open to amateurs and professionals. What are the advantages and disadvantages of this?

3 Amateurs and professionals often differ in their approach to sport. Discuss the differences with regard to:

> **i** attitude to sport;
>
> **ii** time devoted to sport;
>
> **iii** rewards.

4 "The Olympic Games have often been troubled by political problems." Use three examples from different Olympic Games to illustrate this statement.

5 Some amateur clubs employ a 'professional'. Explain what this term means and how a professional can be important to a club.

6 Give the name and venue of two international sports events that have taken place since 1990.

7 State three advantages and three disadvantages, to a city or country, of staging a major sports event.

8 List three ways in which an amateur may receive financial assistance.

9 Name and describe three major causes of change in sport since 1945.

10 Name one sport and describe a significant change that has taken place within it in recent years.

# 9 Providing for Sport

In Britain, individuals, groups and clubs have developed their particular sports in their own way. They have had little to do with other sports. This freedom means that the overall development of sport has not been controlled at all.

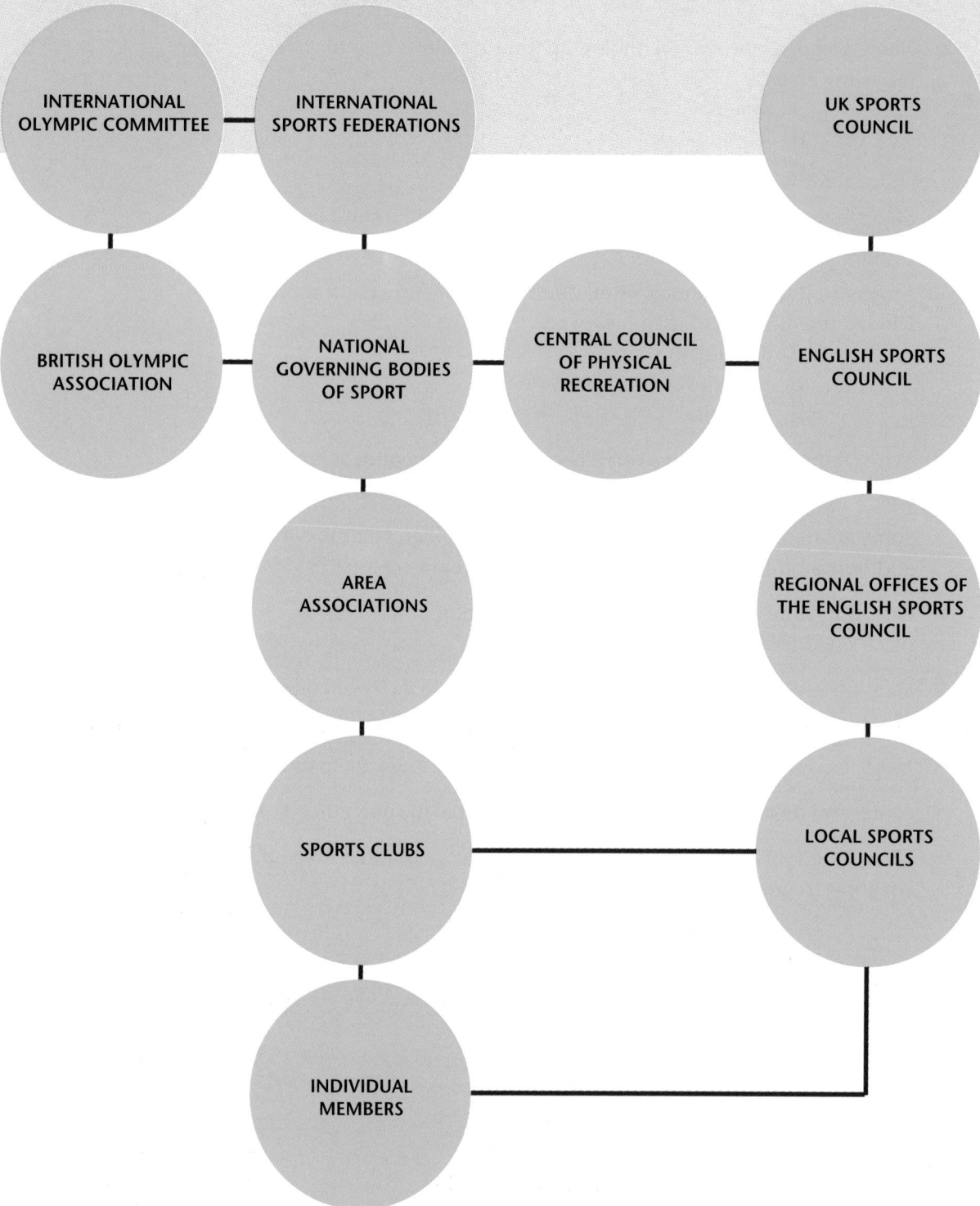

**The structure of sport in Britain**

The sports clubs and their governing bodies have protected their independence. The Government has rarely been involved directly at either national or local levels.

The only serious attempt to develop a national sports policy came with the setting up of the Sports Council. Today it is the clubs and their governing bodies who are at the heart of sport in Britain.

# What are the Sports Councils?
page 166

- UK Sports Council looks after UK sport;
- there are Sports Councils in England, Scotland, Wales and Northern Ireland;
- there are regional offices in England;
- there are local sports councils.

# What are the national governing bodies of sport? page 168

- they control their own sports

# What is the Central Council of Physical Recreation? page 169

- it represents the governing bodies

# Other major organisations page 170
## National Coaching Foundation

- it develops coaching

## British Sports Association for the Disabled

- it supports people with disabilities

## Women's Sports Foundation

- it supports women

## National Playing Fields Association

- it deals with outdoor playing areas

## Countryside Commission

- it looks after the countryside

# Who controls international sport?
page 172

## International Sports Federations

- control their own sports worldwide

## International Olympic Committee

- controls all Olympic matters

## British Olympic Association

- promotes the Olympics

# Who provides sports facilities?
page 174

Sports facilities are provided by three different sectors (or, parts) of society:
- the public sector, in which the government and local authorities provide the facilities for the community;
- the private sector, in which companies provide facilities mainly to make a profit;
- the voluntary sector, in which clubs and governing bodies provide facilities for their members.

# Funding for sport – an overview page 178

The Sports Council made a dramatic impact on the provision of sports facilities. Regional offices were set up to find out what was needed in different areas of the country. Regional Councils for Sport and Recreation (now abolished) and local sports councils were also set up to give advice. The national sports centres were developed as centres of excellence by the Sports Councils.

# What are the Sports Councils?

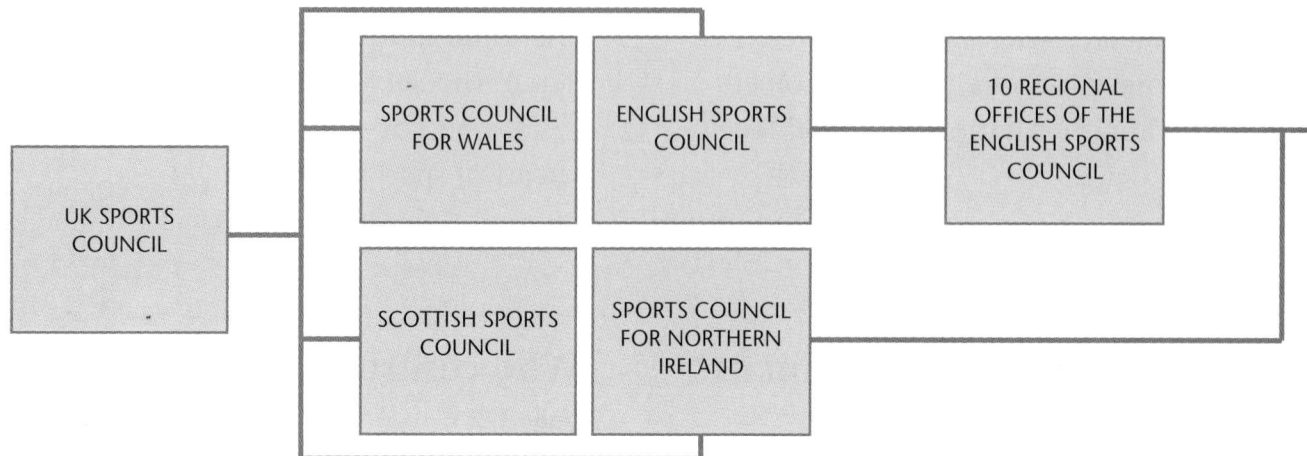

The Sports Council was an independent body founded by **Royal Charter** in 1972. In 1997, major changes were made to this organisation.

## How are the Sports Councils organised?

The UK Sports Council looks after sport in Great Britain and Northern Ireland. It has responsibility for international affairs and for attracting major events to the UK. It supports excellence and a British Academy of Sport and it organises doping control. The English Sports Council now only has responsibility for its own country, like the other three national Sports Councils.

## Who are the members?

The UK Sports Council and the English Sports Council are made up of members chosen by the Secretary of State for National Heritage. The Secretaries of State for Scotland, Wales and Northern Ireland choose members for their own Sports Councils. There are also full time staff to carry out the policies of each Sports Council.

## The regional offices

The English Sports Council has a London headquarters. There are ten regional offices. They have two main tasks:
- to promote Sports Council policy at local level;
- to help the Sports Council keep in touch with needs at grass roots levels.

Until 1996, the regional offices worked closely with Regional Councils for Sport and Recreation. They have since been abolished and replaced by informal advisory groups.

## The local sports councils

Local sports councils are encouraged by the Sports Councils, but they have no direct control over them. These councils bring together all the local people, clubs and groups interested in sport to exchange views, discuss problems and draw up plans for the future. They are only advisory but help local sports developments to be made in the best interests of the community.

> **◐ KEY POINT**
>
> The Sports Councils try to co-ordinate all the different organisations involved in developing sport.

LOCAL SPORTS COUNCILS

# What do the Sports Councils do?

The Royal Charter given to the Sports Council in 1972 set out its aims. These four main 'charter' aims of the Sports Councils are still:

- to increase participation in sport and physical recreation;
- to increase the quantity and quality of sports facilities;
- to raise standards of performance;
- to provide information for and about sport.

The Sports Councils give grants to the national governing bodies to run programmes in order to meet these aims. The Councils run campaigns to encourage participation, give grants for new facilities, run national sports centres and provide information. They also work in many other ways to improve British sport and physical recreation. For example, they are responsible for giving out the money for sport from the National Lottery.

The Sports Councils produce strategy documents to explain how they will achieve their aims in the future. In 1993, they published 'Sport in the nineties: new horizons'. This describes their vision of everyone being able to take part and reach their full potential in sport. To turn this vision into practice, there are aims based on two key principles which have been called the sports development **continuum** and sports **equity**.

## Sports development continuum

This is to offer everyone the chance to improve their skills and take part in sport and physical recreation. There are four different stages of development:

- foundation – young people are taught P.E. and learn basic sports skills;
- participation – everyone is able to take part in the sport of their choice;
- performance – those interested have the chance to improve their sporting ability;
- **excellence** – talented performers can develop sporting excellence.

## Sports equity

This is to protect sport and sportspeople from harmful influences. It is about:

- fairness in sport;
- enabling all to take part;
- recognising problems and taking action;
- changing the culture of sport so that age, race, gender or ability does not stop anyone from taking part.

Today, the emphasis is on three key programmes. These are help for young people, the support of excellence and the use of National Lottery funds to improve facilities and support top sportspeople.

# Who pays for the Sports Councils?

- The Government gives a grant to each Sports Council.
- National Lottery money given out by the English Sports Council will be about £300 million in 1996/7.
- Sponsorship from commercial companies supports development programmes.

# What are the national governing bodies of sport?

The national governing bodies of sport:
- are voluntary organisations with democratic constitutions;
- have members from clubs elected to make decisions;
- use mainly unpaid volunteers;
- have full time paid officials to run the body;
- are independent of the Government;
- are usually members of the C.C.P.R.

## What do national governing bodies do?

The national governing bodies:
- run the sport smoothly;
- promote development of the sport;
- organise competitions and events;
- select teams at all levels;
- arrange coaching and training;
- organise award schemes;
- enforce rules and laws;
- see that they meet the rules of their international federation;
- negotiate with television and sponsoring companies.

## Who pays for the national governing bodies?

The national governing bodies are paid for by:
- members' subscriptions;
- companies (through sponsorship);
- companies (for television rights);
- grants from the Sports Councils, National Lottery, Foundation for Sport and the Arts;
- profits from spectator events;
- partnerships with central government and local authorities.

## How do area sports associations fit in?

Governing bodies are responsible for sport throughout the country. Those that have large numbers of member clubs need to split the country up into smaller areas, for example the Essex Netball Association. These area associations carry out the policy of the national body. They organise coaching, training and competitions for clubs and individuals in their own area.

> **KEY POINT**
>
> The national governing bodies support the sports clubs. Together they make sure we can take part in sport.

## Organising for excellence

Top sportspeople now get grants from the National Lottery

Many different organisations help sportspeople develop excellence:
- the Sports Councils give grants to the governing bodies, run national sports centres and pay for support services such as sports science and sports medicine;
- the governing bodies run training and coaching schemes at the highest level. They have priority use of the national sports centres for their top sportspeople;
- the Sports Aid Foundation provides financial help for the best amateur sportspeople;
- the National Coaching Foundation runs the Champion Coaching scheme to help 11 – 16 year olds;
- the Government, in 'Raising the Game', emphasised the importance of encouraging excellence. It proposed the setting up of a National Academy of Sport.

# What is the Central Council of Physical Recreation?

**The C.C.P.R. helps develop sport**

The Central Council of Physical Recreation (C.C.P.R.):
- is an independent **voluntary body**;
- its officials are elected by the members;
- its members are mainly governing bodies. They are split up into six divisions based on their interests: movement and dance, games and sports, major spectator sports, outdoor pursuits, water recreation and interested organisations;
- it was formed in 1935, to develop sport and physical recreation;
- in 1972 its staff and assets (including the national sports centres) were transferred to the Sports Council. The governing bodies, however, decided to keep the C.C.P.R. and their independence from the Sports Council.

## What does the Central Council of Physical Recreation do?

The C.C.P.R. has two main objectives:
- to improve and develop sport and physical recreation;
- to support the work of the governing bodies.

The C.C.P.R:
- allows governing bodies to meet to discuss common problems and the best way to develop their sports;
- runs campaigns, for example against the loss of school playing fields;
- advises Government, local authorities and Sports Councils on sporting matters;
- gives advice on sports sponsorship, through its close links with the Institute of Sports Sponsorship;
- helps professional sport through the Institute of Professional Sport;
- runs the Community Sport Leaders Award scheme (C.S.L.A.).

## Who pays for the Central Council of Physical Recreation?

The C.C.P.R. is paid for by:
- the English Sports Council;
- **donations** from its governing body members;
- sponsorship from companies;
- sale of publications and research materials.

> **◯ KEY POINT**
>
> The C.C.P.R. is the voice of the governing bodies and, therefore, of the sports clubs.

**The C.C.P.R. helps develop recreation opportunities**

> **◯ EXTENSION**
>
> COMMUNITY SPORTS LEADERS AWARD (C.S.L.A.)
>
> The C.S.L.A:
> - is a training award started in 1982;
> - aims to develop leadership, responsibility and self confidence amongst voluntary helpers in sports and youth clubs;
> - has awards at four levels – junior, preliminary, basic expedition training, higher;
> - is financed by the British Sports Trust with donations from companies.

# Other major organisations

## What is the National Coaching Foundation?

The National Coaching Foundation (N.C.F.):
- is an independent **charity**, which was founded in 1983;
- includes members from C.C.P.R., BOA.

## What does the National Coaching Foundation do?

The N.C.F:
- co-ordinates coaching and coach education;
- provides a network of ten Coaching Development Officers in regions of England;
- improves the skill and knowledge of coaches;
- helps coaches through introductory courses, key courses and advanced workshops;
- runs the Diploma in Professional Studies for experienced coaches;
- works closely with all four Sports Councils and the governing bodies;
- organises the Champion Coaching scheme for young people.

## Who pays for the National Coaching Foundation?

The N.C.F. is paid for by:
- the Sports Councils;
- members' **subscriptions**;
- profit from trading.

## What is the British Sports Association for the Disabled?

The British Sports Association for the Disabled (B.S.A.D.):
- is a national voluntary body, which was founded in 1961;
- is run by a committee and a national advisory council;
- works with groups involved with people with disabilities, governing bodies and the Sports Councils.

## What does the British Sports Association for the Disabled do?

B.S.A.D:
- provides opportunities for people with disabilities to take part in sport and physical recreation;
- organises programmes and championships at all levels;
- promotes the sporting achievements of people with disabilities;
- provides advice on all sporting matters to do with people with disabilities.

## Who pays for the British Sports Association for the Disabled?

The B.S.A.D. is paid for by:
- the Sports Councils;
- local authorities;
- charitable trusts;
- companies (through sponsorship).

**➲ EXTENSION**

CHAMPION COACHING

This scheme is run by the N.C.F. It links together local authorities, governing bodies, schools and sports clubs. It aims to give 11 – 16 year olds coaching opportunities in after school hours. This is to help them move from school sport to junior clubs and squads.

## What is the Women's Sports Foundation?

The Women's Sports Foundation (W.S.F.) is:
- a national voluntary organisation, which was founded in 1984.

## What does the Women's Sports Foundation do?

The W.S.F:
- supports women involved in sport at every level;
- raises awareness of problems in women's sport;
- encourages better access to sport for women;
- promotes the achievements of women in sport;
- challenges inequality in sport;
- works closely with the Sports Councils.

## Who pays for the Women's Sports Foundation?

The W.S.F. is paid for by:
- members' subscriptions;
- the English Sports Council.

## What is the National Playing Fields Association?

The National Playing Fields Association (N.P.F.A.):
- is a national, independent charity, which was founded in 1925;
- is open to membership by both individuals and organisations;
- is run by a council and trustees.

## What does the National Playing Fields Association do?

The N.P.F.A:
- acquires, protects and improves playing fields, playgrounds and play spaces;
- works for those who need play areas most, that is children of all ages and people with disabilities;
- runs 2,000 play areas across the UK.

## Who pays for the National Playing Fields Association?

The N.P.F.A. is paid for by:
- the public (through appeals);
- supporters (through donations);
- sales of publications and technical advice.

## What is the Countryside Commission?

The Countryside Commission (C.C.) is:
- an independent, **public agency**, which was established in 1968;
- run by commissioners chosen by the Government.

## What does the Countryside Commission do?

The C.C:
- looks after and improves the countryside in England;
- runs the National Parks of England;
- develops access for outdoor activities;
- works with many organisations like the Ramblers Association;
- advises the Government on all countryside matters.

## Who pays for the Countryside Commission?

The C.C. is paid for by:
- the Government.

---

### ⮕ EXTENSION

SPORT: RAISING THE GAME
In 1995 the Government set out its plans for the future of British sport. It encouraged schools to increase the amount of time for sport outside of lessons and set up a new 'Sportsmark' for schools, promoting sport effectively. It promoted closer links between sports clubs and schools. It introduced the idea of a National Academy of Sport to be the pinnacle of a national network of centres of excellence.

# Who controls international sport?

The International Sports Federation (I.S.F.), and the International Olympic Committee (I.O.C.) control international sport. The British Olympic Association (B.O.A.) promotes the Olympics in Britain.

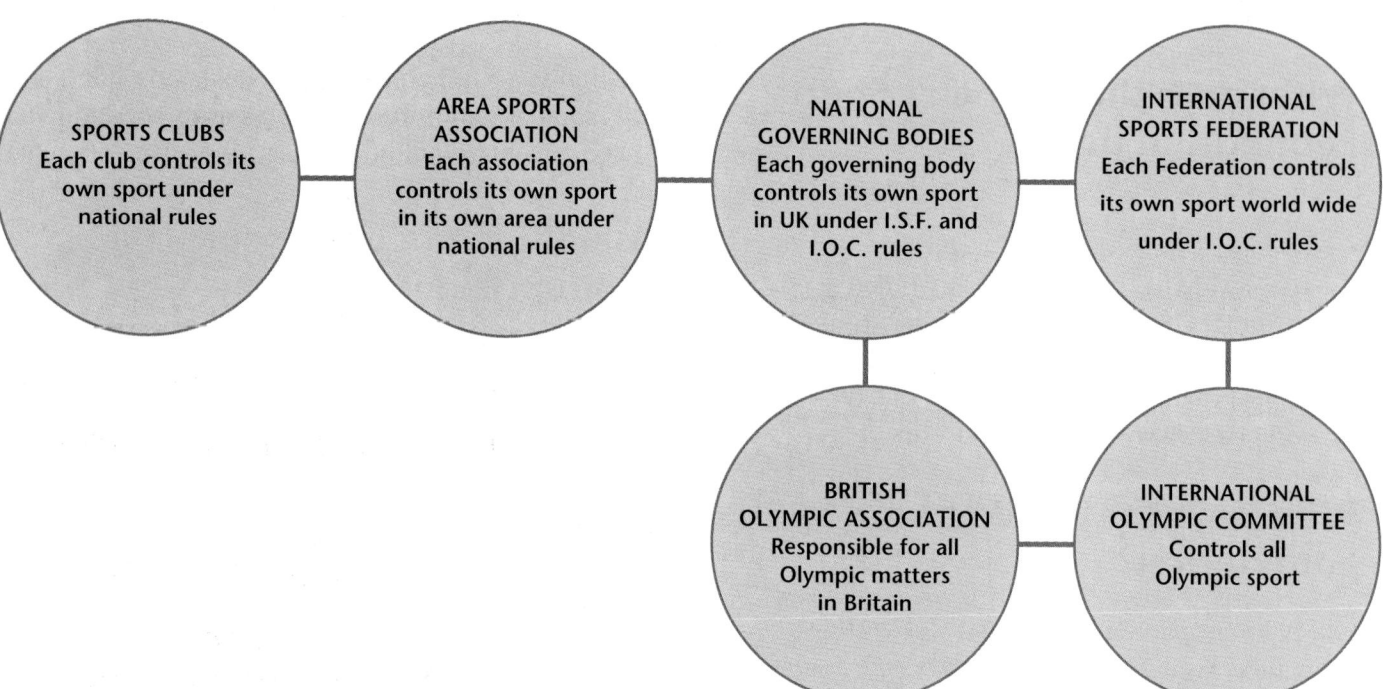

## What are the International Sports Federations?

The International Sports Federations (I.S.F.):
- are independent organisations;
- are responsible for their sport world wide;
- have members who are representatives of governing bodies in countries where the sport is played.

## What do the International Sports Federations do?

The I.S.F.s:
- encourage the world wide development of their sport;
- make sure their rules agree with the rules of the International Olympic Committee (I.O.C.);
- control all their international fixtures and competitions;
- enforce and change the rules of their sport.

## Who pays for the International Sports Federations?

The I.S.F.s are paid for by:
- companies (for televising major championships and international fixtures);
- companies (through sponsorship of events);
- payments from national governing body members.

> **KEY POINT**
>
> International Sports Federations organise international sport, apart from the Olympics. All countries want to take part in international sport. This puts the I.S.F.s in a very powerful position.

# International Olympic Committee

The International Olympic Committee (I.O.C.):
- is an independent club of non-elected members, which was founded in 1894;
- has a membership of about 90 people;
- allows its members themselves to elect new members.

## What does the International Olympic Committee do?

The I.O.C:
- is in complete control of everything to do with the Olympic Games;
- works through National Olympic Committees. They are found in all countries competing in the Olympics;

The aims of the I.O.C. are:
- to promote the physical and moral side of sport;
- to educate young people, through sport, in order to encourage better understanding and friendship and build a more peaceful world;
- to spread the Olympic principles throughout the world, in order to create international good will;
- to bring sportspeople together every four years at the Olympic Games.

## Who pays for the International Olympic Committee?

The I.O.C. is paid for by:
- companies (for television rights);
- companies (for being official sponsors of the games).

# British Olympic Association

The British Olympic Association (B.O.A.):
- is an independent voluntary organisation, which was founded in 1905;
- is the National Olympic Committee of the UK;
- has as members representatives from all Olympic sports;
- allows its members to elect a committee to make decisions;
- is totally independent of Government and politics.

## What does the British Olympic Association do?

The B.O.A:
- develops interest throughout the UK in the Olympics;
- runs the British Olympic Medical Centre;
- helps the governing bodies of Olympic sports to prepare their teams;
- organises the British team for each Olympic Games.

Sending teams to the Olympics is very complicated and expensive. The B.O.A. is responsible for travel, transport, insurance, health care, accommodation, food, training, publicity and all documents. It is also responsible for the behaviour of the team.

## Who pays for the British Olympic Association?

The B.O.A. is paid for by:
- the public (through the British Olympic Appeal);
- companies (through sponsorship);
- companies (for being official B.O.A. sponsors).

> ### ⟳ KEY POINT
>
> The International Olympic Committee is all powerful in decisions about the Olympic Games and the Olympic sports.

# Who provides sports facilities?

## Who provides sports facilities in the public sector?

Sports facilities are provided by the public sector, private sector and voluntary sector.

## The Government

The Government:
- pays directly for facilities for the armed forces;
- gives grants to the Sports Councils for running national sports centres;
- pays for the Countryside Commission which runs the national parks.

## National sports centres

There are twelve national sports centres managed by the four Sports Councils.

National team training and competition, together with the training of leaders and officials, is given priority.

The following are national sports centres and their specialist facilities:

| | | |
|---|---|---|
| *England* | Crystal Palace | Athletics, swimming and diving |
| | Bisham Abbey | Tennis |
| | Lilleshall Hall | Football, gymnastics |
| | Holme Pierrepont | Water sports |
| | Plas y Brenin | Outdoor activities |
| | Manchester | Cycling |
| *Scotland* | Cumbrae | Water sports |
| | Inverclyde | All purpose |
| | Glenmore Lodge | Outdoor activities |
| *Wales* | Cardiff | All purpose |
| | Plas Menai | Outdoor activities |
| *N. Ireland* | Tollymore | Outdoor activities |

## National parks

The seven national parks of England are Dartmoor, Exmoor, the Lake District, North Yorkshire Moors, Northumberland, the Peak District and the Yorkshire Dales. The Norfolk and Suffolk Broads and the New Forest have similar status. They provide a wide range of opportunities for outdoor recreation.

## Local authorities

Wherever we live, local authorities supply us with a variety of services such as education, street cleaning and leisure. If we live in a large city area, it is likely that all these services will be provided by one authority. In other areas there may be a county council responsible for major services such as education, with a district or town council providing others. In all areas there are small town or parish councils responsible for halls and open spaces.

## What are leisure and recreation departments?

Local authorities have departments to deal with their services. The policy of each department is decided by a committee of elected councillors. In other words, the councillors decide what should happen. Professional staff in the department then carry out this policy. Most local authorities have a department responsible for leisure and recreation. Their committee will decide, for example, if a new swimming pool should be built.

**Local authorities supply us with leisure services**

# What is provided?

Local authorities provide various sports facilities:

- sports facilities for education must be provided by law;
- facilities for general leisure are not compulsory although sports centres, swimming pools and recreation grounds are usually provided;
- all facilities need qualified staff, good equipment and regular maintenance;
- leisure and recreation departments need activity programmes which people find attractive, accessible and affordable.

## Dual use

**Dual use** is the use of school sports facilities by local clubs and groups in the evenings, at weekends and during the holidays.

## Joint provision

Schools are designed with purpose built sports facilities to be used by the school and the community.

The Sports Councils give grants to build **joint provision** facilities.

Both types of arrangements are supported by the Sports Councils who often pay for staff to manage the community use of the facilities.

> ### ⤵ KEY POINT
>
> Local authorities are the largest providers of sports facilities for the community in their areas.

# Who provides sports facilities in the private sector?

**PRIVATE SECTOR**

**COMMERCIAL VENTURES**

**FACILITIES FOR EMPLOYEES**

**SPECIALIST FACILITIES (FOR THE PUBLIC TO USE AT A PRICE)**

**FACILITIES FOR TOP SPORTSPEOPLE (TO PERFORM FOR THE PUBLIC)**

- In the past, all large companies had social clubs;

- they provided a range of sport and social activities;

- this was free but only for employees and their families;

- companies hoped it would encourage people to stay with them;

- the upkeep of the buildings, courts, pitches and greens was paid for by the companies. It was expensive;

- today, companies are more likely to make arrangements with sports centres for special rates for employees or introductory fitness courses.

- commercial organisations may step in where there is a need but no facilities;

- facilities are usually modern, friendly and expensive;

- they provide good sporting value for money;

- attractive social activities are also offered;

- specialist facilities need to attract customers and make a profit to stay in business;

- examples include health and fitness centres, golf driving ranges, ten pin bowling halls, ice rinks and tennis courts.

- top sportspeople perform for spectators;

- vast crowds pay to see high quality sports;

- facilities are usually purpose built for the sporting activity;

- at race tracks, dogs and horses race for their owners and to provide betting on the result;

- major team sports attract loyal fans who watch regularly. Individual sports like athletics, golf, tennis, gymnastics and boxing also attract large crowds.

## EXTENSION

THE TAYLOR REPORT

This was a report into the reasons for the Hillsborough football tragedy. In 1989, 95 fans were crushed to death during an FA Cup Semi-final. The report suggested ways to improve the safety at football grounds. It recommended that Football League grounds should become all-seater, fencing be safer and policing and medical facilities be improved. The Football Trust gives grants to help with the cost of these improvements.

# Who provides sports facilities in the voluntary sector?

**FACILITIES**

**VOLUNTARY SECTOR**

**NATIONAL GOVERNING BODIES**

**COMMUNITY ASSOCIATIONS**

**SPORTS CLUBS**

## Sports clubs

Taking part in sport for many adults means belonging to a local club. There are sports clubs in every town. Usually they are run by enthusiasts and concentrate on one sport.

Sports clubs need facilities. Those that have been going for many years may own their own facilities, for example golf clubs, tennis and cricket clubs. Clubs that are new or do not have the money will be able to hire facilities. These may be at the local sports centre, school, playing field or church hall.

## Community associations

Not everyone wants to join a sports club in order to carry on with their sport. Sometimes groups of people in a village or part of a town get together to provide a variety of physical recreation for their own local community.

These community associations need facilities. The village green may be available for cricket in the summer and hockey in the winter. Village and church halls can provide facilities for a number of indoor sports like table tennis and badminton. Other facilities can be hired if necessary.

## National governing bodies

Some national governing bodies have magnificent facilities, for example the Rugby Football Union's ground at Twickenham. Most governing bodies formed recently have no facilities of their own. Many use the facilities provided by the national sports centres.

Some governing bodies have close historical links with an established club and use their facilities for its major events, for example the Marylebone Cricket Club (M.C.C.) at Lords. The Football Association does not own its own ground but uses Wembley Stadium, which is run by a private company. Athletics and swimming do not have their own national facilities and neither do many other major sports.

## KEY POINT

Facilities cost money to buy or to build. The cost of running the facilities is also very important.

# Funding for sport – an overview

To understand funding for sport, we need to look at why sport needs money and where the money comes from.

## How important is spending on sport?

Today, sport and physical recreation are an important part of British life. Surveys show that around 36 million people, that is about two out of every three people, take part in sport and physical recreation at least once a month.

Sport is valuable to society for economic reasons:

- sport provides jobs for nearly 500,000 people;
- sport pays £3.6 billion in taxation;
- sport attracts £9.75 billion of people's spending.

## Why does sport need money?

We all need clothing, equipment, facilities and opportunities in order to take part in sport.

We might also need teaching, training, coaching and competition.

When we are at school, many of these things are provided without cost. As adults we will have to pay for them.

Professional sportspeople expect to be able to pay their living, training and competition expenses. In addition they will expect payment and rewards for performing.

Clubs and governing bodies need to pay for running costs, facilities, events, competitions and development projects.

Local authorities need to provide the leisure facilities for the community.

> **◯ KEY POINT**
>
> Today, there is a change in funding for sport. There is less direct financial support from the Government. Sport is moving towards self help. In the future it will have to rely more on organisations which give grants and partnerships with business.

# Funding for sport

## Public sector

### Local authorities

**Money comes in from**

- the Government;
- council tax;
- business rates;
- grants from – National Lottery, Foundation for Sport and the Arts, Sports Councils;
- partnerships with business;
- charges for sports facilities.

**Money goes out for**

- education facilities, equipment, staff for schools, youth clubs, adult education;
- local sport facilities such as pools, sports centres, playing fields;
- grants to local sports clubs or groups.

### Central Government

**Money comes in from**

- taxes;
- betting duties.

**Money goes out for**

- local authorities;
- grants to – Sports Councils, Countryside Commission, Inner city areas;
- Sportsmatch sponsorship;
- Armed Services sport.

# Do we have enough money for sport?

Although very large sums of money are involved, there is still not enough to go around. The National Lottery has millions of pounds a week to give out, but it still cannot satisfy everyone. In fact it is now clear that many other fund raising organisations are collecting less money as a direct result of the lottery. Organisations who want grants from the National Lottery must raise some of the money themselves before being helped. This self help aims to get more money into sport. Self help is now an important part of most grants.

# Where does money for sport come from?

Money comes into sport in many different ways. For example, large amounts are given out by the National Lottery, the Sports Councils give grants to governing bodies and there is much sponsorship by companies. At present they all work independently of one another. There is no national co-ordination to decide on long term goals.

We can say that money comes from three different sectors of society. In the same way, facilities are provided by the three different sectors:

- in the **public sector**, the Government and local authorities provide a service to the **community**;
- in the **private sector**, companies work for **profit**;
- in the **voluntary sector**, clubs and governing bodies provide sporting opportunities for their **members**.

## Private sector

**Money comes in from**
- profit from running business, including National Lottery profit;
- spectators (paying to watch);
- merchandising.

**Money goes out for**
- direct sponsorship of individuals, teams and governing bodies;
- sponsorship (through the Sports Aid Foundation);
- pools company money to the Foundation for Sports and the Arts and the Football Trust;
- payment for television rights;
- National Lottery grants;
- operating sports facilities.

## Voluntary sector

**Money comes in from**
- grants from Central Government (Sportsmatch and inner city funds);
- local authority;
- Sports Councils;
- governing bodies;
- National Lottery;
- Foundation for Sport and the Arts;
- charitable trusts;
- companies (sponsorship);
- subscriptions;
- fund raising.

**Money goes out for**
- basic running costs;
- development expenses.

# Sports funding and the public sector: the Government

The Government raises money through taxes. There are taxes on personal earnings, on business profits, on sales of goods (called V.A.T.) and many other taxes. Gambling is also taxed. So whether someone buys a National Lottery ticket, does the football pools or bets on horses, they will be paying taxes to the Government.

**Local authority money for sport goes to schools and the community**

## Who gets Government money for sport?

**Local authorities.** They get a 'Revenue Support Grant' to help provide local services, including education and leisure.
**Sports Councils.** Get an annual grant from the Government. In turn, they give grants to national governing bodies.
**Countryside Commission.** Its costs are paid for by the Department for the Environment.
**The Sportsmatch scheme.** This is a 'grass roots' sponsorship scheme. For some types of sponsorship (mainly new schemes) the Government will give the same amount as the sponsor. This means that sport gets twice as much money.
**Inner city areas.** The Government supports a number of schemes paid for by a special fund. The aim is to help economic development and the quality of life in run down areas. Some sports organisations and local authorities have produced schemes which qualify for grants.
**Armed services.** Physical fitness is essential for the armed forces. The Government funds all facilities, equipment and clothing.

> ### ⊙ EXTENSION
>
> GOVERNMENT POLICY AND SPORTS FUNDING
> In recent years there has been less direct Government spending on sport:
> * the Sports Councils grants have been reduced each year since 1993–4. They are now expected to raise money and reduce their own running costs;
> * capital funding for sport (that is money for building) went down from £300 million in 1988 to £125 million in 1992;
> * help for local authorities with capital funding has been gradually reduced.
>
> Local authorities, organisations and clubs are now all expected to find more of the money they need. They are being encouraged to:
> * develop links with companies who will provide funding;
> * apply for grants from the Sports Councils, Sportsmatch, National Lottery, Foundation for Sport and the Arts;
> * run their affairs as cost effectively as possible.

# Sports funding and the public sector: local authorities

Local authorities receive a 'Revenue Support Grant' from the Government. They also raise money through  the council tax and business rates. Today, local authorities often do not have enough money themselves to build facilities. They usually look for partnerships with grant giving organisations like the Sports Councils, National Lottery, Foundation for Sport and the Arts or business.

# Who gets local authority money for sport?

Local authorities fund sport by building new facilities, improving old ones and paying for the running costs of activities in education and the community.

## Education

The facilities for physical education in schools must be provided for by law. The local authority may also provide money for sporting facilities for youth clubs and adult education. Apart from the facilities, the local authority pays for the costs of staffing and equipment.

## Community

This money goes to the leisure and recreation department. Much of the money is spent on building and maintaining the indoor and outdoor facilities. Some money may pay the salaries and costs of sports development officers and programmes. There are often small grants available to local clubs.

## ⟳ EXTENSION

COMPULSORY COMPETITIVE TENDERING (C.C.T.)
The Government wanted to find out if local authorities were the best people to run community sports facilities. The Government thought other organisations might be able to run them more cheaply and so they introduced **Compulsory Competitive Tendering** (C.C.T.). This meant that local authorities had to set out detailed plans for running their sports facilities. Commercial companies were then able to offer to run the facilities. The local authorities' leisure departments were also allowed to bid for the work. The contract to run the facilities was given on the basis of high quality service at a competitive price. This is not privatisation. The facilities are still owned by the local authority who decide how the facility will be run.

## ⟳ KEY POINT

The money that local authorities spend on sport is very important. They provide over £1 billion each year.

## Sports funding and the private sector: companies

The main purpose of running a business is to make a profit. There are very many businesses involved in sport – companies making sports goods, shops selling sportswear and fitness clubs offering facilities. Professional sport today relies less on spectators paying to see the event than in the past. The sale of television rights and profits from selling merchandise (goods linked to the sport) are now very important.

### ⊙ KEY POINT

Spectator sport as we know it today, could not exist without sponsorship from commercial companies.

Sports grounds have been improved in recent years

### ⊙ EXTENSION

THE FOOTBALL TRUST
The Football Trust is a non-profit making organisation, which was founded in 1975. It is run by trustees from the Football Association and organisations which are linked to football.
**What does the Football Trust do?**
The Football Trust supports football at all levels. It helps professional clubs carry out safety improvements to grounds. These were recommended by the Taylor Report following the Hillsborough tragedy. The Football Trust gives grants to football clubs, leagues and teams. Grants are given for ground improvement, safety work, spectator facilities, pitches and changing rooms.
**Who pays for the Football Trust?**
Football pools companies pay for the Football Trust.

## Who gets company money for sport?

- individuals, teams, governing bodies and professional sports organisations receive sponsorship;
- the Sports Aid Foundation (S.A.F.) receives sponsorship from companies;
- the Foundation for Sport and the Arts (F.S.A.) gets money from the football pools companies;
- the National Lottery gets money from the general public;
- the Football Trust receives money from the football pools companies;
- governing bodies of sport and other sports organisations receive payment for the right to televise major events and to be official sponsors;
- local authorities get money through partnerships with business.

# Sports funding and the private sector: the National Lottery and the Foundation for Sport and the Arts

Private sector sports funding comes from the National Lottery and the Foundation for Sport and the Arts, as well as from companies.

## What is the National Lottery?

The National Lottery:
- is a lottery started by the government in 1994;
- is run by 'Camelot', a commercial company.

## What does the National Lottery do?

The National Lottery:
- gives money to five good causes – sport, the arts, heritage, charities and the Millennium Fund;
- gives each of the five good causes 20% of the 'available' money. This is the money left after prizes (50%), tax (12%), retailers' commission (5%), and operators' costs and profits (5%) have been taken away from the sales figures;
- awards for sport are distributed by the four national Sports Councils;
- grants have been concentrated on new and improved facilities. Normally grants are not given for running and maintaining facilities;
- rule changes in 1996 allowed 'talent funds' to be set up to give grants to top sportspeople and to help sports coaching and talent spotting projects;
- only provides part of the total cost of any project. It prefers at least half of the cost to be raised in other ways;
- funding is only available to sports recognised by the Sports Councils.

## Who pays for the National Lottery?

The general public pay by buying weekly lottery tickets and scratch cards.

## What is the Foundation for Sport and the Arts?

The Foundation for Sport and the Arts (F.S.A.) is:
- an independent, non-profit making organisation, founded in 1991;
- controlled by trustees from the pools companies, the arts and sport.

## What does the Foundation for Sport and the Arts do?

The F.S.A:
- aims to improve the quality of life of the community generally;
- gives about two-thirds of its money to sport and physical recreation and one third to the arts;
- originally gave capital grants for new buildings, improvements and equipment. With the National Lottery funding these items, it has moved further towards giving grants for running costs;
- supports the Sports Aid Foundation (S.A.F.);
- works closely with the Sports Councils.

## Who pays for the Foundation for Sport and the Arts?

The football pools companies pay for the F.S.A.

# Sports funding and the voluntary sector: clubs

Clubs need money to run their day to day affairs. They may also raise money to try to improve the club.

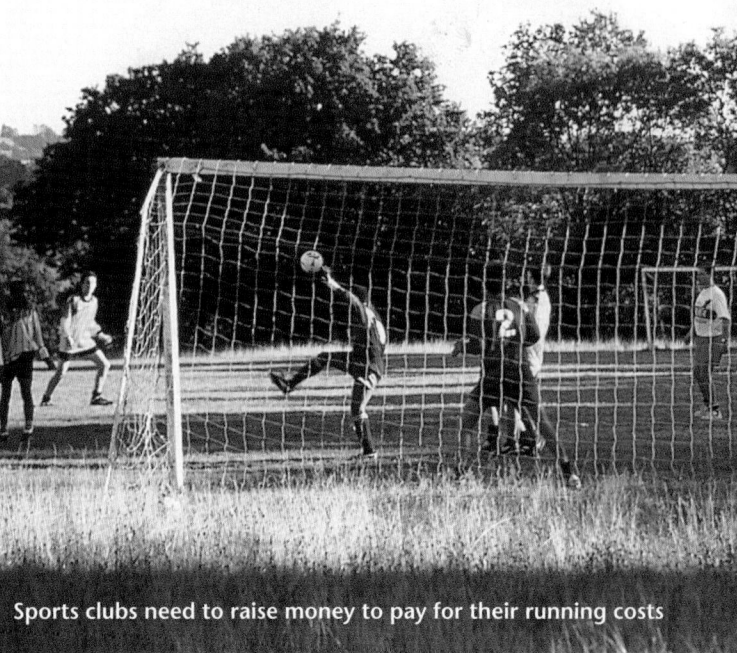

Sports clubs need to raise money to pay for their running costs

## Basic running costs

Traditionally sports clubs have been self-sufficient. In other words, they have been able to raise enough money from their members to pay the costs of their sport. These costs include such things as facilities, equipment, clothing, organising events and taking part in competitions as well as day to day expenses. Clubs raise this money by:

- collecting membership subscriptions;
- charging fees for taking part in the sport;
- running fund-raising events such as discos, raffles, quiz nights;
- organising sponsored activities such as runs and swims.

The money raised in this way is not very great but usually enough to cover the basic costs of the club.

## Development costs

If a club wanted to build new facilities, improve what they have or start any other major development programme, they would need a lot more money. In order to raise this money they would need outside help. These organisations give money to sport:

- Central Government (through Sportsmatch and the Inner Cities Fund);
- local authorities;
- Sports Councils;
- governing bodies;
- National Lottery;
- Foundation for Sport and the Arts;
- charitable trusts
- companies (through sponsorship).

### ⏩ EXTENSION

THE SPORTSMATCH SCHEME
The Government funds the Sportsmatch scheme. It encourages business sponsorship of 'grass roots' sport by matching the amount of money put in by the sponsor. The scheme is run by the Institute of Sports Sponsorship. Since 1992 more than £10 million of new money has gone to sport in this way. Over 500 companies and 50 sports have been involved. Projects must be new schemes for existing sponsors or completely new sponsors. They must show that the activity could not happen without the sponsorship.

## Sports funding and the voluntary sector: governing bodies

Governing bodies of sport are voluntary bodies. They need money for many purposes. These include:

### Basic running costs

- organisation of events and competitions;
- costs of providing training and coaching;
- achievement schemes for young people;
- supporting area organisations;
- upkeep of their own facilities;
- general administration.

### Development costs

Governing bodies always need more money to improve their sport. This includes building and running new facilities and developing new schemes for different ages and abilities.

> ⟳ **KEY POINT**
>
> Sports clubs and governing bodies need to raise money to pay for their running costs and the development of their activities.

## Where do governing bodies get their money from?

Governing bodies can raise money in various ways:

- all clubs and organisations pay membership fees to their governing body;
- governing bodies can apply for grants to the same organisations as the sports clubs, i.e. the Sports Councils, the National Lottery, the Foundation for Sport and the Arts and charitable trusts. They can work in partnership with the Government (through Sportsmatch and the Inner Cities Fund) and local authorities;
- governing bodies can get sponsorship from companies;
- some governing bodies run sports which are very popular and attract large crowds at major events and championships. Examples include the Football Association Cup Finals, Rugby Football Union international matches and the Wimbledon Tennis Championships. They are able to sell the television rights for these events and make a profit.

# How is a sports club organised and financed?

Sports clubs exist because enthusiastic people have got together in the past to enjoy their sport together. However, enthusiasm is not enough to keep a club going. To be successful, a club needs members, a committee, a constitution, facilities and finance.

There are three essential jobs:
- *Chairperson* – controls commitee meetings and acts as the club's representative;
- *Secretary* – deals with the day-to-day business; arranges meetings;
- *Treasurer* – deals with all the finances.

## Members

should be:
- enthusiastic about their sport;
- happy to take part with others;
- willing to pay their share of the costs;
- able to accept club rules;
- available to play, organise, coach or be officials at competitions.

## Commitee members

should be:
- willing to take on jobs;
- ready to work on a commitee;
- able to make decisions for the club;
- elected by the members at the Annual General Meeting (AGM).

## Finance

A club will need to pay for:
- hire or upkeep of facilities;
- team clothing and equipment;
- training and competition costs;
- office expenses.

It can raise money through:
- fees and subscriptions;
- fund raising;
- grants and sponsorship.

## Constitution

This sets out the rules of the club which explain:
- how you become a member;
- how people are elected to jobs;
- how fees can be charged;
- what happens if members break the rules;
- how the club can be changed.

## Facilities

- these are needed for playing, training, meetings and social events;
- the needs of the club will depend on the type of activity and size of the club;
- they might be owned or hired.

> **KEY POINT**
>
> Clubs are usually small, facilities basic, the organisation simple and money limited.

# Questions

## Providing for Sport

1 Explain ways in which a governing body of sport can encourage more people to take part.

2 Name an award scheme and describe what it involves.

3 Sports clubs are always in need of funds. Describe three ways in which a club might raise its income.

4 Describe how a sports club might be organised. Use the following headings:
    **i** members;
    **ii** constitution;
    **iii** facilities;
    **iv** finance.

5 Describe the main purpose of the Sports Councils, campaigns and policies.

6 Explain the functions of the new UK Sports Council.

7 What do the letters C.C.P.R. stand for? List this organisation's two main objectives.

8 Name two national sports centres and list the activities in which they specialise.

9 Name the organisation which controls the Olympic Games.

10 Name one national governing body of sport.

# 10 Taking Part in Sport

Different people take part in sport for different reasons. The following are questions which affect how, and whether, each of us takes part in sport.

Society is made up of all sorts of different types of people, for example: men, women, people from different ethnic groups, able-bodied people, people with disabilities, people of different ages. If we belong to a particular group/groups of people, there may be a number of barriers to taking part in sport.

## Home influences page 192

- What influence do our parents, friends and peers have?
- What effect does our social class, financial situation and environment have?

## Leisure time page 190

- How much time do we have for leisure activities?

## Benefits page 191

- Do we know what the benefits of sport are?

## School influences
page 194

- How does the status of P.E. in our school affect us?
- How do our P.E. lessons affect us?

Opportunities to take part in sport are not equal, some groups of people will have more than others.

This is a complex issue and, in order to be able to understand it properly, we need to understand why people take part in sports.

*"Sport enhances community spirit, equality of opportunity, personal development and social integration... Sport should provide a context where everyone can come together on equal terms to participate and reach their full potential regardless of race, social class, gender, age, ability or religious belief."*

Sports Council ('Sport in the 90s – New Horizons')

## Gender and sport page 198
## Black and ethnic minorities and sport page 199
## Disability and sport page 200
## Older people and sport page 201

• Are we influenced by our gender, race, culture, disability, age?

## School and community links page 196

• Do we know where to find centres and clubs?

## Careers in sport
page 202

• Would we like to work in sport?

## National campaigns page 197

• Do national campaigns help to get us involved in sport?

# Leisure time

If we listed all of the things we did during any one day we would end up with a very long list, which included many different activities. Our lists would be different but some activities, for example sleeping, would be on everybody's list.

We can put most of our activities under the headings of bodily needs, work, duties and leisure time.

We have to do many things to stay healthy. These include sleeping, eating and washing. Taking care of our bodily needs takes time.

It is necessary for us to work to earn a living. Some unemployed people (most of these are women) do not earn money but look after their home and care for children. This is also work. Pupils might consider time at school as work. Some activities are closely linked to work, such as travelling to work. Work takes time.

There are a number of things which we feel we have to do. These include duties towards our family and home. Many things may be called duties, for example washing up, or taking the dog for a walk. Our duties take time.

If we take out of our day the time used up for bodily needs, our duties and for work and work related activities, we are left with free time for leisure activities. This is the time in which we have the greatest choice about what we do. During our leisure time we can take part in sport and physical recreation.

## Patterns of work

Most people work regular hours and this sets the pattern for their lives. For people who work regular hours, weekends, evenings and holidays are the time for leisure. Working long hours or overtime will reduce our leisure time. People on night work and shift work may have to take their leisure time when other people are working. Our duties take time.

In the last fifty years there has been a great increase in the time people have available for leisure. Leisure time

**During our leisure time we can choose our activities**

will continue to grow for almost all of us. There are many reasons for this:

- working careers have got shorter as we continue our education longer and retire earlier;
- we live longer in retirement;
- paid holidays have increased;
- working hours have got shorter;
- housework takes less time;
- unemployment, short-time and part-time work have increased.

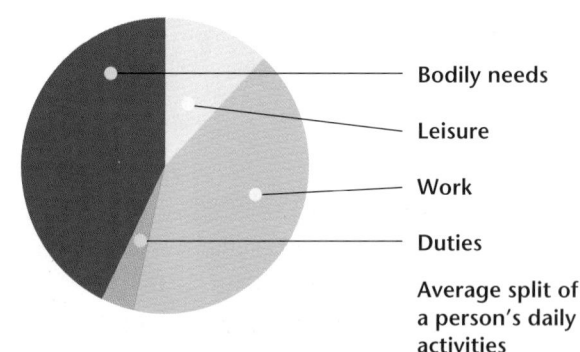

Bodily needs

Leisure

Work

Duties

**Average split of a person's daily activities**

> **○ KEY POINT**
>
> We all have leisure time. What we do during this time depends on what matters to us and what our interests are. We may decide to take part in sport or physical recreation. Our decision will depend on what we think the benefits are.

# Benefits

It is, of course, quite right that we should be free to choose our own leisure time activities. We may be bee keepers, stamp collectors, or voluntary hospital workers. All these activities have great value. Physical recreation and sport are different and offer other benefits.

> **KEY POINT**
>
> We take part in sport for many different reasons. We can put these reasons into four different categories – 'enjoyment', 'health', 'social' and 'work'.

## Enjoyment

For most of us, enjoyment is the main reason why we take part in sport and physical recreation. We enjoy activities for different reasons. Dance can be enjoyed for the experience of moving to the music. Some players enjoy using up energy and aggression in activities such as judo. Archers get pleasure from being able to hit the target. The thrill of going at speed over land, water and snow attracts racing car drivers, canoeists and skiers. Some people enjoy achievement, for example winning a match, recording a personal best or representing their area.

## Health

Taking part in physical activity helps us to maintain good health. We need to keep our bodies fit for the daily demands of life. The more vigorous the activity, the greater the physical benefits.

Exercise is vital in weight control. Unfit, overweight people are more likely to have poor health compared with those who exercise regularly.

Stress is one of the greatest challenges to health today. Physical activity helps us feel and look good, improving our self-image whereas worrying can make us ill. Physical recreation will not solve our worries but it will help us to relax for a while, perhaps allowing us a fresh look at our problems.

**Dance can be enjoyed for the experience of moving to the music**

## Social

We all need daily contact with other people. Physical recreation gives us the opportunity to meet and talk to others. We have the activity as a common interest. This helps to stimulate conversation and encourages friendships to develop. Many activities take place in sports centres and clubs. We may attend regularly and develop an interest in a group or club. Many people like being part of a team and play together. Others work together to run the affairs of a club.

## Work

A few very talented sportspeople can earn a living as professional sportspeople. Many more are able to make some money from sport as part-time professionals.

# Home influences

## Family

How and whether we take part in sport is influenced by several factors. Our family is a very important influence on us. If our parents play sport regularly then we will be brought up in a sporting atmosphere. Sporting parents and older brothers and sisters provide us with role models to follow. Sometimes children with famous sporting parents will follow in their footsteps. (This is not easy to do and many will decide to do something completely different.) Family influences can also be negative if there is little interest or encouragement to do sport.

**Our family influences our participation in sport**

## Friends and peers

Our peers are those people who are the same age as us. Our friends are our peers.

What our friends do in their leisure time will usually affect us. Friends often have similar interests. We all need friends and if our friends are not interested in sport, we may find ourselves dropping out of sport too. On the other hand, if our friends take part in sport and enjoy it we might be willing to give it a try. In school, peer pressure can be very strong.

**From a young age, our friends and peers influence us to take part**

# What effect does our social class, financial situation and environment have?

## Social class

Social class refers to a number of factors including type of employment, income level and family background. Our social class can affect the type of activity we take part in. For example, a middle class person who is well off, lives in the country and owns their own horse, is more likely to be involved in riding sports than someone who lives in a city and has a lower family income. Research shows that fewer working class people take part in sport than people from other social classes. This is because people from other social classes have more time, money and opportunities to take part in sport.

**Four-week participation rates for all sports activities by socio-economic group and sex: Great Britain, 1993**

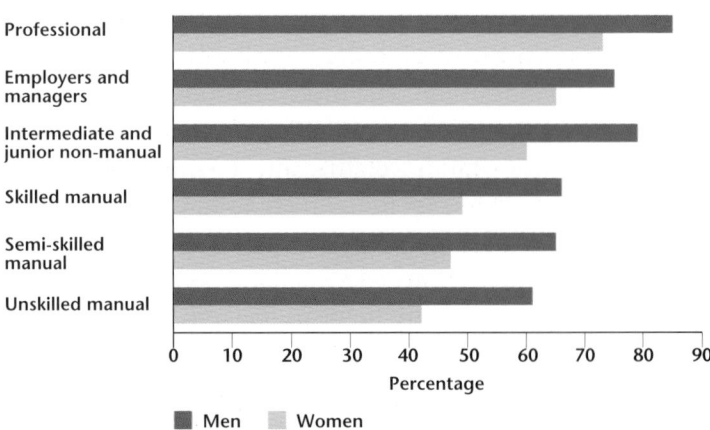

**Ref: General Household Survey**

Our financial situation affects what activities we
do in our leisure time

## Financial situation

The amount of money coming in to our family affects
our standard of living and all the activities we do in
our leisure time. Even for school P.E. we need quite a
lot of sports clothing and equipment. Playing sport
outside school time means we will have to pay even
more for equipment, the hire of facilities and the costs
of joining a club or centre. At a higher level we may
need to pay travelling costs, training fees and all the
expenses of competition. Although help is available
to meet some of these costs, we are affected by our
parents' ability to pay for our sport. If sports
opportunities at school are reduced, children will miss
out if their parents cannot afford the fees at sports
centres and clubs.

> **⮕ KEY POINT**
>
> How and whether we take part in sport as an
> adult is affected by our family background,
> our finances, our friends and peers, our
> social class and where we live.

## Environment

Where we live affects
some of the sports we can take part in. Obviously, if
we live near the sea, a large lake, or river, there will be
greater opportunities to learn water sports. Country
areas might provide opportunities for outdoor
activities, but they may be a long way from leisure
centres and swimming pools. Inner City areas will be
short of open space but are more likely to have many
indoor facilities within travelling distance. Also these
areas, because of their high population, may attract
both commercial and private sports clubs. In some
parts of the country, there is a tradition for a
particular local sport. For example, Highland wrestling
in Scotland.

We may need transport to get to facilities in order
to play sport. If our parents do not have a car we will
have to find the money for public transport.

# School influences

We are affected by our experiences of Physical Education (P.E.) in school and also by the importance given to P.E. by the school.

## Changes in education

In recent years, there have been a number of changes in education which have had an effect on P.E. in school.

### The National Curriculum

P.E. is a foundation subject in the National Curriculum. Targets have been set for each age group. The sports taught are chosen by the P.E. department from different categories. There are checks to make sure pupils achieve their targets. P.E. teachers decide on the best teaching methods. This has given P.E. equal status with other foundation subjects.

**Time for P.E. has been cut in many schools**

**P.E. teachers influence our interest in sport**

## Time given to P.E.

By law, schools have to teach the subjects of the National Curriculum. This means there is a lot of pressure to fit all the subjects into the school curriculum. As a result, time for P.E. has been cut in many schools.

## Local management of schools

Management of schools has been moved from the local authority to school governors. The governors decide which school sports facilities can be booked by the local community. They also decide what to charge. **Local management of schools** means that more facilities may be made available but it may lead to higher fees. Schools now have to pay for all sports facilities outside of school, including transport. Swimming in particular has been reduced because of this change.

## Open enrolment

**Open enrolment** means that schools are in competition with one another to attract pupils. The standard of P.E. in the school and the number of out of school activities will help the school's reputation. As a result P.E. in schools is especially important in attracting pupils.

## Examinations in P.E.

It is now possible to gain P.E. qualifications at both GCSE and A level. This has given P.E. equal status with other examination subjects.

# How do our P.E. lessons affect us?

P.E. has the same aim as other subjects on the school curriculum, in that it aims to contribute to the general education of all children. It does this by using physical activities of many kinds in P.E. lessons. Good P.E. lessons in school will encourage us to take part in sport after leaving school. There are three major factors which influence whether we take part in sport after we have left.

## Skills

P.E. teachers teach all pupils the basic skills of a variety of different activities. During our years at school we develop these skills so that we can take part confidently in the activities. Teachers may also improve our abilities through coaching and training during after school practices. Sometimes they will send pupils to local sports clubs or centres of excellence. In school there will usually be an opportunity to try for achievement awards in different sports.

## Health

P.E. teachers explain the value of regular exercise for health and fitness. They go through the important principles involved in training for different sports, in both theory and practice. We learn safe practices for all activities together with advice for avoiding and, if necessary, dealing with injuries.

## Attitude

P.E. teachers try to develop in their pupils a positive attitude towards an active lifestyle. They explain the advantages of life long involvement in physical recreation. The attitude and experience of the P.E. staff is all important as P.E. teachers are important **role models** for pupils.

## Research

The National Survey of Young People and Sport reported in 1994 that most young people thought that sport was fun and that it kept them fit.

> ⊙ **KEY POINT**
>
> P.E. teachers and the lessons they teach have an important effect on our interest in sport as adults.

*"I'd never have won my gold medal without first being interested in sport through P.E. at school. It's obvious that school P.E. is the only way we can ensure that all children learn the basics, so they can develop in their own way and in their chosen activity later. The road to gold begins at school."*

**Tessa Sanderson**

# School and community links

Even if the school P.E. programme is very good, the school-community link is vital in helping young people continue with physical recreation after leaving school. Pupils need to be introduced to the sports clubs, activity groups and leisure centres in their local community before they leave school. It helps if the community uses school facilities regularly.

To help bridge the school-community gap, schools could:

- bring club members, centre managers and others involved in community sport into schools;
- arrange for pupils to visit the clubs, centres and other facilities in the area;
- explain how to find out about other sports not taught at school.

To help bridge the school-community gap, clubs and centres could:

- run special introductory courses for young people at school;
- ensure the clubs and centres are welcoming to young people;
- provide coaching and training for young people;
- help young people with the costs.

Local authorities have helped bridge the school-club gap by appointing sports development officers. Their role is to organise activities and encourage participation out of school time in centres and clubs.

**You can play sport in most youth clubs**

## KEY POINT

We need to leave school with:

- sound basic sports skills;
- a wide experience of different activities;
- a good understanding of the link between health and exercise;
- a positive attitude towards physical recreation;
- knowledge of local sporting opportunities.

## EXTENSION

**The National Junior Sports Programme**

This programme was started in 1996 by the Sports Council and the Youth Sports Trust (a charity aiming to improve sports provision for young people). It aims to give better sporting opportunities to young people aged from four to 18 by getting schools, local authorities, governing bodies, sports clubs and youth organisations to work together. The programme is as follows:

- TOP play for four–nine year olds to develop basic skills in schools;
- TOP sport for seven–11 year olds to introduce mini-games in schools;
- champion coaching for 11–14 year olds, to improve ability after school;
- TOP clubs to help all clubs establish junior sections.

The cost is £14 million. This money comes from the national lottery, the English Sports Council, the Youth Sports Trust and sponsorship.

# National campaigns

Here we look at national campaigns, who they have helped and who they have missed out.

## 'Sport for All'?

The Sport for All campaign was launched by the Sports Council in 1972 and is still going strong. Its main aims are to:
- increase participation;
- improve performance at all levels;
- establish the idea that sports provision is a social service;
- promote good health through physical activity;
- improve quality of life.

'Sport for All' encourages everyone to take part in sport

## Special campaigns

At different times the Sport for All campaign has focused on different themes.

| | | |
|---|---|---|
| 1975 | **Sport for all the Family** | Encouraged activities for the whole family. |
| 1978 | **Come Alive** | Emphasised good health through regular exercise. |
| 1981 | **Disabled People** | Promoted sport for people with disabilities. |
| 1983 | **50+ All to Play For** | Encouraged older people to take part in physical recreation. |
| 1985 | **Ever thought of Sport?** | Focused on the 13 – 24 year olds who were missing out on sport. |
| 1987 | **What's your Sport?** | Produced detailed information about where to take part in sport. |
| 1990 | **Women in Sport** | Concentrated on the needs of women. |
| 1991 | **Year of Sport** | Coincided with a number of international events in the UK. |

## Who has missed out?

Although more facilities have been provided and levels of participation have increased, not everyone has benefited. Research has shown that some groups have missed out:
- low paid and unskilled workers;
- ethnic minorities;
- school leavers;
- parents of young children;
- women generally;
- unemployed young people.

Today the Sports Councils are encouraging participation at the local level by:
- promoting school-club links;
- paying for sports development officers;
- funding local schemes to improve participation, especially for those missing out.

National campaigns need very strong links between the national message and local clubs to be successful.

# Gender and sport

Today it is possible for women to take part in almost any sport as social changes have gradually given them more and more opportunities to control their own lives. This was not so in the past as many sports were not open to women. The history of sport is mainly the history of men's sport.

**Men/women participation rates**

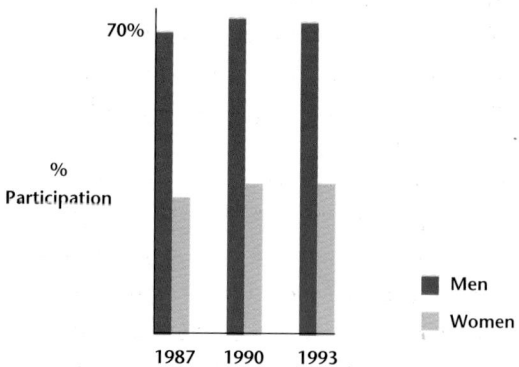

Ref: General Household Survey

## What needs to be changed?

**Stereotyping** means having a fixed image of a group of people. Girls in the past were encouraged to play with dolls, to learn to cook and to keep themselves clean. In contrast boys were encouraged to play ball games, to climb trees and to get covered in mud. Children were, and are, brought up to fit into these **gender** stereotypes, or stereotypes for the different sexes. As a result, boys had greater opportunities to develop the skills of sports and the confidence that goes with them. Boys think a lot of their peers who are good at sport. Sport has high status for them. In contrast many girls have been turned off P.E. at school and so do not consider sporting achievement to be important. Some of these gender stereotypes are gradually being broken down.

Male, female stereotypes continue into adult life. Some sports are still seen as unsuitable for women. Women do not think that playing sport will make them attractive to men. Married women are expected to take responsibility for the home and children. This reduces the time and energy they have for sport. Sport for the mother is a low priority in family life. They do not always have an independent income to spend on sport or their own transport.

Some sports are still seen as 'unsuitable' for women

## What is being done?

The Sports Council has targeted women in a number of campaigns. In 1993 it published a policy and framework for action:

- to improve girls' skills and to develop a positive attitude to an active life;
- to increase the opportunities for women to take part in sport;
- to increase the opportunities for women to improve their level of performance;
- to increase the number of women involved in the organisation of sport;
- to encourage all organisations to have equal opportunities;
- to improve communication about women in sport.

### ⊙ KEY POINT

The Sports Councils aim to increase the involvement of women in sport at all levels and in all roles.

The Women's Sports Foundation supports women's sport (see page 171).

# Black and ethnic minorities and sport

In our multicultural society, people of all races and ethnic backgrounds take part in sport at all levels. As a result of this, we often assume that they face no problems in sport. However, there is discrimination and disadvantage in sport as there is in everyday life.

## What needs to be changed?

**Racism** means not treating people of different races equally. Racists often hold stereotyped views about people from different ethnic backgrounds. Stereotypes lead to sporting myths about what different people can and can't do. One example of a racist sporting myth is 'Black people can't swim at top levels'. This is nonsense.

Personal racism is seen when black or **ethnic minority** people are made to feel unwelcome by individuals at a sports club. Institutional racism is racism perpetrated by an organisation/organisations, rather than particular individuals. This kind of racism can often be seen in a lack of understanding, or a lack of willingness to understand and respond to, the problems faced by black people and ethnic minorities in an organisation. Racism is a major problem in spite of the efforts of many committed people who work to eliminate racial inequality.

**Racism can lead to sporting myths**

Socio-economic factors are things such as employment, pay and social class. In this country, black people and people from ethnic minority groups are over-represented amongst the unemployed and the poorly paid. One result of this is that more black people and ethnic minority people have less money to spend on sport and other leisure activities.

There are many different **cultures** in Britain, each with their own sets of beliefs about many important areas. Some of these beliefs will impact on sport. For example, some women may not take part in mixed sports for religious reasons. Some people think this needs to change, but others disagree.

## What is being done?

In 1994, the Sports Council published a policy and objectives.

Sports Council aim: To work towards the elimination of racial disadvantage and discrimination in order to achieve better quality sport for black and ethnic minority people.

They have six main objectives:

- to raise awareness of racial inequality in sport;
- to increase the number of black and ethnic minority decision makers in sport;
- to increase the number of black and ethnic minority people involved in sports organisation;
- to improve skill and develop a positive attitude to an active life for young black and ethnic minority people;
- to increase opportunities for black and ethnic minority people to take part in sport;
- to increase opportunities to improve the level of performance of black and ethnic minority people.

In 1993, the Professional Footballers' Association and the Commission for Racial Equality set up a 'Kick Racism out of Football' campaign, financed by the Football Trust.

# Disability and sport

People with disabilities have much to offer the world of sport. As well as the top disabled sportspeople, there are many ordinary disabled people who can and do benefit from sport. Sport allows everybody to stay healthy and to meet people. However, people with disabilities do face serious obstacles to participation in sport.

Success is important for all sportspeople

## What needs to be changed?

It is not always possible for disabled people to get to events. Transport to facilities may be difficult and there may not be suitable doors and ramps at entrances to buildings. There are also difficulties in taking part in the full range of sports and activities, both indoor and outdoor.

Plans for facilities, funding and events do not always take account of the needs of competitors and spectators with disabilities. Planning should include training for people to work with sports people with disabilities.

Sports centres and clubs do not make provision automatically for everyone, including people with disabilities. Governing bodies do not usually hold separate events for disabled people within their championships.

## What is being done?

In 1993 the Sports Council published a policy and action plan.

Sports Council aim: To ensure equality of opportunity for people with disabilities to take part in sport and recreation at the level of their choice. They have seven main objectives:

- to raise the profile of people with disabilities in sport;
- to make sure plans for sport include the needs of people with disabilities;
- to provide opportunities for people with disabilities to take part in sport;
- to improve access to sport for people with disabilities;
- to encourage involvement for people with disabilities in international sport;
- to use all resources and to seek extra finance;
- to make sure sport meets the needs of people with disabilities.

Full details of British Sports Association for Disabled (B.S.A.D.) are given in chapter 9.

British sportspeople won many medals at the Atlanta Paralympics. They showed that, given the right opportunities and support, people with disabilities can excel at sport

# Older people and sport

In general, people are less physically active as they get older. The General Household Survey confirms this trend (see chart below). The Allied Dunbar National Fitness Survey in 1992 showed that activity levels for older people were well below those necessary to improve health and well being.

## What needs to be changed?

If older people have not exercised for a long time it is hard to get their bodies working again. Some may not have had the opportunity to learn skills when they were young. Others may have had illnesses which mean they have to be cautious when exercising.

Older people living on pensions may only have a limited amount of money for leisure spending. Most sports centres do offer older people special rates, especially if they come along at off peak times.

Older people are less likely to be able to afford to run a car and may find it difficult to get to sports facilities.

Sport in the media is dominated by young people but in many clubs veteran teams start at 35 or 40. There is not enough publicity for older people who achieve at a high standard.

## What is being done?

In 1983 the Sports Council started its campaign 'Sport for All – 50 plus all to play for.' It is still going. It encourages older people to take part in sport. It emphasises not just the health benefits but also the social benefits of an active life style. Sport provides the opportunity for people to meet. In 1994 new guidelines were produced for leaders.

Local authority leisure and recreation departments usually offer a full range of activities for the 50 plus age group.

### ● KEY POINT

Time will tell if today's more active younger people are able to bring their positive attitude to sport into their own old age.

**Four-week participation rates for sports, games and physical activities by age: Great Britain, 1993**

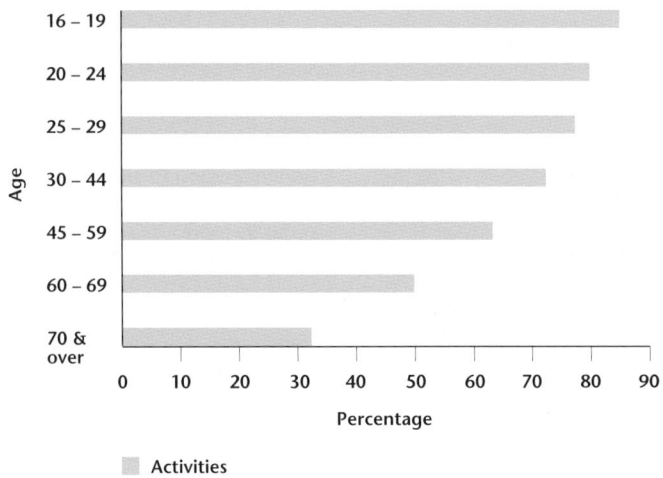

■ Activities

**Ref: General Household Survey**

**There is not enough publicity for older people who achieve at a high standard**

# Careers in sport

When we talk about careers in sport we usually think of the glamorous lifestyle of some of the top sports stars. These sportspeople have outstanding ability. We must remember they are the lucky few. The rewards for the majority of professional sportspeople are much smaller.

> ⭕ **KEY POINT**
>
> There are many careers in sport apart from performing. Most of these jobs do not make the headlines, although they are essential to sport.

Racing car drivers could not race without the team of people who support them

## Sport as a career

| Performer | Working with performers | Science and health | Organisation | Media | Business | Practical work |
|---|---|---|---|---|---|---|
| Basketball | P.E. teacher | Sports doctor | Centre manager | Journalist | Manufacturing | Groundsman |
| Boxing | Trainer | Physiotherapist | Leisure officer | Commentator | Retail | Mechanic |
| Cricket | Coach | Sports psychologist | Administrator | T.V. presenter | Sales | Stable hand |
| Cycling | Instructor | Dietician | Sports development officer | | Agent | Match official |
| Darts | Team manager | Sport and exercise adviser | | | | |
| Equestrian | | | | | | |
| Football | | | | | | |
| Golf | | | | | | |
| Motor racing | | | | | | |
| Rugby | | | | | | |
| Snooker | | | | | | |
| Tennis | | | | | | |

**Performer**
Job description: Playing sport at a high level.
Main quality: Outstanding ability.

**Working with performers**
Job description: Developing sports skills in others.
Main quality: Ability to analyse and improve skill.

**Science and health**
Job description: Improving sports performance.
Main quality: Understanding of sports medicine.

**Organisation**
Job description: Organising sporting activities.
Main quality: Motivating others to take part.

**Media**
Job description: Describing sport.
Main quality: Communication skills.

**Business**
Job description: Applying business understanding to sport.
Main quality: Ability to see potential for profit in sport.

**Practical work**
Job description: Doing practical work of a high standard.
Main quality: High level practical skill.

# Questions

## Taking Part in Sport

1 What is meant by the term 'leisure'?

2 What is 'physical recreation'?

3 The National Junior Sports Programme was launched in 1996.
Who started it and what does it involve?

4 It has been suggested that women are disadvantaged when taking part in sport on an equal basis with men.
   **a** What kind of disadvantages do women need to overcome?
   **b** What steps are being taken to try and improve this situation?

5 Imagine that you are a sports centre manager. How might you provide suitable opportunities for the following groups:
   **i** people with disabilities;
   **ii** older people;
   **iii** women.

6 Many young people leave school at 16 and fail to continue playing sport.
   **a** Suggest two reasons for this.
   **b** How might this trend be stopped?

7 List two different reasons why people take part in physical activity during their leisure time.

8 Name one physical activity that takes place in the countryside.

9 Name two aspects of sport (other than performing) which offer career prospects.

10 Schools can encourage participation in a wide range of physical activities or concentrate on only a few. Decide which approach you favour and explain your reasons.

# 11 Sport as a Spectacle

Sport has always been a spectacle. Today,
television and sponsorship greatly influence
our view of sport.

£

SPONSORSHIP

Johnnie Walker Classic

16
Johnnie Walker
Classic
PAR   4
YDS  359
MTS  328

## Sponsorship
**page 206**

Sports sponsorship is an agreement
between a commercial company
and an individual, team or sport.
The sportspeople agree that in return
for payment they will advertise the
names of the sponsors. The detailed
arrangements about the advertising
are worked out by the sponsors
and the sport. The sponsors also try
to make their potential customers
feel good about them sponsoring
sport. Sport is attractive to sponsors
because it involves young people
and exciting action.

£

TV

## The media page 212

Sport is always worth reporting. At its best it is full of drama, tension and
excitement. By its very nature there will be winners and losers. Through the media
we share in their happiness and their pain, we know their successes and their
disappointments. Uncertainty accompanies sport, often to the finish, and keeps
hope alive until the very end. Above all, sport is about people. For the media,
sport makes bold headlines, good stories and wonderful pictures.

**SPORT**

## £ Sport, sponsorship and television – the future? page 215

Governing bodies need to control the demands of television producers and commercial sponsors who want sport to become increasingly like entertainment. The traditional idea of sport as being recreational has almost disappeared at the highest level. Today, professional sport is fast becoming part of show business and demands stars and performances.

Governing bodies are in danger of losing control of their sports. They have become dependent on money from sponsors and television. They know that television coverage is essential for major events. Without television coverage there would be no sponsors, which would mean no money available to attract top sportspeople. Without this money there would be no event!

## Television page 214

The sport we see on our television screens has been brought to us only after a lot of negotiation between many groups of people. These include the sportspeople involved, the governing bodies of sport, the sponsoring companies and people who work in television, such as producers, editors, presenters and commentators. The television companies need to keep the viewer happy, the sponsors require plenty of publicity, the governing bodies expect a good picture of the sport and the sportspeople want good publicity, a winning performance, and money. The viewer hopes to be entertained.

# Sponsorship

Companies exist in order to make profits. They do not have to make donations to charity or to sponsor sport, although many do so.

Sponsorship is an investment. The company expects to get something back in return. Sponsorship helps the company to sell its products. The company wants to have an impact on likely customers. The impact comes through the link between the sporting activity and the product. The aim is to improve the business of the company.

Donations are different from sponsorship, they are gifts. The company chooses to give money to sport. The company benefits by being seen to care about the community. There is no direct commercial advantage in giving money in this way.

Sports sponsorship can work by promoting a sales message, or by promoting a feeling.

Exciting sports attract a lot of sponsorship

## Promoting a sales message

At its simplest, sponsoring sport gives a company a chance to put over a sales message such as 'Buy our clothing'. Sportstars are linked with a particular company's sportswear. A team wears shirts with a company's name for all to see. Advertising hoardings at a televised sports event are caught by the cameras. A competition may carry the sponsor's name, for example the Carling Premier League or Cornhill Test Matches. Sponsorship aims to put the company's name in front of the public so that it is remembered.

## Promoting a feeling

At another level, selling a product can be a more subtle process. Sponsorship is not linked directly to sales at all. Instead it tries to make the likely customer feel happy about the sponsoring company and their product. If the name of a company was on your favourite player, you might, without realising it, also feel good about the company.

In this way, a company can transfer some of the values of the team or player to its products. If the player or team is successful then this success is good for the sponsor company also.

High level sport, in general, is played by young people, who bring energy, enthusiasm, excitement and skill to the activity. These qualities make sport a very helpful partner when marketing a product. Sponsorship is about getting the spectators to enjoy the sporting event and, therefore, to be likely to buy the sponsor's product.

## ⊙ KEY POINT

Sports sponsorship means that a company gives financial help in return for linking their name with an individual, a team or a sport in general.

## ⊙ EXTENSION

HOW HAS SPONSORSHIP GROWN?
Over the past 15 years sports sponsorship has grown each year. In 1985 it was worth £129 million. In the ten years leading up to 1995 it more than doubled to £285 million. The number of new deals increased from 818 in 1994 to 939 in 1995. There is no one area of sports sponsorship which is responsible for this growth alone. The alcoholic drinks industry had easily the most new deals but in fact this year it had fewer new deals than in the previous year. The soft drinks industry and sports goods and clothing manufacturers had a large increase in the number of new deals in 1995 compared to 1994. There were seven deals worth more than £5 million each. The record figures for 1995 included a large number of smaller sports sponsorships which resulted from the Government's Sportsmatch scheme (see page 180).

## Deciding on sponsorship

When a company looks at sponsoring a sport, it must consider the following questions:

- Will our product go well with the sport?
- Is the public interested in the sport?
- Will the individual, team or event be seen on television?
- Will there be publicity on radio or in the newspapers?
- Will lots of people attend the event?
- Will the team or individual win?

**Advertising is all around at popular sports events**

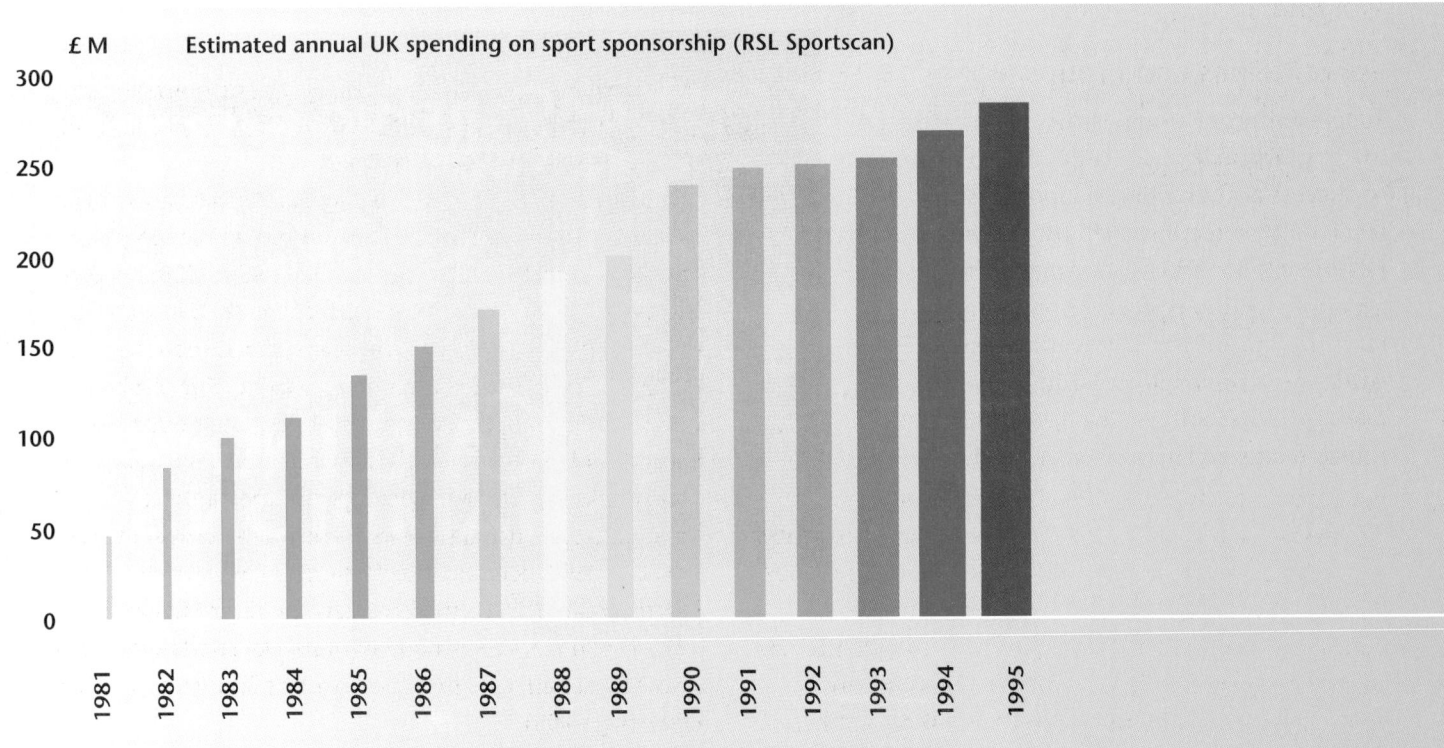

**£ M      Estimated annual UK spending on sport sponsorship (RSL Sportscan)**

# Who receives sponsorship in sport?

Today, sponsorship is available throughout the sporting world. It is not only the stars of sport who are sponsored. Local teams and individuals can also find sponsors, often from the local community. Sponsorship is received by: individual sportspeople, sports teams and groups, governing bodies, coaching and achievement schemes, sporting events.

## Individual sportspeople

World champions and Olympic gold medallists can choose their sponsors. Successful sportspeople are in great demand. Sponsors hope that we will link the name of their product with sporting excellence. We forget sometimes that players advertise one product rather than another because of the money they are paid.

Sponsorship, for professional sportspeople, adds money to their income from sport.

For younger up and coming sportspeople it enables them to buy the best equipment and helps with training, competition and travelling costs. Top amateurs rely on sponsorship to pay living expenses. They can then give up work or work part time. Money is also available for equipment, clothing, travel, accommodation and the expenses of training and competition.

## Sports teams and groups

Successful professional sports teams attract a lot of sponsorship. Sponsors like to be linked to success and excellence. Sponsorship received by a team is used by the organisation responsible for the team. Amateur teams who are sponsored may get equipment and clothing, training and travelling expenses paid. Sometimes sponsorship is given to teams at different age levels. Sponsorship of junior teams gives sponsors a good name.

## Governing bodies

Governing bodies receive sponsorship to develop the sport generally, for events and special projects.

## Coaching and achievement schemes

Most children are very happy to win a competition or achieve a standard in sport. Many sponsors support achievement schemes for young people. Sponsors pay all the costs of running the scheme, including badges and certificates. They get publicity when the badges and certificates go home. They hope to get credit for encouraging young people to take part in sport and improve their ability.

## Sporting events

International matches and championship finals are very popular with sponsors. These events are televised and the sponsor is guaranteed good publicity. Sponsors pay for the administration, organisation and expenses of the event. This allows the sport to keep any profit from television fees or gate money. Sometimes companies sponsor a league or cup competition which takes place over a period of time. Most major events depend on sponsorship in order to take place. Local events are also sponsored, with companies benefiting from local publicity.

Sponsors look for successful teams

*"I will always be grateful for the financial backing I received when it was needed. I hope the S.A.F. gets the funds necessary to keep up the good work."*

*Sally Gunnell*

# Which organisations assist sponsorship of sport?

The Sports Aid Foundation and the Institute of Sports Sponsorship were set up to assist sponsorship of sport.

## The Sports Aid Foundation

The Sports Aid Foundation (S.A.F.) is:
* an independent non-profit making company set up in 1976;
* managed by trustees and governors.

## What does the Sports Aid Foundation do?

The S.A.F.:
* raises sponsorship money from companies;
* gives grants to top British amateur sportspeople;
* helps sportspeople with disabilities and talented youngsters through the S.A.F. Charitable Trust;
* was set up originally to enable our top amateurs to compete against state or college sponsored sportspeople, its slogan being 'Giving Britons a better sporting chance';
* at the Atlanta Olympics, many of the team members had received grants, including the gold medalist rowers Steve Redgrave and Matthew Pinsent.

## Who pays for the Sports Aid Foundation?

The S.A.F. is paid for by:
* the Foundation for Sport and the Arts;
* sponsoring companies;
* donations from individuals and organisations.

## The Institute of Sports Sponsorship

The Institute of Sports Sponsorship (I.S.S.)is:
* a national non-profit making organisation, formed in 1985;
* a group of companies who are sponsors of sport;
* run by a committee representing the member companies.

## What does the Institute of Sports Sponsorship do?

The I.S.S:
* helps increase sports sponsorship by bringing together sponsors and sports;
* protects the traditional nature of sport;
* helps companies get a fair return on their sponsorship;
* has strong links with the Sports Councils, Central Council for Physical Recreation (C.C.P.R.) and governing bodies;
* runs the Sportsmatch scheme with the Government.

## Who pays for the Institute of Sports Sponsorship?

The I.S.S. is paid for by:
* member companies

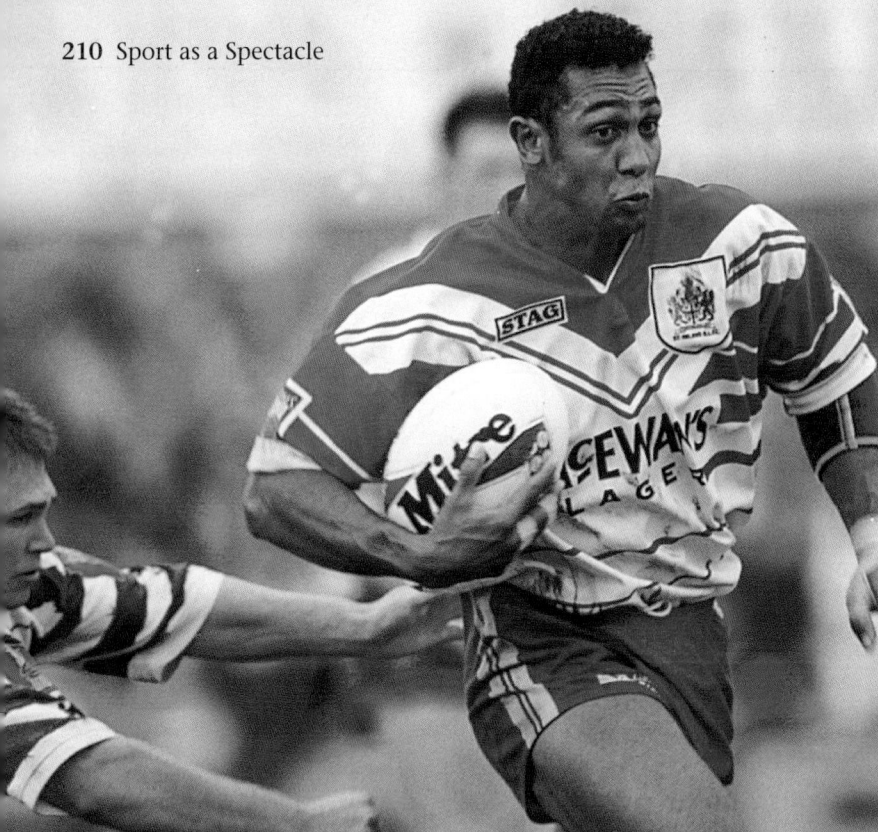

**Modern rugby attracts many sponsors**

# What advantages and disadvantages are there in sports sponsorship?

There are advantages and disadvantages to sports sponsorship for both the sports and the sponsoring companies themselves.

## Advantages for sport

For professional sportspeople and organisations sponsorship is just another part of their income.

For amateur sportspeople, sponsorship may:
* allow them to give up their jobs and train full time;
* pay day-to-day living expenses;
* pay for clothing and equipment;
* pay for costs of training and competition.

For amateur organisations, sponsorship money can be used to:
* fund the running of events;
* improve facilities;
* organise coaching and training schemes.

## Disadvantages for sport

The disadvantages of sponsorship for sport are that:
* once sponsorship is accepted, the sport comes to rely on it. If sponsorship is removed, there may be financial problems for sport. This gives the sponsor a powerful hold on the sport;
* sponsors may be able to change the sport. For example, professional rugby league has been changed to a summer game and completely reorganised;
* some sports have little television appeal and so attract little sponsorship. They may find it hard to develop their sport without money from sponsorship;
* governing bodies make agreements with sponsors. These agreements affect their sportspeople. They may be forced to wear the sponsor's clothing or use the sponsor's equipment. Their name will also be linked to the sponsor without them being consulted first.

## Advantages for the sponsor

The advantages of sponsorship for the sponsor are:
* sponsorship advertises the name of their product;
* sponsorship links the product with a popular activity;
* sponsorship provides exposure on television whenever the sport is seen;
* sponsorship ensures the use of the sponsor's name in the media;
* sponsorship improves a company's reputation because the company is supporting British sport;
* sponsorship transfers the spectator's good feeling about the sport to the sponsor company's product;
* sponsorship reduces tax on the company, depending how they give the money to sport.

## Disadvantages for the sponsor

The sponsor has difficulty in deciding whether or not the sponsorship has been good value for money. The questions to be asked include:

- has the sportsperson, team or event been successful?
- has the publicity been good in the media, especially television?
- does the public link the sponsor with the sport?
- does the public feel good about the sponsor?
- have sales increased ?

Sponsorship agreements last for a period of time, sometimes years. Sponsors sign agreements. They cannot pull out quickly if things go wrong. From time to time the action of the sportsperson or team brings bad publicity. This can happen because of their sporting behaviour or their behaviour in their private lives. The sponsor may want to withdraw its sponsorship.

Sponsors need successful people. Regular losers and weak teams attract few sponsors.

**EXTENSION**

SPORT AND TOBACCO SPONSORSHIP
- when television advertisements for cigarettes were banned, tobacco companies found they could get around the ban by sponsoring sport;
- tobacco companies continue to sponsor sport;
- smoking is a health risk. Sport keeps us healthy, therefore smoking and sport cannot go together;
- others argue that sport should accept sponsorship from any company. After all, it is accepted from companies which make alcohol and weapons.

**Sponsors need successful people**

# The media

When we talk about the media, we are referring to all the different ways that are used to bring us stories, news, action and information.

## Books

Successful books on sport are usually the life stories of current sports stars. At regular intervals, the histories of individual sports or their clubs are published in great detail. Coaching and training books help us to improve our sporting performance. Novels based on sport are much harder to find.

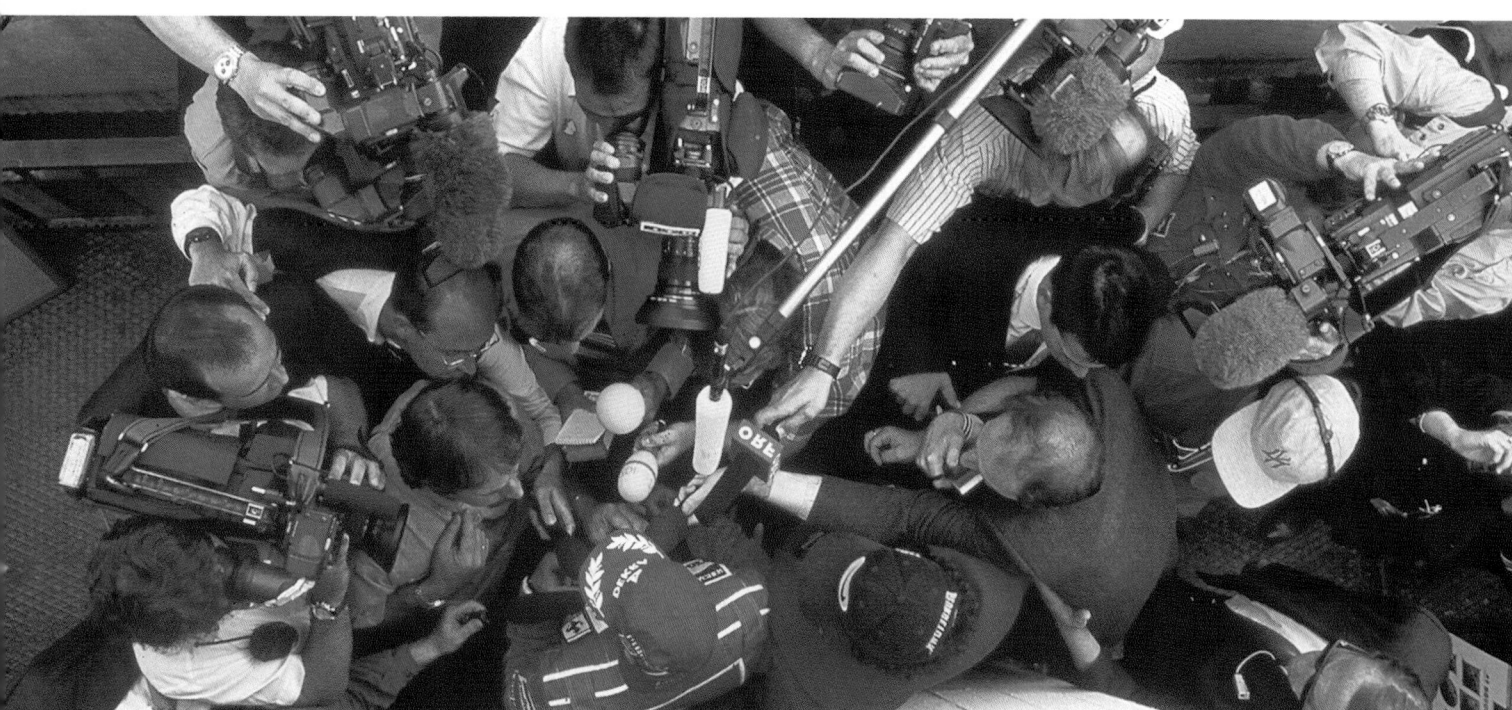

The media bring us stories, news, action and information

## Magazines

If we walk into any newsagent we will find dozens of magazines about sport. There is a wide choice of reading which ranges from major activities like tennis to minority sports like the triathlon. Within the covers are packed pages of pictures, stories and news about particular sports. General sports magazines are very much rarer and in the past have not been successful over a long period.

## Newspapers

All national newspapers give several pages to sport and employ a large number of sports journalists. However, there is no national newspaper devoted to sport in Britain. The aim of editors is to sell more newspapers. This is reflected in the sports pages. Some newspapers carry more details about the private lives of the sports stars than they do about the sport itself. Newspapers are good at building stars up when they are successful. However, they are even better at knocking them down when they fail. Today, newspapers play a major part in forming our views about sport. The way sports writers present sport, and the pictures they use, affect how we think about sport. In the 1996 European Football Championships, some newspapers talked about a football war between England and Germany. Many ordinary people thought this was going too far.

## Radio

Before television, the great advantage of radio was that it reported events live. The commentator described the action as it happened and the listeners felt they were there. In spite of television, radio still has its place today. From the radio companies' points of view, it is much cheaper to report on radio, and uses a much smaller team of people. For the listener, radios are much cheaper and more mobile than televisions. This gives radio its great advantage – we can do other things at the same time as listening to the match, race or competition. It allows us to keep in touch with the sporting action, particularly when the event takes some time to complete, for example cricket matches and tennis championships.

**The media can make successful sportspeople into stars**

## Film and video

Sport, being dramatic, full of heroic triumph and tragic tears, should make fabulous material for films. However, it seldom does.

'Total Sport' magazine in 1996 limited the top five sports films to:

1. Hoop Dreams (1995, Basketball)
2. Raging Bull (1980, Boxing)
3. The Club (1980, Australian Football)
4. The Hustler (1961, Pool)
5. Slap Shot (1977, Ice Hockey)

Video collections of great sporting occasions and outstanding individual performances are very popular. We can relive past glories whenever we like, in the comfort of our own homes. There are also instructional videos for improving our sporting performances and to help coaches.

## Computer – CD Roms and the Internet

CD Roms contain a wealth of information about a whole range of subjects. For example, we can find out every detail about the modern Olympic games from just one disc. Through the Internet, we can get information on sporting subjects from around the world. If we want information from, for example, the Australian Academy of Sport, we can get it almost instantly on the Internet. Future developments in this area are likely to be staggering.

> ### ⟳ KEY POINT
>
> There are four main types of media:
> - magazines, books and newspapers;
> - radio;
> - television, film, video;
> - computer – CD Roms and the Internet.

# Television

Whether you love sport or hate it, you certainly can't get away from it on television! An ever increasing number of hours are devoted to sports of very many different kinds. This is because sport is immensely popular and relatively cheap to produce for television. International sport does not have a language barrier either.

In the past, governing bodies were not interested in having their sport shown on television. They were worried it would reduce the number of spectators going to the events. The payment for television rights at this time did not compensate for this loss of gate money. This situation was changed by a number of factors. Colour television pictures made sport look far more exciting as better cameras and other new technology improved the quality of the coverage. The banning of direct cigarette advertising on television forced tobacco companies to advertise in other ways. Cigarette companies decided to use sponsorship of sport as a method of advertising to get around this ban. As a result, money for sponsorship and television rights greatly increased.

> ### ⊙ KEY POINT
>
> Today, most people experience sport through television, rather than taking part in it or watching events live. This emphasises the importance of sport on television.

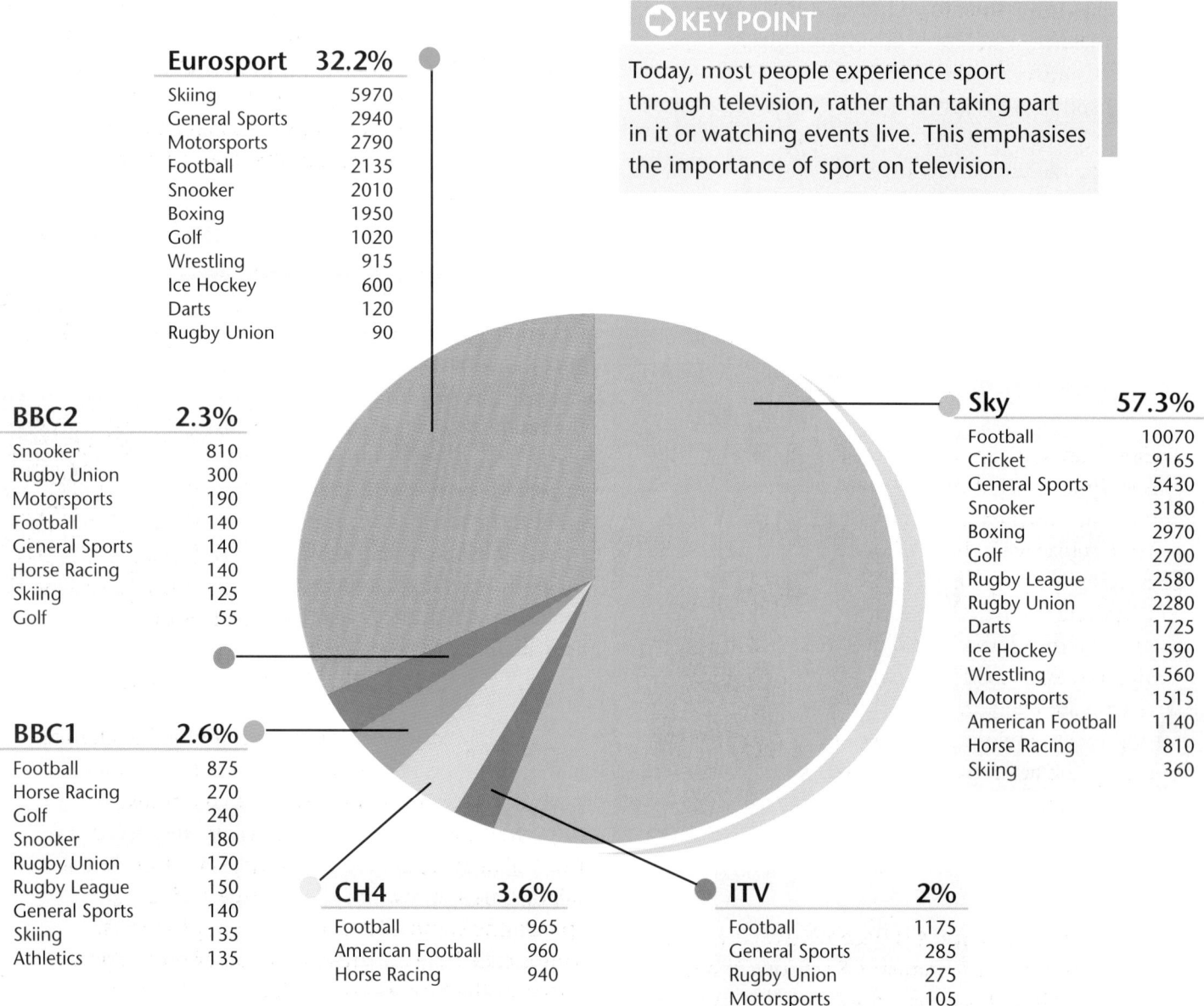

**Eurosport   32.2%**

| | |
|---|---|
| Skiing | 5970 |
| General Sports | 2940 |
| Motorsports | 2790 |
| Football | 2135 |
| Snooker | 2010 |
| Boxing | 1950 |
| Golf | 1020 |
| Wrestling | 915 |
| Ice Hockey | 600 |
| Darts | 120 |
| Rugby Union | 90 |

**BBC2   2.3%**

| | |
|---|---|
| Snooker | 810 |
| Rugby Union | 300 |
| Motorsports | 190 |
| Football | 140 |
| General Sports | 140 |
| Horse Racing | 140 |
| Skiing | 125 |
| Golf | 55 |

**BBC1   2.6%**

| | |
|---|---|
| Football | 875 |
| Horse Racing | 270 |
| Golf | 240 |
| Snooker | 180 |
| Rugby Union | 170 |
| Rugby League | 150 |
| General Sports | 140 |
| Skiing | 135 |
| Athletics | 135 |

**Sky   57.3%**

| | |
|---|---|
| Football | 10070 |
| Cricket | 9165 |
| General Sports | 5430 |
| Snooker | 3180 |
| Boxing | 2970 |
| Golf | 2700 |
| Rugby League | 2580 |
| Rugby Union | 2280 |
| Darts | 1725 |
| Ice Hockey | 1590 |
| Wrestling | 1560 |
| Motorsports | 1515 |
| American Football | 1140 |
| Horse Racing | 810 |
| Skiing | 360 |

**CH4   3.6%**

| | |
|---|---|
| Football | 965 |
| American Football | 960 |
| Horse Racing | 940 |

**ITV   2%**

| | |
|---|---|
| Football | 1175 |
| General Sports | 285 |
| Rugby Union | 275 |
| Motorsports | 105 |

**TV coverage (minutes of sport) – December 1995**

**Horse racing is a popular televised sport**

# Satellite television

Satellite television has had a great impact on sport. It allows us to watch sports events live from around the world. It also gives us the choice of a large number of channels. This has resulted in many minor sports being seen regularly on television. Today people are worried that more and more of the major sports events are being bought and shown 'live and exclusive' by satellite television. This is because the satellite television companies are able to offer sport more money than the other television companies. The Government decided some years ago that a number of events including the FA Cup Final, the Scottish FA Cup Final, the Derby, cricket test matches and Wimbledon, are too important to the nation to be sold exclusively to one company. Of course, satellite sport is not free. It is only available if you have the money to spend on the equipment and the monthly payments to the company.

## How is sport shown on television?

Sport on television appears in many different forms. We can watch live events as they take place and then see the edited highlights later. News programmes bring the results of major events like Olympic finals, as well as the latest stories. Sports quizzes, documentaries and magazine programmes are also popular. There seems to be no limit to the amount of analysis, discussion and interviewing which we can see on some sporting subjects. Television also supplies sports information such as results, and it provides reports throughout the day and night on Ceefax and Teletext.

# Sport, sponsorship and television – the future?

Today, television, sport and sponsorship are very closely linked. What brings them together is money. Television wants to show major events because they are so popular with the public. The television companies are prepared to pay vast sums of money to win exclusive rights. This money is usually paid to the governing bodies of sport. At the same time, companies want to sponsor the sports and sports stars who are likely to be seen on television. This is to improve the sales of their products. Vast sums of money are again paid to the sports organisations and their stars.

**High level sport today is show business**

## Sport and commercialisation

Sponsorship and television have combined to change sport and its performers into a product to be sold. Sport is used to make money. Sport is not just important for its own sake, it has become a business. Control of sport has moved away from those people taking part and towards the managers of sport, sponsoring companies and television producers. This is called the commercialisation of sport. Sport today, at the highest level, is like show business with, its stars, very high salaries and need for spectacular performances.

**KEY POINT**

Professional sport is becoming a part of the entertainment industry. Sponsorship and television have turned sport at this level into a business.

## Who controls what we watch?

The governing bodies of sport are responsible for everything to do with their sport. However, the money paid by the television and sponsoring companies is so great that these companies can make their influence felt on the governing bodies. This is because the governing bodies have come to rely on money from television coverage and sponsorship to run their sport. Without this money they would be in financial trouble.

Many people believe that decisions are often made in the interests of sponsors and television producers. Governing bodies have been willing to change their sport to meet the new requirements. For example, some Football League matches have been moved from their traditional place on Saturday afternoons to Sunday and Monday. Sport on television is now an important part of the entertainment industry and has to respond to influences outside sport itself.

## How do sports programmes affect our opinions about sport?

Television presenters, commentators, producers and editors aim to attract us and keep us watching their own programmes. In doing so they influence our opinions. The way sport is presented on television affects our views about it. For example, a team may win a match well, but if the presenters concentrate on poor decisions by officials or bad behaviour by players they can change the emphasis of the match. So called experts may praise a particular player or highlight a skill. We must remember that these are only opinions and we should make up our own minds. Sport on television can also reinforce stereotypes. In the past, sport on television was dominated by young, able bodied, male sportspeople. Today, older people, people with disabilities and women are seen much more often. However, some commentators still comment on the appearance of sportswomen and whether or not they are married rather than their sporting achievements.

⊙ KEY POINT

Sponsorship money gives sponsoring companies a powerful hold over sport.

## How does television affect sport?

Television benefits sport in the following ways:
- sport increases in popularity. This is especially true when a national team or an individual does very well in international sport;
- large amounts of money come into sport from the sponsors and television companies. This money can be used to pay those taking part and to help the development of the sport;
- some sports have been saved from economic collapse by money from the sponsors and television companies. It has been needed because costs have increased but crowds have decreased. Most sport has come to rely on sponsorship money. This makes it open to pressure from sponsors;
- television increases the rewards for both individuals and teams. This in turn raises the standards of performance.

The way sport is presented on television affects our views about it

It is difficult to televise squash

Sport has been changed because of television. Not everyone welcomes all of the changes that have occurred. Television causes the following problems for sport:

- rule changes have made some sports more exciting for the television audience. Examples include one day cricket, tie breaks in tennis and penalty shoot outs in football;
- changes have been made in clothing. For example, in some competitions cricketers wear multi-coloured clothes and not the traditional white;
- starting times of events have been altered to increase the number of viewers. Matches in the 1994 Football World Cup in the USA were played in the heat of the day to ensure prime time viewing in Europe;
- complete control and reorganisation of rugby league has passed to the sponsors. The company decided to form new league teams and play the game in the summer;
- the authority of officials can be undermined when their decisions are examined in detail. They make decisions instantly without the help of replays and many different camera angles. Constant criticism of officials is not good for sport. Ways need to be found to help them make good decisions;
- domination of television by a few of the most popular sports can lead to the impression that others are of little importance;

- the emphasis on winning produces sportspeople and teams who are desperate for success. This might encourage sportspeople to take part too often, to play when injured, to resort to unsporting play or to cheat by using drugs;
- some sports have great difficulty in making their sport attractive for television. For example, squash is very popular at club level but is only rarely seen on television. Television has tried to cover squash through using all-glass courts, special balls for the cameras to pick up and different scoring;
- loss of television coverage has had disastrous effects on some sports in the past, for example table tennis and darts;
- there will be bad publicity for sport when such things as violence, drug abuse or personal problems make all the headlines.

**Loss of TV coverage of darts has had disastrous effects for the sport**

## How does television influence us?

Television viewers are affected by televised sport in a number of ways. The vast amount of sport on the different channels means that we all know more about what is going on in the world of sport. This means that we have more detailed knowledge about our own favourite sports and also a better understanding of all the new and less popular sports.

Sports stars can act as an inspiration for us all and as role models for young people. We hope that they will combine the highest skill with good personal behaviour, but this is not always the case.

The gap between the top sports people and us, the viewers, is getting wider. The level of skill is now far beyond that of the casual performer. The financial rewards and lifestyle of top sports people are far different from those of ordinary people.

**Television
shows sport
as a spectacle**

## How does television influence people to watch, or take part in, sport?

The answer is that we are not sure. We can claim that television increases our interest in sport of all types. This has been true of sports such as snooker and show jumping in the past. Sports from abroad, like American football and Sumo wrestling, have also become popular. Major events like World Championships attract huge television audiences. On the other hand, we can say that many of us would rather watch sport in the comfort of our homes than go to an event. Good television coverage of sports means that there will be little reason for us to go and watch it take place. This has been accepted for example in football. Part of the television payments to televise the matches live goes to compensate the clubs for the reduced gate money.

Television certainly encourages us to be a nation of sportswatchers. It seems less likely that it will inspire us to put on our sports kits and take part.

# Questions

## Sport as a Spectacle

1 List and describe the types of sponsorship available to sports clubs.

2 How might television affect the running and organisation of international sports events? Give two examples in your answer.

3 Give the main reason for each of the following:
   **a** sponsoring sport;
   **b** being sponsored.

4 List the ways in which television promotes physical recreation.

5 It is said that there is too much sport on television. What might be the effects of too much television coverage?

6 **a** Name two forms of media other than television.
   **b** Explain in detail two harmful and two beneficial effects that the media has on sport.

7 How do some sports performers become 'stars'?

8 Cigarette companies sponsor many sports. Give four arguments for or against their involvement in sports sponsorship.

9 Explain why a sponsor is more likely to sponsor sport rather than arts or environmental projects.

10 What is meant by the term 'armchair critic' of sport?

# Glossary

**ability**: qualities we have as a person which we have inherited from parents.

**active stretching**: extending limbs rhythmically beyond normal range. Thorough warm up essential.

**adenosine triphosphate (ATP)**: chemical substance which provides all energy needs of body. Must be reformed constantly.

**aerobic capacity** (cardio-respiratory endurance or stamina): ability of heart and lung system to cope with activity over period of time.

**aerobic system**: energy system we use when enough oxygen available to satisfy demands of working muscles.

**aerobic threshold**: minimum rate at which heart must work in order to improve aerobic fitness.

**aggression**: in sport, intention to dominate others forcefully.

**agility**: ability to change direction of body at speed.

**amateurs**: people who take part in sport for enjoyment.

**anaerobic endurance**: see muscular endurance.

**anaerobic threshold**: minimum rate at which heart must work in order to improve anaerobic fitness.

**antagonists**: muscles which work together with prime mover to control movement at joint. As prime mover contracts, antagonist relaxes.

**appendicular skeleton**: part of skeleton made up of arms, shoulder girdle, legs and hip girdle.

**arousal**: intensity of desire to become involved in sporting situation.

**atrophy**: loss of muscle mass due to physical inactivity.

**autonomic nervous system**: part of nervous system which automatically controls many of bodily functions, for example digestion.

**axial skeleton**: part of skeleton made up of skull, vertebral column, ribs and sternum.

**balance**: ability to retain equilibrium whether stationary or moving.

**basal metabolic rate**: amount of energy we use to keep body alive and healthy.

**blood pressure**: force of blood against walls of artery caused by heart pumping blood around body.

**body build**: ability to carry correct amount of body fat and muscle.

**body composition**: relationship between fat and lean tissue in body.

**body size**: relationship between height and weight.

**body type**: use of somatotyping to describe body shape using terms endomorph, mesomorph and ectomorph.

**carbohydrate loading**: eating greater amount of carbohydrate before endurance events. Increases amount of glycogen available to work muscles.

**cardio respiratory endurance**: see aerobic capacity.

**cartilage**: tough layer of tissue covering and protecting ends of bones. Also a shock absorbing disc between bones at a joint.

**central nervous system (C.N.S.)**: made up of brain and spinal cord. C.N.S. analyses information, makes decisions and starts action.

**charity**: organisation set up to help a good cause financially. Many sports organisations are registered charities.

**choice reaction time**: ability to choose an action and perform it as quickly as possible.

**cholesterol**: fat like substance found in blood. Can build up on artery walls.

**chronic injuries**: injuries which have not been given enough time to heal. Will reoccur on a regular basis unless sufficient time given for repair.

**closed skills**: skills not affected by sporting environment, for example gymnastic vault.

**commercialisation**: use of any activity for business purposes and financial gain.

**compulsory competitive tendering**: companies allowed to bid in order to run sports facilities owned by local authorities.

**concentric contraction**: isotonic contraction in which muscle shortens.

**coordination**: ability to perform complex movements easily.

**creatine phosphate system**: system which provides energy instantly but is used up quickly (immediate energy system).

**decision making**: we make sense of what is happening around us by using perception and memory. We use this process to make decisions.

**dehydration**: loss of body fluids, usually when working extremely hard in hot conditions.

**donations**: in sport, gifts to sporting individuals, teams or groups.

**doping**: use of illegal drugs to obtain unfair advantage in sport.

**dual use**: use of school sports facilities by local community during out of school hours.

**eccentric contraction**: isotonic contraction in which muscle lengthens whilst under tension.

**ectomorph**: body type with little fat or muscle and a narrow shape.

**eligibility**: qualifications we need to take part in organised sporting activities.

**endocrine glands**: glands which produce hormones and release them into bloodstream when required.

**endomorph**: a body type, fat and pear shaped.

**energy equation**: diet, weight and energy needs are linked together. Changing one will affect the others, for example if we eat more we will gain weight unless we increase our exercise.

**enzyme**: chemicals produced in body which help in many bodily processes.

**ethnic minority**: relatively small group of people in a society who differ from majority because of race, religion or culture.

**etiquette**: special ways we are expected to behave in our sport.

**excellence**: in sport, performance at the highest level.

**exercise**: physical activity aimed at improving health.

**expiration**: breathing air and waste products out from lungs.

**exteroceptors**: organs which get information from outside body, for example from eyes.

**extroverts**: people who are confident and socially outgoing.

**fartlek**: speed play – method of training in which we vary pace and training conditions.

**fast twitch**: muscle fibres which we use for anaerobic work. They provide fast, powerful contractions but tire easily.

**fatigue**: tiredness as a result of physical activity, caused by a build up of lactic acid in body.

**feedback**: information about outcome of performance.

**fixators**: muscles which steady parts of body to give prime movers firm base on which to work.

**flexibility**: range of limb movement about a joint (mobility, suppleness).

**formations**: positions that games players take up on field of play at different times.

**games**: physical activities involving competition between opponents and played within fixed rules.

**gender**: being male or female.

**glucose**: simple type of sugar which is used for energy in body.

**glycogen**: chemical substance we use to store glucose in body.

**health related fitness**: fitness we need for good health.

**health**: state of being physically, socially and mentally sound and free from diseases.

**hip girdle**: bones of pelvis and fused vertebrae of sacrum and coccyx.

**hormones**: chemical messengers produced by endocrine glands and sent around body.

**hygiene**: way we use good personal habits to keep ourselves clean and healthy.

**hypertrophy**: growth of muscles as result of regular physical activity.

**industrialisation**: change from a farming economy to one based on industrial production in towns and cities.

**information processing model**: theory about how we perform skills, with brain acting as computer.

**input**: all information about a situation. We get this from senses.

**inspiration**: breathing air into lungs.

**interoceptors**: organs which get information from other organs inside body, for example digestive system.

**introverts**: people who lack confidence and are socially shy.

**isokinetic contraction**: special form of isotonic contraction where muscle tension is high throughout movement.

**isometric contraction**: muscular contraction which results in no movement at joint.

**isotonic contraction**: muscular contraction which causes movement at joint. The movement can be concentric or eccentric.

**joint provision**: schools are designed with purpose built sports facilities for use by school and community.

**kinaesthetic sense**: our ability to know where our body parts are at any moment.

**knowledge of performance**: form of feedback which tells us how well we have performed.

**knowledge of results**: form of feedback which tells us the outcome of performance.

**lactic acid**: waste product of muscular action which builds up if oxygen is not available.

**lactic acid system**: provides energy to working muscle when oxygen not immediately available (short term energy system). Lactic acid builds up in working muscles.

**leisure time**: free time after we have taken care of our bodily needs, our work and our duties.

**lever**: rigid bar that moves about a fixed point. Bones act as levers in body.

**ligament**: band of fibre joining bone to bone and stabilising movement at joint.

**limited channel capacity**: brain can only deal with limited amount of information at a time. Too much information will overload it.

**maximum strength**: maximum force that can be applied by a muscle group to an immovable object.

**media**: different ways that are used to bring us stories, news, action and information, for example television, radio and newspapers.

**memory**: process which helps us store and recall past events.

**mesomorph**: body type, muscular and wedge shaped.

**motivation**: determination to achieve certain goals. Intrinsic motivation comes from inner drives. External motivation comes from rewards and outside pressures.

**motor nerves**: carry information to effector organs from central nervous system.

**muscle tone**: slight, constant contraction of skeletal muscles.

**muscular endurance**: ability of muscle or muscle group to work very hard for limited period of time (anaerobic endurance).

**muscular power**: ability to contract muscles with speed and force in one explosive act.

**nutrients**: basic elements of food which provide nourishment for body.

**obesity**: we are obese if we are more than 20% over standard weight for our height.

**open skills**: skills which are affected by whole sporting environment, for example hockey.

**ossification**: growth and development of bones.

**output**: actions decided by central nervous system.

**overload**: principle of training which states that we must work our body systems harder than normal to improve them.

**over training**: continuing to train when body needs rest and time to recover.

**over-use injuries**: caused by using a part of body incorrectly over long period of time.

**oxygen debt**: the way we pay back oxygen deficit built up during anaerobic exercise, once exercise stops.

**oxygen deficit**: build up of lactic acid during exercise when insufficient oxygen available.

**Paralympics**: Olympic Games for people with disabilities.

**passive stretching**: using partner to slowly and carefully extend our limbs beyond normal range.

**patronage**: arrangement in which wealthy people supported talented people who were poor.

**perception**: the way we sort out information we receive, using our experience.

**periodisation**: method of dividing training programme into different parts.

**peripheral nervous system**: nerves and sense organs which send information to central nervous system and also send orders to working muscles.

**personality**: our unique qualities as a person, our character and temperament.

**physical education**: a National Curriculum subject which uses physical activities for educational purposes.

**physical recreation**: physical activity enjoyed in our leisure time.

**plyometrics**: training method using explosive movements to develop muscular power, for example, bounding and hopping.

**PNF stretching**: muscles are stretched immediately after being contracted.

**posture**: way in which body parts are positioned in relation to one another.

**pressure points**: blood flow can be stopped at points near surface of body where arteries pass over bones.

**prime movers**: muscles which are responsible for movement at joints.

**professionals**: people who take part in sport for payment.

**progression**: principle of training which states that amount of work we do must be increased in gradual way for improvement to take place.

**proprioceptors**: organs which tell us where our body parts are positioned. Found in muscles, tendons and joints.

**public schools**: private and independent education system for people able and willing to pay.

**pulmonary circulation**: movement of deoxygenated blood from heart to lungs. In the lungs, carbon dioxide is exchanged for oxygen and oxygenated blood returns to heart.

**pulse**: beating of heart which is felt at arteries near surface of body.

**racism**: discrimination against individuals or groups of people on the grounds of race.

**reaction time**: ability to react to a stimulus quickly.

**recreation**: a way of relaxing and enjoying ourselves during leisure time.

**repetition maximum (RM)**: the maximum weight we can lift a specified number of times, for example 1RM is the maximum weight we can lift once.

**residual volume**: amount of air left in lungs after we breathe out as hard as possible.

**resistance**: weight or load against which muscles have to work.

**reversibility**: principle of training which states that any effects of training are not permanent and will be lost when training stops.

**role models**: individuals who set standards of behaviour and achievement for young people. Role models can be good or bad.

**scholarships**: in sport, money and support offered to talented sportspeople whilst they study.

**selective attention**: ability to choose important information out of all input from our senses.

**sensory nerves**: carry information from receptor organs to central nervous system.

**set**: certain number of repetitions performed in succession when training, for example, one set = ten repetitions.

**shoulder girdle**: made up of two clavicle and two scapula bones.

**skills**: ability to choose and perform right techniques at right time, efficiently, successfully and consistently.

**slow twitch**: muscle fibres designed for aerobic work. Provide slower, less powerful contractions than fast twitch muscle fibres but can keep working for long periods.

**specificity**: principle of training which states that training must closely resemble sporting activity for improvement to take place.

**speed**: ability to move all or part of body as quickly as possible.

**sponsorship**: in sport, a company gives financial support in return for linking their name with an individual, a team, or a sport in general.

**sport related fitness**: level of fitness necessary for success in a specific sport.

**sport**: skilful physical activity in which we take part to meet particular challenge.

**static stretching**: slowly stretching limbs beyond normal range and holding position for short period of time.

**stereotyping**: having fixed image of a group of people.

**strategies**: long term plans for success in sport.

**strength**: ability of muscle or group of muscles to overcome force or resistance.

**stretching**: extending movement of limbs about joints.

**stroke volume**: amount of blood pumped out by heart in each contraction.

**synergists**: muscles which reduce unnecessary movement at joint when prime mover contracts.

**synovial joint**: joint containing synovial fluid which allows wide range of movement.

**systemic circulation**: movement of oxygenated blood from heart to working muscles and other body organs and return of deoxygenated blood to heart.

**tactics**: methods we use to put strategies into practice in a game, race or other sporting event.

**technique**: basic movements in sport. We usually combine number of different techniques into pattern of movement called skill.

**tedium**: principle of training which states we must vary training methods to prevent boredom and over-use injuries.

**tendons**: strong, fibrous tissue which joins muscle to bone.

**tidal volume**: amount of air breathed in and out during normal breathing.

**tissue (hard tissue, soft tissue)**: one of materials of body, for example soft tissue (skin, muscles, ligaments, tendons and cartilage) and hard tissue (bones and teeth).

**training threshold**: minimum rate at which heart must work in order to bring about specific fitness improvements.

**training zone**: range of heart rate within which specific training effect will take place.

**training**: regular physical exercise aimed at specific improvements.

**transfer of skills**: we can learn techniques and skills more easily if we have learnt similar techniques and skills in the past. Transfer can be negative and can interfere with our skill learning.

**trust funds**: arrangement for amateur sportspeople to receive payment but retain their amateur status.

**vertebral column**: vertebrae of spine which protect spinal cord.

**vital capacity**: maximum amount of air we breath out after we breath in deeply.

**VO₂ max**: maximum amount of oxygen that can be transported to and used by muscles during exercise in one minute.

**voluntary body**: in sport, an independent organisation formed by individuals interested in one or more sports.

# Index

abdominal curl test 58
abduction 16
active stretching 62
adduction 16
adenosine triphosphate (ATP) 44, 46, 82
adolescence 83
aerobic capacity 50, 52, 54-55
aerobic system 42-43, 46-47
aerobic threshold 47, 48
age 30, 189, 201
aggression 95
agility 51, 53, 65
alcohol 105, 116, 119
Allied Dunbar National Fitness Survey 201
alternate hand wall toss test, 66
amateurs 154-159
anaerobic endurance 58
anaerobic system 46, 47
anaerobic threshold 47, 48
ancient Olympics 140, 146-147, 154
antagonists 22
apartheid 150, 151
appendicular skeleton 12
armed services 180
arousal 92, 94
arteries 28
associative stage of skill learning 86, 96
attitude 195
autonomic nervous system 37
autonomous stage of skill learning 86, 96
axial skeleton 12
balance 51, 53, 68
balanced diet 106
ball and socket joint 15
benefits of sport 188, 191
black and ethnic minorities 189, 199
Black power 151
bleeding 135
blood pressure 30, 81, 117
blood 28-29
body build 50, 52, 59-61
body composition 60, 61
body size 60, 61
body systems and exercise 40
body systems 8-9
body type 59, 61
bone growth 11
bone injuries 138
bone types 10
bones 81
boycott 151, 152
brain 36
breathing 33, 132
British Olympic Association (B.O.A.) 172-173
British Sports Association for the
Disabled (B.S.A.D) 170, 200
broad jump 57
bruises 137
capillaries 28
carbohydrate loading 113
carbohydrates 106, 110
cardiac muscle 18
care of our body 104-122
careers 189, 202
cartilage 11, 13
Central Council of Physical Recreation (C.C.P.R.) 169
central government 145, 174, 179, 180
central nervous system 36
Champion coaching 168, 170, 196
childhood 83
choice reaction time 67

circuit training 71, 78
circulatory system and exercise 31
circulatory system, 9, 26-31
clothing 129, 161
coaches 99
coaching 161
cognitive stage of skill learning 86, 96
collagen fibres 11
college scholarships 156
Coma report 110
commercialisation 145, 215
communications 162
community associations 177
Community Sports Leaders Award (C.S.L.A.) 169
competitions 126
competitive sport 100
compulsory competitive tendering 181
concentric contraction 20
concussion 1320
conditioned reflexes 37
condyloid joint 15
continuous training 71, 76
Cooper 12 minute run 55
coordination 51, 53, 66
Countryside Commission 171, 180
cramp 137
creatine phosphate system 42-43, 44
creatine phosphate 82
de Coubertin, Pierre 148
decision making 90, 91
diet 30
digestive system and exercise 39
digestive system 8, 39
disability 189, 200
dislocations 138
donations 206
doping classes 120-121
doping methods 121
D.R.A.B.C. 131
drug testing 119, 122
drugs 105, 118-122
dual use 175
dynamometer 56
eccentric contraction 20
ectomorph 59
education 145, 181, 194
effector organs 36
eligibility 157
embryo 11
emergency procedures 125, 131, 135
endomorph 59
energy and exercise 42-48
energy for sport 112
energy in food 111
energy 111
environment 193
equipment 124, 126, 129, 161
etiquette 129
evaluating 89, 102
examinations 194
excellence 168
excretory system 8, 39
exercise 30
experience 86, 97
explosive strength 82
extension 16
extensors 22
extroverts 94
facilities 126, 161, 165, 174-177
family 192
fartlek training 71, 76
fast twitch muscle fibre 21, 64, 81
fats 107, 110
feedback 86, 90, 91, 97

feet 115
fibre 109, 110
financial situation 193
fitness and exercise 53
fitness training 98
fitness 71, 75, 128
F.I.T.T. 70, 74
fixators 22
flat bones 11
flexibility 50, 52, 62-63
flexion 16
flexors 22
food 104
Football trust 182
formations 101
Foundation for Sport and the Arts (F.S.A.) 183
fractures 138
freely movable joints 14
frequency 70, 74
friends 192
funding for sport 165, 178-186
gambling 142
game plan 101
games 98
gender and sport 189-198
gentleman amateurs 141, 154
gliding joint 15
glycogen 45, 82, 112
goal setting 93
governing bodies 185-205
Grace, W.G. 155
guidance 86, 97
haemoglobin 81
hard tissue injuries 138
H.A.R.M. 137
Harvard step test 55
Health and Safety at Work Act 1974 126
health related fitness 50, 86
health 52, 104, 128, 191, 195
healthy diet 110
heart 26, 81
heat exhaustion 133
heatstroke 133
hinge joint 15
hip girdle 12
history of sport 140, 142-145
home influences 188, 193
hormonal system 8, 38
hormonal system and exercise 38
host city 153
hyaline cartilage 14, 15
hygiene 114-115
hyperextension 16
hypothermia 133
Illinois agility run 65
immovable joints 14
industrialisation 142
information processing model 90
inner city areas 180
input 90
Institute of Sports Sponsorship (I.S.S.) 209
intensity 70, 74
International Olympic Committee (I.O.C.) 118, 156
157, 172-173
international sport 172-173
International Sports Federation (I.S.F.) 157, 172-173
interval training 71, 77
introverts 94
inverted u 92
irregular bones 11
isokinetic contraction 21
isometric contraction 20, 21
isotonic contraction 20
joint injuries 138

joint provision 175
juggling test 66
kinaesthetic sense 67
knowledge of performance 91
knowledge of results 91
lactic acid system 42-43, 45
lactic acid 45, 47, 82
leisure and recreation departments 175, 201
leisure 189, 190
leverage 24
ligaments 14, 81
local authorities 175, 178, 181
local community 181
local management of schools 194
long bones 11
long term effects of aerobic training 81
long term effects of anaerobic training 82
long term effects of resistance training 82
lung capacity 34
maximum heart rate (MHR) 48
maximum strength 56
media 145, 205, 212-218
mesomorph 59
minerals 108
motivation 92
motor nerves 36
multi stage fitness test 54
muscle action 20-22
muscle fibres 46
muscle tone 22
muscles 19, 81
muscular endurance 51, 53, 58, 82
muscular power 51, 53, 57
muscular system and exercise 24
muscular system 8, 18-25
National Academy of Sport 168
national campaigns 189, 197
National Coaching Foundation (N.C.F.) 168, 170
National Curriculum 194
national governing bodies 168, 177
National Junior Sports Programme 196
National Lottery 179, 183
national parks 174
National Playing Fields Association (N.P.F.A.) 171
national sports centres 174
National survey of young people and sport 195
nerves 36
nervous system and exercise 37
nervous system 8, 36-37
newspapers 212
officials 99, 127
Olympic Games 141, 148-153, 173
one repetition max test 56
open enrolment 194
open sport 158
ossification 11
output 90
overload 70, 73
overloading 90
over-use injuries 130
Owens, Jesse 149
oxygen debt 45
oxygen deficit 47
P.E. teachers 86, 99
participation in sport 188-202
passive stretching 62
patronage 144
peers 192
perception 86
performing 89, 102
periodisation 74
peripheral nervous system 36
personality 94
Physical education 145, 194-195, 196

physical fitness 50-68
pivot joint 15
planning for safety 124, 126-127
planning 89, 102
plasma 29
platelets 29
plyometrics 71, 80
PNF stretching 63
posture 23
practising 97
press up test 58
P.R.I.C.E.D. 137
prime movers 22
principles of training 70, 72-73
private sector 176, 178, 182-183
professionals 154-159, 191, 202, 208
progression 70, 72
proteins 107
public schools 143, 154
public sector 178, 179, 180-181
pulse 134
racism 199
radio 21
Raising the game 168, 171
reaction time 51, 53, 67
receptor organs 36, 37
red blood cells 29
residual volume 34
respiration 32
respiratory system and exercise 35
respiratory system 8, 32-35
rest 115
reversibility 70, 73
ribs 12
R.I.C.E. 136-137
rules 129
saddle joint 15
safety in sport 124-138
satellite television 215
school and community links 188, 196
school influences 188, 194-195
sensible eating 104, 106-113
sensory nerves 36
set plays 89, 101
shock 132
short bones 11
shoulder girdle 12
shoulder hyperextension test 63
sit and reach test 62
skeletal muscles 18
skeletal system and exercise 16
skeletal system 9-16
skeleton 10
skill development 71, 75
skill in sport 86-102
skill learning 96-97
skill 86, 195
skin 114, 137
skinfold measurement 61
skull 12
sleep 115
slightly movable joints 14
slow twitch muscle fibre 21
S.M.A.R.T.E.R. 93
smoking 30, 105, 117, 211
smooth muscles 18
social change 145
social class 192
soft tissue injuries 136-137
specificity 70, 72
speed 51, 53, 64
spinal cord 13, 36
sponsorship 156, 204-211
Sport for All 197

sport related fitness 51
S.P.O.R.T. 73
sporting machines 160
Sports Aid Foundation (S.A.F.) 156, 209
sports clubs 177, 184, 186
Sports Council 166-167, 180, 197, 198-201
sports development officers 196
sports injury 125, 130-131
sports organisations 165, 166-173
Sportsmatch scheme 180, 184
sportspeople 156
static strength 82
static stretching 62
stereotypes 198, 199
sternum 12
stitch 137
Stork stand 68
strategies 89, 100-101
strength 50, 52, 56-58
stress fractures 138
stress 30
structure of sport 164
synergists 22
synovial fluid 14
synovial joints 14
synovial membrane 14
tactics 89, 100-101
Taylor report 176
teamwork 101
technology 141, 160-162
tedium 70, 73
television 204, 214-218
tendons 22, 81
terrorism 151
Thorpe, Jim 156
tidal volume 34
tobacco sponsorship 211
training effects 71, 81-82
training methods 71, 74-80
training programme planning 70, 74
training zones 48
training 47, 161, 128
transport 143
trust funds 156
twentieth century sport 144-145
unconsciousness 132
valves 28
veins 28
vertebrae 13
vertebral column 13
vertebral disc 13
vertical jump 57
Victorian times 143, 154
violence in sport 142
vital capacity 34
vitamins 108, 110
VO₂ max 34, 47, 48, 54, 81
voluntary sector 177, 179, 184-186
warm down 71, 75, 98, 128
warm up 71, 75, 98, 128
water 109
weather 127
weight gain 112
weight loss 112
weight training 71, 79
white blood cells 29
Women's Sports Foundation (W.S.F.) 171